162-0

IMAGINE A SEASON IN WHICH THE TWINS NEVER LOSE

DAVE WRIGHT

TRIUMPH
B O O K S

Library of Congress Cataloging-in-Publication Data

Wright, Dave, 1953-
  162–0 : imagine a season in which the Twins never lose / Dave Wright.
    p. cm.
  ISBN 978-1-60078-326-5
  1. Minnesota Twins (Baseball team)—Anecdotes. I. Title. II. Title:
One hundred sixty two to zero.
  GV875.M55W75 2010
  796.3570776—dc22

                                    2009049277

This book is available in quantity at special discounts for your group or organization. For further information, contact:

Triumph Books
542 South Dearborn Street
Suite 750
Chicago, Illinois 60605
(312) 939–3330
Fax (312) 663–3557
www.triumphbooks.com

Printed in U.S.A.

ISBN: 978-1-60078-326-5

Editorial and page production by Red Line Editorial

Photos courtesy of AP Images and Getty Images unless indicated otherwise

CONTENTS

INTRODUCTION

In the history of Major League Baseball, there have only been 18 nine-inning perfect games—affairs where one team never reached base at all. This is a fact the Minnesota Twins know well since they were on the losing end of two such efforts. (The only other team to suffer this fate, oddly, is the Los Angeles Dodgers.)

Human nature dictates we will make mistakes and have off nights. (The 2009 World Series champion New York Yankees, for example, were shut out just once at home all season—by the Washington Nationals, who finished with baseball's worst record.)

Thus, the idea of a perfect season—a campaign where a team goes all the way through without losing a single game—is, of course, ludicrous. Or is it?

We decided to take the approach of taking the top win for 162 game dates on the calendar. A 162-game season broke nicely into 27-games-per-month segments. This gave room for off-days, something that occurs during the course of the regular season. As all good managers do, we improvised at times. When the 2009 Twins won a playoff game against Detroit to win the AL Central title, a 163rd game was quickly added to the mix.

Since the idea is to win it all, we added four World Series victories at the end. Here, there had to be adjustments made for dates because of when games occurred. It adds up to 167 games in all, featuring all the key players who came to Minnesota and made an impact in some way, shape, or form.

This book is a fantasy that contains real people in starring roles—including such legendary former players as Rod Carew, Harmon Killebrew, Tony Oliva, Kirby Puckett, Bert Blyleven, Frank Viola,

Brad Radke, and Kent Hrbek, all of whom had long, terrific careers with the Twins. There are tales about guys like Dave Goltz, Roy Smalley, and Larry Hisle, who were solid performers here before moving on elsewhere. There are games where Lyman Bostock and Bill Campbell—two bright lights during their brief time here—rose to the forefront. The hometown guys who got away but eventually came home—Dave Winfield, Paul Molitor, and Jack Morris—are on hand as well. And we haven't forgotten the recent generation of players, including Johan Santana, Joe Mauer, Justin Morneau, and Joe Nathan.

Then there are the lesser-remembered names who had a few big moments during their time here. Included in the book is the story of Pete Redfern's impressive 1976 debut in front of his family in California, Steve Luebber's near no-hitter in Texas, and Ken Landreaux's record-tying three triples in one game. Then there are the tales of some long-forgotten names. Are there many diehard fans who remember Tom Tischinski and Hal Haydel? Both ended up the unexpected heroes of wins that are retold here.

Once the germ of the idea was in place, the trick was to find the games. Although they rarely occur any more (and are never scheduled), some notable doubleheader sweeps were used. Since the game in question had to be a victory, it eliminated such important events in team history as the first games ever played at Met Stadium and the Metrodome, both of which ended up losses. So did the final game at Met Stadium. So did such in-between events as the famous July 4, 1973, game when Eddie Bane, who had been drafted No. 1 just a month before, debuted before a full house at Met Stadium. Bane pitched very well, going seven strong innings, but Kansas City rallied to win the game.

Although it wasn't a requirement, it turns out there is a game from each of the Twins' first 49 seasons. Some years, naturally, inspired more games than others. Statisticians will note 1967—when the Twins were involved in a frenetic four- (and, for a long time, five-) team scramble for the AL pennant—ended up placing eight regular-season games into this volume. There are eight seasons that earned just one notice. Some of them—such as Cesar Tovar's 1968 game in which he became one of the few players to appear at all nine positions in the course of a game—are among the most famous in team history.

As for opponents, the combined Kansas City/Oakland A's franchise earned the top spot with 21 appearances. This makes sense when you consider the Twins were lumped for years with the A's in the same division. The White Sox earned the second spot with 20 games, while the combined Senators/Rangers' franchise came in for 17 games. And so it went, right through 10 wins over the hated Yankees to a single win over Tampa Bay and an interleague win over the Dodgers.

Finally, to anticipate a query, there were many other games that could have been chosen over the ones that ended up here. And you'll get no disagreement from this corner if you think we missed a sure bet. But such is the nature of baseball. Let the arguments begin.

A Good (But Harrowing) Start for the New Boss

The day started well for new Twins manager Ron Gardenhire. Sixty residents of his hometown of Okmulgee, Okla., descended upon Kansas City's Kaufmann Stadium to wish their favorite son good luck in his first major league game as Tom Kelly's replacement. Some three hours later, Gardenhire and his fellow Oklahomans' hearts were still beating fast. The Twins slapped five home runs but needed a terrific Torii Hunter catch in shallow center field to hold off the Royals for an 8–6 win.

"I don't know if Nervous Nelly is the right word but I couldn't sit down," Gardenhire said after his first game. "It was very exciting."

The excitement started when Jacque Jones drove the season's second pitch over the fence in right-center field. Later in the first inning, David Ortiz went deep. Brian Buchanan, whose appearance in the lineup was perhaps the most interesting decision of Gardenhire's first regular-season day on the job, followed suit the next inning. Alas, starter Brad Radke didn't have it and was chased in the fifth inning, giving all up six Kansas City runs. At that point, the Twins' longball bats returned. Hunter hit a solo shot in the sixth and Jones drilled a three-run shot to center in the seventh to put the Twins back ahead for good.

> ## At a Glance
>
> **WP:** Romero (1–0)
>
> **S:** Guardado (1)
>
> **HR:** Jones 2 (2), Ortiz (1), Buchanan (1), Hunter (1)
>
> **Key stat:** Multi-homer opening day for Jones

However, Gardenhire quickly found out that nothing that day would be easy. It was still 8–6 in the ninth inning when new closer Eddie Guardado entered and re-tired the first two batters he faced. He then walked Carlos Febles and ex-Twin Chuck Knoblauch to bring the winning run to the plate in the form of Neifi Perez. When Gardenhire first saw Perez's liner head toward Hunter, he assumed it was an easy out. The ball hit a wind pocket, however, and suddenly tailed down. Fortunately, Hunter was tearing in at full speed and made a knee-high catch to end the game.

Later, when he started to breathe again, Gardenhire was told that Major League Baseball wanted the official lineup cards for all Opening Day games. "They'll have to find it if they want it," he said. "If they want a copy, they can have a copy. I'm keeping the original." —𝚖—

In front of 60 family members and friends from Oklahoma, Ron Gardenhire's career got off to a solid start with an 8–6 win on the road over the Kansas City Royals on April 1, 2002. Gardenhire didn't get thrown out of his first game, but that inaugural toss eventually came.

A Wild Afternoon in the Metrodome

The 12,256 fans on hand at the Metrodome on this afternoon had good reason to expect to see a high-scoring game. The Twins and Tigers had scored 30 runs between them in splitting the first two games of the season. But nobody was prepared for what happened on this day, including a two-inning segment in which a combined 17 runs were scored. By the time the calculators had finished spinning, the Twins had a 16–7 victory that reminded third base coach Scott Ullger of his minor league days. "This was like a Pacific Coast League game," said Ullger, who managed in that league for three seasons. "You score a couple of touchdowns, kick a couple of extra points and hold on."

Dave Hollins' two-run homer in the second inning wasn't much of a cushion for Minnesota starting pitcher Frankie Rodriguez. Cecil Fielder's three-run homer capped a six-run third inning that also ended Rodriguez's workday. His replacement—Pat Mahomes—became the pitching story of the day when he retired Mark Lewis on a groundout to end the inning and started a 4 1/3-inning scoreless effort that would finish with his gaining the victory.

> ## At a Glance
> **WP:** Mahomes (1–0)
> **HR:** Hollins (1)
> **Key stats:** Coomer 3-for-4, 3 RBIs

Down 6–2, the Twins chased Scott Aldred with five runs in the bottom of the third inning. Catcher Mike Durant made a successful major league debut with a leadoff single. Three more singles, a walk, an error and a sacrifice fly followed. Roberto Kelly then singled sharply to produce two more runs and the comeback was complete. In case the Tigers had any ideas of returning the favor, the Twins combined doubles by Chuck Knoblauch and Ron Coomer, a walk, a sacrifice fly, a pair of Detroit errors and another Durant single the next inning for six more runs.

Things mercifully settled down from there and the Twins eased their way home, finishing the opening series with a team batting average of .377.

FUN WHILE IT LASTED

For Durant, that Wednesday afternoon game would be about as good as it ever got in what amounted to a short stay in the big leagues. Called up from the minors because of an injury to Matt Walbeck, Durant stayed with the team until mid-June. He returned for a brief spell in July and again in September. But he recorded his last big league hit on June 8 before going hitless in his final 22 at-bats and finishing with a lifetime big league batting average of .210. —

Living Up to Expectations

It was The Kid's first game back in town since playing for his dad's Air Freight Unlimited amateur team. But Joe Mauer, described by Torii Hunter as "20 going on 30," seemed impervious to it all. He seemed blissfully unaware that, when he stepped behind the plate to open the season against the Indians, he would be only the fifth 20-year-old catcher in a major league game in the past 40 years. The list of predecessors at that tender age behind the plate included a Hall of Famer (Johnny Bench), another guy who may get there some day (Ivan Rodriguez), Bob Didier and, ironically, a former Twin (Butch Wynegar).

Instead of worrying about history, Mauer's biggest concern hours before game time was helping out his mother, Theresa, who had managed to get 929 tickets for the game but suddenly needed four more.

The dutiful son took care of his mom's request and then went to work. In addition to taking over behind the plate and guiding a pitching staff that had won 90 games the year before, Mauer was facing a rugged customer on the mound: CC Sabathia.

Although he had come in with much hype after being the first player taken overall in the 2001 draft, Mauer won his teammates over early with his calm, no-nonsense demeanor.

Mauer's story was one of many plots this Opening Day. Although the team had won its second straight division title in 2003, the Twins had shown little offense when they lost their first-round playoff series to the Yankees. The final game—an 8–1 loss at home—made for a rough winter, and the team seemed anxious to make amends right away.

Sabathia, however, had other plans. The 6-foot-7 southpaw gave up two hits and fanned nine batters. Meanwhile, Minnesota starter Brad Radke was suffering from a bad case of homeritis. Travis Hafner hit a pair of longballs and Jody Gerut hit one. Fortunately, all three home runs were solo shots and it was only 4–0 when Sabathia left the game in favor of the Indians' bullpen.

At a Glance

WP: Rincon (1–0)

HR: Stewart (1)

Key stats: Mauer 2-for-3 with 2 BBs in first MLB game; Stewart 3-run HR wins it

Relieved they could see the ball again, the Twins began bashing it. Mauer, who had walked earlier, led off with another free pass. Cristian Guzman singled him to third. Shannon Stewart's grounder moved Guzman to second, and both runners came home on Michael Cuddyer's single. Later, Corey Koskie doubled and Torii Hunter singled to get two more runs and send the game into extra innings. Mauer singled to open the ninth but was left stranded. With one out in the 11th inning, Matthew LeCroy walked. Mauer doubled his major league hit total with another single, and one out later, Chad Durbin, a free-agent pickup over the winter, tried to sneak a fastball past Stewart. Instead, Stewart snuck it over the left-field fence for the game-winning blow.

As for Mauer, he finished his first big league game by going 2-for-3 with two walks, drawing praise from players on both sides for his poise behind the plate. It would not be the last time this would occur.

A SHORT BUT MEMORABLE SEASON

Unfortunately, Mauer's first season in the majors didn't last long. The night after his successful debut, Mauer heard something "pop" in his left knee while he chased a foul ball. He had surgery to repair a medial meniscus tear on April 8 and, after a short stint in the minors, returned to the major leagues on June 2. He hit his first career big league homer a few days later and rattled off a four-hit game against Kansas City on July 7. But the knee was still sore and he finally shut it down for good in mid-July. In 35 games, he hit .308 (33-for-107) with eight doubles, six home runs, and 17 RBIs. It was enough to be named the team's top rookie in a vote of the local media. Two years later, he would become the first catcher in 64 years to win a batting crown when he hit .347. He won a second batting title in 2008 with a .328 mark. He had offseason surgery that caused him to miss spring training and the start of the 2009 season. After rehabbing in Florida, he returned to town to make his debut with the team against Kansas City on May 1. It didn't take long to get acclimated. Sidney Ponson's third pitch to Mauer disappeared over the left field fence. By the time the weekend series was over, Mauer had gone 7-for-10 and the Kid was back. By the end of the season, batting title No. 3 was in his hand, earned with a .365 average. —⁓—

Joe Mauer

Few players have ever lived up their hype better than the St. Paul native who was the top amateur draft pick in the country in 2001. It took him just 2½ years to advance to big leagues. When he arrived in 2004, he singled twice in his first major league game. Unfortunately, a knee injury in his second big league game held him to just 35 games that season. Once healthy, he has been sensational, becoming the only AL catcher to win a batting title (he has now done it three times in five seasons), setting a new record with a .365 mark in 2009.

Born to Hit

Every major league team has them—the players who, in the view of their fans, should be enshrined in Cooperstown. Perhaps the two most noteworthy Twins in this department both took center stage in the team's 1973 season opener, an 8–3 victory over the Oakland A's, the defending World Series champions. Bert Blyleven, who would go on to win 20 games in a season for the only time in his career, gave himself a nifty gift for his 22nd birthday, a complete-game 10-hitter. On this night, he had to share the spotlight with the man who many feel that, if his knees could have stayed sound, would have been a slam-dunk for the Hall.

Tony Oliva had already won three batting titles and been named American League Player of the Year twice. However, a fourth operation on his right knee had left Oliva a shadow of his old form. But the man could still hit. His two-run homer in the first inning was the first longball struck by a player in the

Injuries that shortened his career by several years were probably the only things keeping Tony Oliva from a place in the Hall of Fame.

American League's newfangled designated hitter position. Hitting fourth (in part because Harmon Killebrew was out of action with a sore knee), Oliva took Catfish Hunter out of the yard for a two-run shot that started the Twins on their way to ruining the night for 38,207 Oakland patrons. Oliva had company rounding the bases. Jim Holt hit a solo homer and Larry Hisle, making his debut as the leadoff batter, had four hits and also left the yard.

Oliva later singled and drove in three runs total. But he sounded like he was still adjusting to his new gig. "I like getting the hits but being the designated hitter is tough. You get cold sitting on the bench. When the other players grab their gloves to go play defense, you want to go with them," he told reporters afterward.

As it turned out, Oliva adjusted very nicely to the DH role. He played more than 400 games in that role over the next four seasons before retiring after the 1976 season with a .304 career batting average. Once the DH became part of the American League rulebook, Oliva never played in the field again.

> ## At a Glance
>
> **WP:** Blyleven (1–0)
>
> **HR:** Oliva (1), Holt (1), Hisle (1)
>
> **Key stats:** Oliva hits first HR by Twins DH; Blyleven CG; Hisle 4-for-5

A CAMEO ROLE AT SECOND BASE . . . AND ONE LAST NIGHT OF GLORY

Gene Mauch became the Twins' manager in 1976. Mauch was an innovative guy, and he liked to get as much offense as he could possibly muster. At the start of the 1976 season, Oliva's knees were so bad that he couldn't even handle the regular DH role early in the season. So, Mauch penciled him in the starting lineup four times as the leadoff hitter playing second base. It was always a road game so there was no danger of Oliva ever having to go into the field. Unfortunately, the experiment didn't go very well. Oliva went 0-for-3 with a walk in a game at Boston. On that occasion, Jerry Terrell, who was playing second base in the field that day, ran for him. Oliva's knees improved enough that he could DH a few games here and there. But he was hitting just .140 when he faced the league's best known pitcher, Detroit's Mark Fidrych, on July 20 at Met Stadium. For one night, the old touch returned. Fidrych pitched a complete game in an 8–3 win but Oliva went 4-for-4 and drove in a run. In the ninth inning, after Oliva's fourth single, Fidrych tipped his cap toward first base.

A reporter approached Fidrych later and asked him why he tipped his cap to Oliva.

"Who's Oliva?" Fidrych asked.

"The guy who got the four hits," came the reply.

"Oh, that guy," Fidrych said. "He's good." —∞—

Making Friends on Day 1

It was one of those small transactions that didn't draw a lot of attention. As the 1970 spring training camp was winding down, the Twins made a deal with the Washington Senators, sending them two pitchers (Joe Grzenda and Charley Walters) who weren't part of new manager Bill Rigney's plans in exchange for an outfielder with the rather unlikely name of Garrabrant Ryerson Alyea. Little did everybody know that Alyea, known to most of the world as Brant, would pay such an impressive first dividend.

The Twins, defending Western Division champs, opened the 1970 season with a 12–0 thumping of the White Sox at Comiskey Park. Right-hander Jim Perry picked up where he had left off in 1969, tossing a six-hitter with six strikeouts for a complete-game win. Alyea, who had hit just .249 in limited action the year before, garnered the majority of the headlines by going 4-for-4 with a pair of home runs and seven RBIs. The latter figure still stands as the most ever for an Opening Day performance.

"I thought I might go to the Twins in 1969 because I heard Billy Martin (the manager that season) liked me and it was clear Ted Williams (Washington's manager) wasn't fond of me," Alyea recalled later. "When Martin was fired in the offseason, I still thought I would get moved but I didn't know where." As it developed, left field was an open spot for the Twins and Alyea was given the first crack at the job. He started modestly, knocking home a run with a first-inning single. He singled again in the fourth to no avail. In the fifth, he ended Tommy John's day with a three-run homer that gave Minnesota a 6–0 lead. Two innings later, Alyea hit another three-run shot as part of six-pack inning that put the game away. White Sox manager Don Gutteridge was suitably impressed. "We have a book on Alyea," he told reporters after the game. "But today, we were looking at the wrong page."

At a Glance

WP: Perry (1–0)

HR: Alyea 2 (2)

Key stats: Alyea sets MLB Opening Day record with 7 RBIs; Perry shutout

SECOND VERSE . . . SAME AS THE FIRST

Alyea had a productive 1970 season, batting .291 with 12 doubles and 16 home runs in just 258 at-bats. He even duplicated his two-homer, seven-RBI effort in a 7–6 win in the first game of a Labor Day doubleheader against Milwaukee. This time, he started fast, nailing Lew Krausse for a grand slam in the first inning. He added a three-run shot in the third and also singled in the seventh inning. In 1971, he got off to another torrid start and was hitting .333 on May 9. But he fell into an awful slump and finished the season at .177. Oakland acquired him in the offseason. In 1972, he managed just nine hits in 50 at-bats and disappeared from the MLB scene for good. —ᴍ—

There's No Place Like Dome for Gladden

During his long run as manager of the Minnesota Twins, Tom Kelly was renowned for his droll way of phrasing his thoughts. He tended to understate and underplay wins and losses together. Thus, several heads looked up with surprise when he told reporters near the end of the 1988 spring training camp, "We're a little better than we were last year."

After all, the 1987 team had won the first World Series title in club history, blowing out Detroit in five games and then outlasting St. Louis in an exhausting seven-game set.

The one constant of that team was its repeated success at the Metrodome. The Twins had a league-best 56–25 win-loss mark there that season, adding six straight postseason triumphs to the log.

After opening the season with a pair of losses at New York, the club returned to its old lair and picked up where it had left off. In front of the largest home crowd in team history, the Twins defeated Toronto 6–3.

Bert Blyleven was his usual solid self on the mound for the Twins, scattering two runs on six hits over six innings before Juan Berenguer and Jeff Reardon finished.

But the night belonged to Minnesota outfielder Dan Gladden, who turned in a remarkable performance that will be remembered for years to come.

All Gladden did on this night was:

- Open the Twins' scoring with a solo home run in the first inning off Toronto's ace, righty Dave Stieb
- Hit an RBI single in the second inning for the team's second run
- Greet Stieb's replacement, Mark Eichhorn, with an RBI double in the seventh
- Greet Eichhorn's replacement, David Wells, with a "pure" steal of home
- Finish off the night (and the Twins' scoring) with a solo home run off Wells in the eighth inning, the first multi-home run game of his career

All in all, it was a rouser of a home opener. Stieb, who had beaten the Twins three times the year before, got off to a bad start by decking Gladden with his first pitch. The outfielder dusted himself off, got up, redirected the next pitch into the left-field seats, and the lively game was on. Still, Minnesota only led 3–2 in the seventh inning when Steve Lombardozzi, the No. 9 hitter, tripled with none out. Eichhorn replaced Stieb, but Gladden tagged a ball to left to make it 4–2. The left fielder was on third base with two outs and Kent Hrbek was at the plate when he got the idea to head home. "I looked in the dugout and Tom didn't say no," Gladden recalled later. "So, I gave Herbie the sign and he nodded back." The next thing anybody knew, Gladden startled Wells by taking off and sliding past Toronto catcher Ernie Whitt easily. It was the Twins' first "pure" steal of home since Rod Carew had done it in 1976.

Things tightened up a bit in the ninth inning when Gladden, of all people, dropped Rick Leach's fly ball for an error and an unearned run that also brought the tying run to the plate. But Reardon retired the veteran Juan Beniquez on a pop-up and the gala affair was over. The Twins were 1–0 at home for 1988. As Tom Brunansky, who had contributed a pair of hits himself to the cause that night, observed, "Magical things seem to happen here."

At a Glance

WP: Blyleven (1–0)

S: Reardon (1)

HR: Gladden 2 (2), Gaetti (1)

Key stats: Gladden 4 hits, steals home

BETTER, AND YET WORSE

In theory, the 1988 Twins had a very good season, winning six more games than they had during their World Series year. They were terrific at home again, going 47–34. But the Oakland A's came out firing, winning 29 of their first 40 games and winning the West by a baker's dozen games. The Twins made a run in late June, coming within four games of the A's after they blanked them twice in a twin bill at Oakland, 11–0 and 5–0. But the A's won six of their next seven games and were never seriously challenged again. —∾—

Did You Know?

Dan Gladden is one of just two players in team history to record more than one "pure" steal of home. Gladden repeated his Opening Night feat in a September game at California. Rod Carew did it five times. Vic Power, Ted Uhlaender, John Roseboro and Rich Becker did it once each.

No Way to Treat a Legend

It had the makings of a rough afternoon for the Twins. For perhaps the first time in major league history, a team had a batting lineup with *fewer* combined years of MLB service than the man who was the opposing starting pitcher. Minnesota's entire batting order totaled of 14 years experience. Their mound opponent for that day, Seattle's Gaylord Perry, was in his 22nd—and final—season as a big league pitcher. To add to the odds, Twins starting pitcher Brad Havens was coming off an Opening Day outing where he had allowed eight runs in 1 1/3 innings.

At a Glance
WP: Havens (1–1)
S: Davis (2)
HR: Bush 2 (2), Castino (2), Gaetti (2)
Key stat: Bush hits 2 of 4 homers off Gaylord Perry

Naturally, the Twins won 6–3.

Most people in baseball agreed that the middle of the Twins' order—Gary Ward, Kent Hrbek, Tom Brunansky and Gary Gaetti—might be inexperienced but had the potential to be explosive. In the first five games of the season, however, the Twins had just three home runs to their credit.

On this Sunday, Randy Bush gave Perry a present he probably didn't appreciate, hitting a pair of home runs. Gaetti and John Castino also took him deep. The four-home-run outburst marked the high-water mark for Perry in a 777-game career with nine different teams. Bush, who had been part of the kiddie corps that had come up to the team the year before, was realistic about his place in the order, telling reporters later, "Our Murderers' Row is hitters 3 through 6. Maybe he relaxed a bit and thought, 'Here's No. 7. I never heard of this guy.'"

Meanwhile, Havens went 7 1/3 innings before giving way to Ron Davis, who earned the save. It would be a rare moment of joy for Havens, who won just five games with an 8.18 ERA for the season. But he would always have this day to savor. —⁓—

Opening in Style

On paper, this looked like a mismatch. The newly minted Minnesota Twins were going to start their history on baseball's most famous playground, New York's Yankee Stadium, against the defending American League champions. To make matters a bit more intimidating, the Yankees were playing their first game for their new manager, Ralph Houk, and seem determined to put the memory of a frustrating 1960 World Series loss to Pittsburgh behind them.

That back story seemed enough to ensure the Twins would get off to a rough start. But Houk seemed to gild the lily by sending out his left-handed ace, Whitey Ford, to the mound. Ford had run roughshod over the Twins in their past life as the Washington Senators, posting a career 24–5 win-loss mark. Meanwhile, the Twins were offering up righty Pedro Ramos, who had suffered 71 losses in the last four seasons, as their first-day choice. Two days before the team's first game, Ramos had gained headlines when he told reporters he was ready to head to his native Cuba to fight for Fidel Castro "if they call me." Later, he told Minnesota manager Cookie Lavagetto he was kidding.

It took a while but the game was a mismatch and it didn't go the way many people thought it would.

For six innings, Ford and Ramos tossed zeroes at each other. In the second inning, the Yankees threatened, putting runners on first and third base with two outs. But Ford, an excellent hitting pitcher (he singled in his next at-bat), grounded out to third baseman Reno Bertoia to end the threat.

For the first six frames Minnesota barely challenged Ford, managing just two hits and getting no runners past second base.

Bob Allison had already had a good trip to New York. The day before the opener, he was a guest on the TV show "Play Your Hunch." Now, he was batting in a ballpark where he always seemed to hit well. Standing at the plate in the scoreless tie in the seventh inning against Ford, Allison played a hunch of his own. With the count 1–0, he guessed he would get a curve ball. He guessed right and whacked it into the left-field seats for the first run in Twins' history. "Maybe I didn't get all of it," he said after the game. "But I got a pretty good piece of it."

Twins	AB	R	H	RBI
Versalles ss	5	1	2	0
Green cf	5	0	0	0
Killebrew 1b	2	0	1	1
Lemon lf	4	0	0	0
Dobbek lf	0	0	0	0
Allison rf	5	1	2	1
Battey c	4	2	1	0
Bertoia 3b	2	2	1	2
Gardner 2b	3	0	1	0
Ramos p	4	0	1	2
Totals	34	6	9	6

Yankees	AB	R	H	RBI
Richardson 2b	4	0	0	0
Lopez lf	4	0	0	0
Berra c	4	0	1	0
Mantle cf	4	0	0	0
Maris rf	3	0	0	0
Skowron 1b	3	0	1	0
Kubek ss	2	0	0	0
Boyer 3b	3	0	0	0
Ford p	2	0	1	0
Terry p	0	0	0	0
Gonder ph	1	0	0	0
Coates p	0	0	0	0
Totals	30	0	3	0

MIN	0 0 0 0 0 0 3 2 1 -	6	9	1
NY	0 0 0 0 0 0 0 0 0 -	0	3	0

Twins	IP	H	R	ER	BB	SO
Ramos W(1-0)	9	3	0	0	1	5

Yankees	IP	H	R	ER	BB	SO
Ford L(0-1)	6.1	5	3	3	3	3
Terry	1.2	3	2	2	1	0
Coates	1	1	1	1	0	0
Totals	9	9	6	6	4	3

E—Minnesota Lemon. DP—Minnesota 1. 2B—Minnesota Battey. HR—Minnesota Allison (1); Bertoia (1). SH—Minnesota Gardner. SF—Minnesota Dobbek. LOB—Minnesota 8; New York 4. SB—Minnesota Versalles 2, Dobbek. Attendance: 14,607.

The Allison homer seemed to unnerve Ford. In quick fashion, Earl Battey doubled and Bertoia coaxed a walk. One out later, Ramos, who was to hit three home runs that season, singled sharply to center field to score two more runs.

As so often happened in games at Yankee Stadium, things fell apart from there. Allison opened the eighth inning with a single off Ralph Terry, who had replaced Ford on the mound. After Battey forced Allison out at second, Bertoia hit the first pitch he saw for a two-run homer, and the rout was on.

The Twins added a run in the ninth inning. Meanwhile, Ramos retired the last 13 batters he faced in a row, and the Twins left Yankee Stadium in a tie for first place. The right-hander walked one and struck out five. New York third baseman Clete Boyer came away impressed. "I only struck out four times all spring and he got me twice," Boyer said to the media after the game. "Boy, he had good stuff."

The joy of the opening-day win lingered for a few days. The team had a scheduled day off and then got rained out of their second game in New York. They went to Baltimore and won the second game in their history as well. The Twins had a good April, winning nine of 15 games played. But an ugly 13-game losing streak in late May and early June sent the team veering in another direction. By season's end, Minnesota's 70–90 win-loss mark was actually three wins worse than the Senators had managed the year before.

Ramos' shutout was the only victory in the nine games Minnesota played that year at Yankee Stadium. (In all, New York won 14 of the 18 meetings between the two teams in 1961.) The Yankees shook it off to record 109 wins and later dusted off Cincinnati in five games in the World Series.

Allison batted only .245 that year but hit 29 home runs and drove in a career-high 105 runs. (He also had 103 walks, a career best.) He stayed with the team for the rest of the decade and would become one of the most popular players in team history. Ramos went on to forge an 11–20 win-loss mark for the year and would be traded prior to the 1962 season. Bertoia became one of the first two players in team history to be traded when he and pitcher Paul Giel were shipped to Kansas City for outfielder Bill Tuttle on June 1. Bertoia would hit one more home run in his major league career and began a teaching/coaching/scouting career the next year.

Still, that unlikely trio (with a little help from Zoilo Versalles, who stole two bases that afternoon in Yankee Stadium) helped the new franchise get off to a memorable start. —⁓—

Turning on a Nemesis

For a decade, he had haunted them. It seemed that all Troy Percival needed to do was step on the mound and the Minnesota Twins turned into little kittens chasing a ball of yarn. In 39 games for the Angels against the Twins, Percival had recorded a victory, 22 saves, 51 strikeouts and a remarkable streak of 40 consecutive scoreless innings. So it didn't seem to bode well for the Twins when Percival, a free agent, defected to Central Division rival Detroit before the start of the 2005 season.

As it turned out, however, this was exactly the tonic the Twins needed. Percival, who had been so good against the Twins in the past, went to the mound to preserve a 4–4 game in the bottom of the ninth inning. But he only retired one of the four batters he faced. The last one—Shannon Stewart—doubled to center field to break the team's longtime jinx. "[Forty] innings' worth of no hits, no runs. Shoot, you start reading about it in the 'Guinness Book of World Records,'" said Minnesota manager Ron Gardenhire. "It's about time we scored a run off that guy."

> ## At a Glance
>
> **WP:** Rincon (1–0)
>
> **HR:** Barlett (1), Cuddyer (1)
>
> **Key stat:** Twins win with first ER ever off Troy Percival (40 IP)

Until the Twins turned on Percival, the story of the night had been the mound return of Joe Mays. Once a prominent member of the starting rotation, Mays had been sidelined Aug. 31, 2003 after undergoing elbow surgery. He wasn't terrific—three earned runs on four hits in five innings—but just seeing him on the mound again seemed to cheer up his teammates.

Four relievers managed to keep the Tigers to a run on three hits from there. Thus, it was a tie game when Lew Ford led off against Percival with a single to center. After a sacrifice bunt and a walk, Stewart slapped the first pitch he saw to center field. The Twins' nightmares about Percival were over.

HISTORY REPEATS ITSELF (SORT OF)

Having taken a decade to score its first ever run off Percival, the Twins got to him again in dramatic fashion during their next encounter 10 days later. Minnesota trailed 4–3 in the top of the ninth inning when Percival entered to attempt the save. Justin Morneau had other ideas, greeting Percival with a booming homer to right field to tie the game. Unfortunately for Minnesota, Percival then returned to form and retired the next six batters he faced. Pudge Rodriguez's homer in the last of the 10th inning made Percival a 5–4 winner. After that, Percival suffered arm problems and only pitched 25 innings for Detroit in 2005. He missed all of 2006 and spent 2007 in St. Louis before returning to the AL as a setup man in Tampa Bay. —

Billy Sweats Out the First Win

Before his first game as the new manager of the Minnesota Twins, Billy Martin said, "I feel like there's a 100-pound weight on my shoulders." The Twins didn't help this feeling with a pair of extra-inning losses to expansion Kansas City to open the 1969 season. They moved to Anaheim Stadium and dropped two more close games, the slowest start in team history. To make matters worse, Rod Carew, Martin's pet project at second base, was unavailable because he was serving a military commitment. One can imagine how heavy the burden seemed to Martin when starting pitcher Dick Woodson was roughed up for three runs in the first inning of Game 5.

Fortunately for Martin, Tom Hall steadied matters with five scoreless innings before things finally began to turn around a bit.

Still, Minnesota trailed 3–1 in the seventh inning when they bunched two singles, a walk, and a pair of fielder's choices for two runs and a 3-all tie. The situation seemed to call for a big blow to turn things around. Fortunately for Martin, he had just the fellow who could do it in Harmon Killebrew, who led off the eighth inning with his first home run of the season to break the tie for good. It was only the second time the Twins had even led in a game in the young season. Leo Cardenas added a sacrifice fly for a run that proved important when ace reliever Ron Perranoski, perhaps unnerved by a rare catcher's interference call against George Mitterwald, suddenly gave up two hits in the ninth that made it 5–4. It was Bob Miller, however, who saved the day by getting Jim Fregosi to ground out to end the game.

Sighed Martin to reporters afterward, "I think the guys will relax now."

As it developed, Martin was right about his team. After struggling to get their first win, the Twins went on a tear, winning their next six games in a row. By the end of May, they had a two-game lead in the newly formed Western Division. —⁓—

Billy Martin

He first came to town as a second baseman, batting .246 on the first Twins' team ever. Later, he returned as a coach and is given credit for helping to nurture Zoilo Versalles through his memorable MVP run in the 1965 season. In 1969, he replaced Cal Ermer and managed the club to a 97–65 win-loss record and the Western Division title.

Carew Sets the Tone, Vets Take It from There

He recorded two hits in his first major league game, but the Twins still lost to Baltimore. The next day, he was hitless in another loss. When Rodney Cline Carew strode to the plate for his first at-bat in the team's home opener, Minnesotans still didn't know much about this 21-year-old kid who had been born in some place called Gatun in the Canal Zone (wherever that was).

All most people knew was owner Calvin Griffith's preseason pronouncement to the St. Paul *Pioneer Press* that "we're taking a big gamble with Carew at second."

On this rainy afternoon, however, they got a snapshot of things to come. Carew was batting fifth in the lineup against Detroit righty Earl Wilson. Minnesota was already leading 1–0 in the first inning when Carew singled sharply to left to score Tony Oliva to make it 2–0. Unfortunately for Carew, that was the end of his good day. Wilson picked him off first base to end the inning.

The Twins' vets took it from there. In the bottom of the sixth, Allison homered to tie the game. Zoilo Versalles, showing some of his 1965 MVP form, then singled and later scored the tiebreaking run. For good measure, Versalles homered in the eighth to finish off the scoring. As he had done in the World Series two years before, Bob Allison made a terrific sliding catch in the left-field corner off Jim Northup in the top of the seventh inning.

At a Glance

WP: Merritt (1–0)

HR: Allison (1), Versalles (1)

Key stat: Carew singles in home debut

A month later, Carew recorded the first of five five-hit games for the Twins, and hit a solid .292 in 137 games in 1967. Two years later, he would win the first of his seven batting titles. Turned out not to be such a gamble after all. ⁓

Did You Know?

For Twins reliever Juan Berenguer, celebrating titles in Detroit was old hat. He was a member of the Detroit team that won the 1984 AL pennant (and later, the World Series). Both clinching games were at Tiger Stadium. Berenguer pitched very well for the Twins in the 1987 AL Championship Series, appearing four times, earning a save and allowing just one run in six innings.

Luck Helps Turn the Tide

It looked like so many other games the Twins had played against the Yankees. Minnesota had jumped to a 4–0 lead after four innings. Johan Santana had allowed two lonely singles and seemed to be rolling. But an infield out and a well-placed Derek Jeter double scored two runs in the fifth. Two innings later, Santana left after giving up two hits. Jeter greeted his replacement, Jesse Crain, with a single to make it 4–4. Two more hits followed. The 4–0 lead was gone and the Metrodome crowd of 42,516 watched in silence.

A feeling of déjà vu had set in as ace Yankee reliever Mariano Rivera entered the game in the last of the ninth inning.

But this was a different day in what proved to be a different season. Luis Castillo, who had tripled and drove home two runs earlier, legged out an infield chopper to start the inning with his fourth hit of the afternoon. Joe Mauer followed with a perfectly placed hit-and-run single to left-center. Hideki Matsui's vain attempt to nail Castillo allowed the alert Mauer to move to second. Still, it looked like it would be the same old ending when Rondell White and Torii Hunter both fanned.

That left it up to Justin Morneau, who had been using the hot-hitting Mauer's bats for a week. The Yankees, fearing a repeat of Castillo's chopper, tightened up defensively on the right side of the infield. Rivera followed instructions and jammed Morneau with his first pitch. But Morneau was ready and looped it softly into right field. It was just far enough to drop in for a hit but not far enough for right fielder Gary Sheffield to do anything but watch as Castillo and Mauer scored easily for a great escape and a 6–5 win.

At a Glance

WP: Rincon (1–0)

Key stat: Morneau 2-run single off Rivera for win

"I just got lucky," Morneau would tell reporters later. Perhaps. But a little luck goes a long way . . . especially against Mariano Rivera and the Yankees. —〰—

Slamming Your Way out of the Blahs

Less than a week into their inaugural season in the American League, the Twins were facing their first serious problem. The team had taken its first loss of the season the day before, 8–0, at Baltimore. But the bigger setback came in the ninth inning of that game when Harmon Killebrew pulled a hamstring running out a grounder. Doc Lentz, the team's trainer, predicted a three-week layoff.

Thus, the team had plenty of reasons to be unexcited about playing a doubleheader on a chilly Sunday afternoon. The top of the first inning, however, changed that view considerably. Zoilo Versalles, Lenny Green (who later homered) and Don Mincher (who had replaced Killebrew in the lineup) all walked against starter Chuck Estrada. Bob Allison, who had been having a terrific week, then drilled a grand slam home run.

Goodbye blahs. Hello 4–0 lead. The Twins added two more before Pedro Ramos got to the mound. In the sixth inning, Allison, who had never homered in Baltimore's Memorial Stadium before, hit a three-run shot that brightened the team's mood even more. Ramos, who had shut out the Yankees to open the season, wasn't as sharp this time, giving up four runs on 12 hits in 6 1/3 innings. Ray Moore finished up for the save and, suddenly, Baltimore became a lovely place to spend a spring afternoon.

At a Glance
W: Ramos (2–0)
S: Moore (1)
HR: Allison 2 (3), Green (1)
Key stats: Allison 2 HRs, career-high 7 RBIs

As for Allison, it would be the high-water mark for RBIs in a game in a 13-year, 1,541-game career. He would go on to record an unusual statistical century hat trick of sorts by finishing the season with 105 RBIs, 103 walks and 100 strikeouts. The only other Twin to do this was the man who didn't play that day. Killebrew did it three times.

THE BIG GUY RECOVERS QUICKLY

When Killebrew suffered his hamstring injury, he said to Lentz, "I'll be able to play the second game of the doubleheader tomorrow, won't I?" Lentz was, well, pessimistic. "Son, if you play at all in the next three weeks, you'll make an awful liar out of a lot of us," he responded.

Killebrew took pleasure in doing just that. He beat Lentz's timetable by a week, returning to the lineup at Los Angeles on April 29. Two days later, he had four hits against the White Sox and was on his way to a big season, finishing with a career best .288 batting average, 42 home runs and 105 RBIs. —⁓—

The Kid Is Going to Be OK

Although he had been in the team's system for two seasons (and had over 100 MLB at-bats), there seemed to be some debate about whether shortstop Zoilo Versalles belonged with the Twins or in the minor leagues. After helping the team to a sweep in the first doubleheader in team history, manager Cookie Lavagetto made his view quite clear. "He's really changed my mind," Lavagetto told reporters after Versalles' two-run home run in the 11th inning gave the Twins a 6–4 win.

It was a game that seemed on the brink of getting away from the Twins. Don Mincher's two RBIs and solo run-scoring hits from Versalles and Bob Allison had staked starter Jack Kralick to a 4–2 lead entering the last of the ninth inning. But the Orioles somehow combined a single, two walks, a ground out, and a wild pitch to score twice to tie the game. Enter rookie pitcher Bill Pleis, who, with runners on first and third, got Dave Philley to pop out to force extra innings.

In the 11th, Reno Bertoia led off with a walk and was bunted to second. Bertoia stayed put as pinch-hitter Ron Henry struck out. Versalles, who already had three hits in the game, then sent a shot down the left-field line that curved inside the foul pole for the game-winning blow. "I lean toward center field so the ball stay in fair territory," he said later.

> ## At a Glance
>
> **WP:** Pleis (1–0)
>
> **S:** Stobbs (1)
>
> **HR:** Mincher (1), Versalles (1)
>
> **Key stats:** Versalles 4-for-6, 3 RBIs, GW 2-run HR

Lavagetto wasn't sure he bought that, but he wasn't complaining. Chuck Stobbs put down the Orioles in the bottom of the inning and some 6½ hours after they started the day, the Twins had a shortstop they felt they could trust and had accomplished something few folks would have believed. Their overall mark of 4–1 put them in first place in the American League.

IT WAS FUN WHILE IT LASTED

The Twins' good start in their new digs lasted for a couple weeks more. Although they did lose their first game at Met Stadium, Minnesota stood 9–6, a mere 1½ games out of first place at the end of April. But they went 10–18 in May and trailed the first-place Tigers by 9½ games after dropping a Memorial Day twin bill to Cleveland. They finished with three fewer wins than the 70 wins they had recorded in their final season in Washington. However, the seeds were in place for improvement. A year later, they jumped to second place, five games behind the champion Yankees. —⁓—

A Grand Way to Hit for the Cycle

The new season was off to a rough start. The combination of having the scheduled opening day battery of pitcher Scott Baker and catcher Joe Mauer sidelined with injuries and a shaky bullpen caused the Twins to drop seven of their first 11 games of the season. It didn't look like the pattern was about to change on this night.

The Angels, a team that was battling its own demons (young pitcher Nick Adenhart had been killed in a car accident the week before and slugger Vladimir Guerrero was out of action with a torn pectoral muscle) broke open a 3-all tie in the seventh inning with five runs. Reliever Jesse Crain was mostly at fault here. He replaced Nick Blackburn and faced six batters. Five of them reached base and four of them scored as part of a five-run inning. The Twins got one of those runs back in the bottom of the seventh, but the Angels regained their five-run advantage in the top of the eighth when ex-Twin Torii Hunter hit a sacrifice fly.

Some in the crowd of 24,168 called it a night and left for home.

But the baseball gods had apparently seen enough misfortune in Minneapolis. In the bottom of the eighth, the Twins cuffed relievers Jose Arredondo and Scot Shields around, causing the exits to suddenly get clogged. After a pair of walks and a pair of singles, Denard Span, who had turned into a very reliable leadoff hitter, doubled up the right-center field alley past Hunter. Suddenly it was 9–7, and people were busy scrambling back to their seats.

Meanwhile, in the Twins dugout, manager Ron Gardenhire was suddenly hopeful. "Those were some great at-bats," he said later.

Reliever Jason Bulger entered and fanned Brandon Harris. Justin Morneau, who was the only Twin with more than one home run on the season, was intentionally walked to load the bases.

Angels	AB	R	H	RBI
Figgins 3b	5	2	3	0
Kendrick 2b	4	0	2	2
Izturis dh	5	1	0	1
Abreu rf	3	1	0	0
Hunter cf	3	1	1	1
Morales 1b	5	1	2	2
Napoli c	4	1	1	1
Rivera lf	4	1	1	0
Aybar ss	5	1	2	2
Totals	**38**	**9**	**12**	**9**

Twins	AB	R	H	RBI
Span cf-lf	5	1	2	2
Harris 2b	4	1	1	2
Casilla 2b	0	0	0	0
Morneau 1b	3	2	0	0
Kubel cf	5	2	4	5
Gomez lf	0	0	0	0
Cuddyer rf	5	1	2	0
Buscher dh	3	0	0	0
Crede 3b	3	1	1	1
Redmond c	4	0	2	1
Morales pr-c	0	1	0	0
Punto ss	3	2	1	0
Totals	**35**	**11**	**13**	**11**

LAA	0	0	0	3	0	5	1	0	-	9	12	1
MIN	1	0	1	0	0	1	1	7	X	-	11	13	1

Angels	IP	H	R	ER	BB	SO
Moseley	3.0	5	2	2	1	1
Speier	2.0	0	0	0	0	4
Rodriguez	1.1	4	2	1	1	0
Arredondo	1.0	1	2	2	1	2
Shields	0.0	2	3	3	1	0
Bulger L(0–1)	0.2	1	2	2	1	1
Totals	**8.0**	**13**	**11**	**10**	**5**	**8**

Twins	IP	H	R	ER	BB	SO
Blackburn	6.1	8	4	4	2	3
Crain	0.1	2	4	4	3	0
Guerrier W(1–0)	1.1	2	1	1	0	2
Nathan S(2)	1.0	0	0	0	0	1
Totals	**9.0**	**12**	**9**	**9**	**5**	**6**

E—Los Angeles Rodriguez; Minnesota Span. 2B—Los Angeles Hunter; Minnesota Kubel, Cuddyer, Span. 3B—Minnesota Kubel. HR—Minnesota Harris (1), Kubel (2). S—Los Angeles Kendrick. SF—Los Angeles Hunter; Minnesota Harris. LOB—Los Angeles 9; Minnesota 6. SB—Los Angeles Izturis, Figgins, Abreu 2; Minnesota Cuddyer. Attendance—24,168.

That brought up Jason Kubel, who was having a wonderful night at the plate. Kubel already had a single, a double, a triple and an RBI on his resume for the night. More importantly, after seeing Bulger toss a curveball on the first pitch that just missed the strike zone, he had an idea what the next pitch would be. Span, standing on second base, had a thought, too. "If you walk Morneau and pitch to Kubel, you're going to get your feelings hurt," he later told reporters.

Bulger, however, had little choice. So, he tried another curve. What happened next was:

1) Kubel took an "easy swing" and drilled the ball into the upper deck in right-center, settling in a couple of rows in front of the Kirby Puckett poster.

2) The grand slam gave the Twins an 11–9 lead and sent the crowd that hung around into hysterics.

3) It was the first cycle by a Twin at the Metrodome in more than two decades. The last Twin to do it? Puckett.

4) It was the first time in Kubel's life that he had hit for a cycle in any game he had ever played.

It also placed Kubel in a very exclusive club. It was just the third time in major league history a player had completed hitting for the cycle with a grand slam home run. (The other two to do it were a pair of shortstops. Tony Lazzeri, a member of baseball's Hall of Fame, did it in 1932 and Miguel Tejada, who might be there himself one day, achieved the same feat in 2001.)

Joe Nathan finished out the ninth with a six-pitch save and, at least for one night, the Twins had stopped the bleeding on what had become a very big sore.

No one was quite ready to say it was the type of game that could turn a season around. Gardenhire, a man who generally had a lot of things to say on many subjects, went the simple route this time when he talked to reporters after the game. "What a great comeback," he said. ―⁓―

The Blade Mows Them Down Easily

Tom Hall had enough to worry about without this. On the morning he was scheduled to start the home opener at Met Stadium, Hall was subject to a controversy over what he should be weighing. Seems owner Calvin Griffith had decided that 140 pounds wasn't enough for Hall's 6-foot frame. "We need him to gain weight to get stronger," Griffith maintained.

But manager Billy Martin had seen Hall when they were together in Denver, and he wasn't worried about such mundane stuff. By the end of this afternoon, everybody knew why. Although the Angels thought Hall might have been doctoring a few pitches, nobody could disagree with the results: a nifty two-hitter in a 6–0 victory that delighted 22,857 fans to no end. Jim Fregosi hit a first-inning triple and Lou Johnson had a seventh-inning single, but that was it for the Angels' offense for the day.

> ### At a Glance
> **WP:** Hall (1–0)
>
> **Key stats:** Hall pitches 2-hitter with 6 Ks

Meanwhile, Cesar Tovar, Tony Oliva, and Harmon Killebrew had two hits each, and the charitable Angels kicked in with three errors as the Twins scored twice each in the fourth, sixth, and eighth innings. Killebrew and Bob Allison also collaborated on an unusual double play in the fourth inning. Fregosi had led off with a walk. Johnson flew out to short left, and Allison's strong throw nailed Fregosi as he headed back to first. It was the type of aggressive defense that Martin had been preaching his team needed to play.

Hall took care of the rest, retiring the last eight batters in a row en route to the first complete game of his career. For one day at least, a 140-pounder threw like a heavyweight.

FOR A WHILE, HE WAS A CUTTING EDGE SORT OF GUY

Minnesota scout Jess Flores once called Tom Hall a "Negro Lefty Gomez." The North Carolinian never matched Gomez's numbers but, for a couple of seasons, he was one of the most versatile pitchers in the game and was a key factor in the Twins' back-to-back Western Division titles in 1969 and 1970. Martin had been his manager in Denver and he knew Hall had a resilient arm. So he had no problem using him in different roles. In 1969, Hall started 18 games and relieved in 13 others, racking up 140 innings and eight wins. The next season, he spent more time in the bullpen but still made 11 starts in 52 games and won 11 games with a nifty 2.55 ERA. When his production fell off the next season, Minnesota traded him to Cincinnati for reliever Wayne Granger. —⁕—

For One Night, He Played Like His Name

It was one of those bargain-basement transactions that looked promising. At 6-foot-3 and 244 pounds, Butch Huskey was a hulk of a guy who looked like he might be the team's answer to a power outage and the DH dilemma. He had hit 52 homers in three full seasons with the Mets and 22 in just 386 at-bats the year before with Seattle and Boston. The Twins signed him as a free agent during the winter. But he was off to a poor start and was hitting just .179 when he singled home the winning run in the bottom of the ninth inning for a victory over the Royals on April 19.

The good feeling carried over to the next game when Huskey went 3-for-4 and was part of an unusual power show in a 9–7 victory over the Royals. Huskey singled to open the second inning and eventually scored as Minnesota took an early 2–0 lead. The Royals came back quickly with three runs in the top of the third inning, but Denny Hocking, who hit just four home runs that season, went deep to tie the game at 3-all. Minnesota led 6–4 in the sixth when Jason Maxwell hit the first of two career home runs with the Twins. Matt Lawton, who did hit a few home runs in his career, followed suit. The next inning, Huskey also went out of the park, giving the Twins four home runs and enough for the victory.

> ## At a Glance
>
> **WP:** Bergman (1–0)
>
> **S:** Wells (2)
>
> **HR:** Hocking (1), Maxwell (1), Lawton (3), Huskey (2)
>
> **Key stats:** Huskey 3-for-4, RBI

Huskey had raised his average 50 points in two nights, giving the team hope he had turned the corner. Unfortunately, things didn't continue to get better for him and Huskey topped out at .246 at the end of May. In mid-July, the Twins sent him and Todd Walker to the Rockies in exchange for first baseman Todd Sears. —⁓—

Streak Stopper

The Twins were off to such a rough start that even perennially optimistic manager Billy Gardner had been reduced to saying, "Hopefully tomorrow." As far as pitcher John Butcher was concerned, more drastic action was needed to get the team going. "Somebody has to throw a M-80 into our dugout right now and wake us up," Butcher said prior to facing the A's.

The right-hander took his own advice, dominating from start to finish with a snappy three-hit, 2–0 complete game that simultaneously ended the Twins' nine-game losing streak and the A's six-game winning streak. Kirby Puckett's two-run single in the fifth inning was the only offense Butcher really needed.

Butcher won 24 games in 2½ seasons with the team. And it seemed like most of them came when the club was reeling with a losing streak. Although this was only his second year with the team, the three-hit gem marked the sixth time he had ended a losing streak of four or more games.

He may never have been more concise. Facing only one batter over the 27-player minimum, Butcher used only 81 pitches to shut down the A's. He walked none, fanned two and was helped by a double play and a caught stealing. It was the type of effort the Twins thought they might get a lot of when they acquired Butcher and Mike Smithson from Texas in a trade for outfielder Gary Ward and minor leaguer Sam Sorce. Although Butcher was a workhorse who started 67 games in his two full seasons with the team, the home-run ball victimized him often.

At a Glance

WP: Butcher (1–1)

Key stats: Butcher 3-hit shutout; Puckett 2-run single

Still, there were days like this one when Butcher showed flashes of brilliance that gave Gardner hope. Unfortunately for Gardner—and Butcher—flashes were all the Twins ever saw. Gardner was fired in June and Butcher was traded to Cleveland a year later.

HE HAD THEIR NUMBER, THOUGH

Butcher finished with an overall win-loss mark of 36–49 and a career ERA of 4.42. But there were two Hall of Famers who were thrilled when he retired from baseball after the 1986 season. Rickey Henderson hit just .200 (3-for-15) against Butcher. But he looked like a power source compared to Reggie Jackson, who managed only a .111 lifetime mark (3-for-27) with no home runs and 13 strikeouts. The latter figure is easily the best individual figure for Butcher, who only had 363 career whiffs in 833 2/3 MLB innings. —∞—

Home Never Felt This Warm in April Before

Rarely had a team been anxious to get home. The Twins opened the 1980 season with a monster 12-game road trip to Oakland, California, and Seattle. They hit .222 as a team, didn't record a save until the final game of the trip and considered themselves fortunate to be just 5–7 when they arrived for their latest home opener ever. The average high in the Twin Cities for April 22 is 62 degrees. On this afternoon, however, temperatures, beer sales, and the Twins' bats soared together.

The team set a record with 61,000 beers sold to 36,628 spectators on an 89-degree day. Owner Calvin Griffith had given in to the times and allowed taped music to be played for the first time. The combination must have had some kind of effect on the Twins. Roy Smalley hit a two-run homer in the first inning and Hosken Powell, off to a flying start, added a solo shot in the fifth. Rick Sofield, who had been hitless in his previous 23 plate appearances, had two hits.

> ## At a Glance
>
> **WP:** Zahn (2–1)
>
> **HR:** Smalley (5), Powell (1), Jackson (1)
>
> **Key Stats:** Powell 3-for-4, 2 RBI; Zahn complete-game 6-hitter

Things went so well that Ron Jackson, who had been 0-for-20 for the season, homered in the eighth inning to cap the day's scoring. Geoff Zahn lowered his ERA to 1.37 with a no-walk, six-hit complete game. As far as manager Gene Mauch was concerned, it was about as perfect a day as possible.

There was, however, one problem. Seems many of the vendors couldn't even get up the ramps to the seats before having to return to get more supplies. By the seventh inning, the place was dry as a bone—no beer could be found anywhere. "We just couldn't keep up," admitted Twins exec Jimmy Robertson later. It was about the only downside to an otherwise glorious day at the ballpark.

THE SECOND ACT WASN'T AS MUCH FUN, BUT IT WAS STILL NOTABLE

The vendors had no trouble with their supplies the next day. But that was about the only thing that went right. Although it was another beautiful day, just 4,772 showed up. The few who came saw history . . . but didn't know it at the time. California's Bruce Kison was on top of his game that day and carried a no-hitter into the ninth inning. The Angels had battered three Twins' pitchers around easily in the first eight innings. In the ninth, an error by Smalley opened the floodgates for seven more runs. All that was left was to see if the team would be no-hit at home for the first time ever. Smalley popped out to start the bottom of the ninth before Ken Landreaux ended the drama with a double to left field.

It turned out to be the first game of a team-record 31-game hitting streak.

—m—

Not Your Standard Night at the Ballpark

It started out like another long night at the Kingdome. The Twins, who had dropped six of their previous seven games, had fallen behind 3–0 in the first inning when starting pitcher Roger Erickson was rocked for five hits. John Castino hit his first home run of the season to lead off the second inning, and Bobby Mitchell, batting just .160 at the time, followed with a double. Ron Washington then singled, and the game turned around in a hurry. Before the inning was done, the Twins had knocked Edwin Nunez out of the box and took off to a totally unexpected 12–4 victory.

At a Glance

WP: Erickson (2–2)

HR: Castino (1), Mitchell (1)

Key stats: Washington 4-for-5; Erickson 13-hitter

There were all sorts of unusual happenings on this night before a sparse house of 5,665 in the Kingdome. Mitchell hit the first home run of his MLB career. Washington, who was starting the season in the majors for the first time in a 12-year career, had four hits. Rob Wilfong, who entered the game with a meager .073 batting average, had three RBIs and a pair of hits. In the first 16 games of the season, Castino, Wilfong, and catcher Butch Wynegar had combined for just six RBIs. On this night, they had eight between them. And so it went. All told, each member of the starting lineup had at least one hit in a season-high 18-hit attack.

Erickson should not be forgotten as part of this unusual equation. He recovered from his tough opening inning to pitch one of the oddest complete games in team history—a 13-hitter with no strikeouts. The 13 hits allowed rank just two short of the team record for any pitcher in a game. Although he allowed hits in every inning except the sixth, he was rarely in danger and there was no consideration of ever taking him out of the game.

All in all, it was an odd night at the ballpark and one of the few pleasurable moments in the 1982 season. —⁓—

Did You Know?

Odd but true: the 13 hits Roger Erickson allowed in that complete game victory were the most he surrendered in a MLB game in his career. It also marked the only complete game of his career in which he did not record a strikeout.

John Castino, the American League Rookie of the Year in 1979, was a key member of the Twins' infield in the early 1980s.

Minnesota 24, Detroit 11

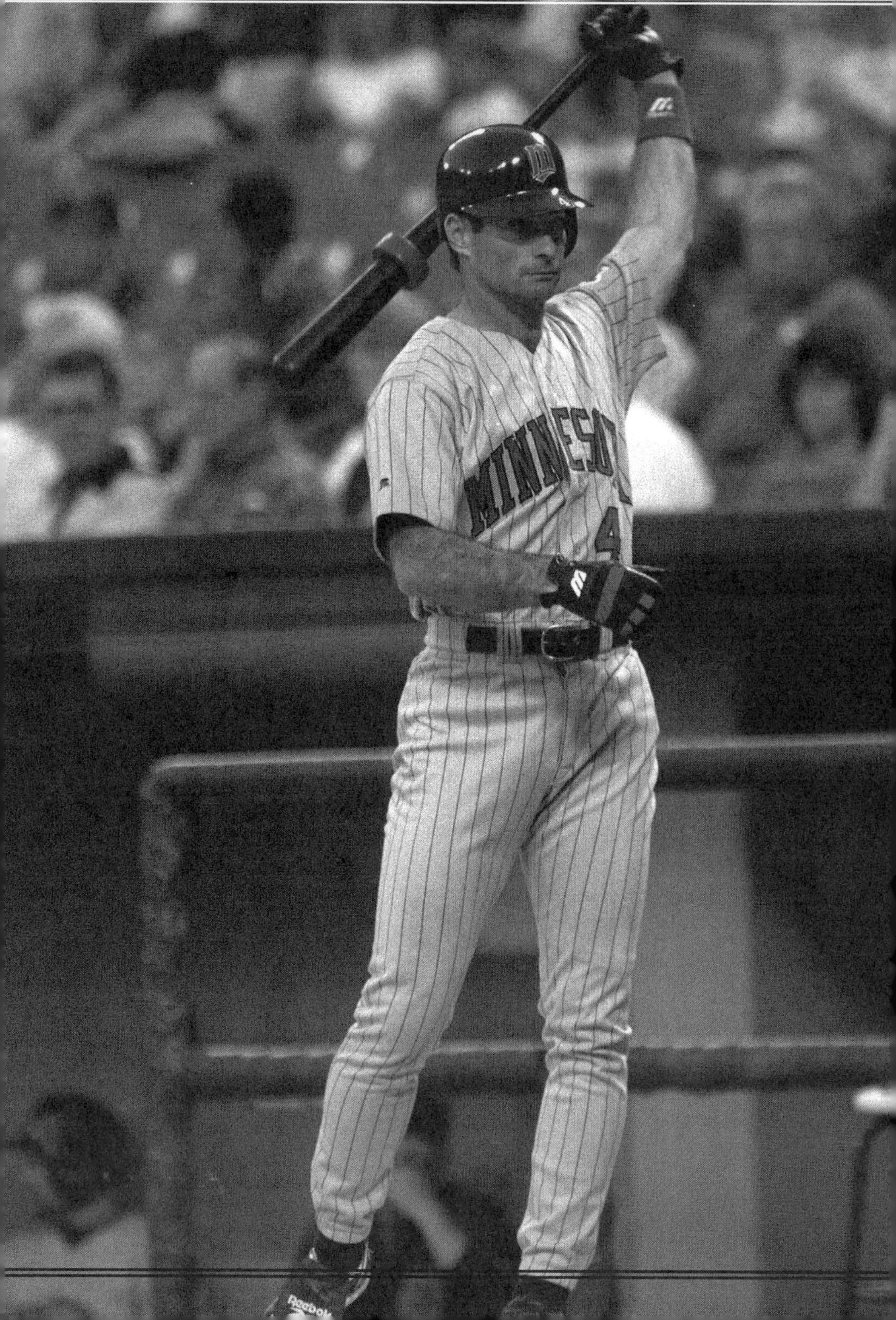

A Wild Day at the Corner

There never was another game like it in the 87 years they played major league baseball at the corner of Michigan and Trumbull. The teams had combined for 53 runs in a three-game series that opened the season at the Metrodome. For a while on this afternoon, it appeared they might match that figure. When all was said and done, the teams combined for 35 runs, 33 hits and 15 walks. The winning pitcher found out about it on TV. The winning team's starting pitcher gave up more runs than any of the losing team's seven pitchers. And the one guy who pitched and emerged scar-free with three scoreless innings didn't figure in the decision.

The score? Minnesota 24, Detroit 11.

Sighed Twins' manager Tom Kelly: "About the only good thing about this game is we won."

That wasn't exactly true, however. Paul Molitor scored five runs and had five RBIs for the only time in his 2,683-game career. (He gave way to pinch-hitter Chip Hale, who promptly hit a three-run home run. Thus, the Twins' designated hitters for the day were a productive 3-for-6 with six runs scored and eight RBIs). Another "M" guy—catcher Greg Myers—had an equally unusual pairing of five, finishing with that total of hits and RBIs. Myers and Marty Cordova each scored three runs in the game. That was only good for third place behind Molitor and Matt Lawton, who crossed home plate four times. It was that kind of day at the old ballpark.

The Twins came out swinging, jumping to a 7–2 lead in the third inning. But that was not enough for starter Frankie Rodriguez. By the end of the third inning, Rodriguez was gone and so was the lead. Detroit had pushed the margin to 10–7, but the Twins regained the lead in the fifth inning on a truly weird play. The bases were loaded when Scott Stahoviak drilled a ball to left-center. Two runners had already

Paul Molitor scored five runs and had five RBIs for the only time in his career during a 24–11 victory over the Detroit Tigers on April 24, 1996.

Twins	AB	R	H	RBI
Knoblauch 2b	0	1	0	0
Reboulet 2b-3b	3	2	0	0
Lawton cf	6	4	4	1
Molitor dh	5	5	2	5
Hale ph-dh-2b	1	1	1	3
Cordova lf	4	3	2	1
Myers c	6	3	5	5
Hollins 3b	4	2	1	2
Durant ph	1	0	0	0
Stahoviak 1b	3	1	1	3
Coomer ph-1b	3	0	1	1
Meares ss	5	2	2	1
Becker rf	5	0	0	0
Totals	**46**	**24**	**19**	**22**

Tigers	AB	R	H	RBI
Curtis cf	3	0	0	1
Hyers lf-1b	4	1	1	0
Fryman 3b	3	2	1	0
Fielder 1b	4	1	2	0
Bautista ph-lf	1	0	0	0
Higginson rf	5	2	4	3
E. Williams dh	5	1	1	3
M. Lewis 2b	5	3	3	3
Flaherty c	5	1	1	1
Trammell ss	3	0	1	0
Gomez ss	0	0	0	0
Totals	**38**	**11**	**14**	**11**

MIN	3	3	1	0	4	3	2	5	3	-	24	19 0
DET	2	0	6	2	0	0	0	0	1	-	11	14 3

Twins	IP	H	R	ER	BB	SO
Rodriguez	2	6	6	6	2	1
Mahomes	0.2	3	2	2	0	0
Bennett W(1–0)	1.1	3	2	2	0	2
Naulty	3	0	0	0	1	4
Parra	2	2	1	1	0	2
Totals	**9**	**14**	**11**	**11**	**3**	**9**

Tigers	IP	H	R	ER	BB	SO
Sodowsky	1.1	2	5	5	3	1
Maxcy	2.2	4	4	4	1	1
Veres L(0–2)	1.1	2	4	3	2	2
Myers	0.2	3	2	2	2	0
R. Lewis	1	1	1	1	1	0
B. Williams	1	4	5	3	2	1
Christopher	1	3	3	3	1	0
Totals	**9**	**19**	**24**	**21**	**12**	**5**

E—Detroit Higginson, Flaherty, Trammell. DP—Minnesota 1. 2B—Minnesota Stahoviak, Myers 2, Lawton; Detroit Higginson 2, Flaherty, Hyers, Trammell. 3B—Minnesota Molitor. HR—Minnesota Molitor (2), Hollins (4), Hale (1); Detroit E. Williams (2), M. Lewis 2 (4). SH—Detroit Curtin. SF—Minnesota Myers; Detroit Curtis. HBP—Minnesota Knoblauch; Detroit—Fryman. LOB—Minnesota 9; Detroit 6. SB—Minnesota Molitor, Meares; Detroit M. Lewis. Attendance—12,189.

scored when Detroit shortstop Alan Trammell took a relay and tried to cut down the tying run at the plate. It was too late for that, so Detroit catcher John Flaherty stepped in front of the plate, grabbed the ball and, seeing Stahoviak heading for third base, threw it in that direction. Good idea. Lousy execution. Third baseman Travis Fryman didn't see the ball coming and left fielder Tim Hyers didn't back up the play. As a result, the ball ended up in the left-field corner as Stahoviak got up and scampered home with the kind of run not seen by most players since their Little League days.

From there, it was all Minnesota. The Twins scored three more in the sixth, two in the seventh, five in the eighth and three more in the ninth.

Dan Naulty, the fourth Twins' pitcher, had been the one hurler of note, tossing three scoreless, hitless innings. But since Erik Bennett, who had been singed for a two-run homer by Mark Lewis in the fourth inning, was the pitcher of record when Stahoviak's mischievous at-bat occurred, he ended up being the winning pitcher. As it turned out, it was one of just two MLB wins for Bennett (his other one, weirdly, came in his next outing three days later in New York). He only appeared in 24 games that season.

The Twins' run total of 24 (as well as the combined figure of 35) still stands as a single-game mark. It is also the most runs the Tigers have allowed in a game since a famous 1912 game when the team was forced to use a bunch of collegians for one day. (The regulars were protesting a suspension handed out to Ty Cobb.) The combined run total was the most in an MLB game since a wind-blown day in 1979 at Chicago's Wrigley Field produced 45 runs.

It was the start of a brief but enjoyable stay in Motown for the Twins. The next day, Stahoviak hit a home run the old-fashioned way and the Twins slammed 15 hits in an easy 11–1 romp to finish off the two-game set. As often happens in baseball, however, things evened out. On the Twins' next visit to Tiger Stadium, they got shut out on consecutive days. —∞—

Did You Know?

After gaining his only career big league victories in consecutive appearances against Detroit and New York, Erik Bennett earned his only big league save in his next outing. On April 29, 1996, he retired all four batters he faced to get the save in an 11–6 victory over Kansas City.

A 7–6–7 Putout at Third Base Helps Save a Win

It has been said that every trip to a major league game may provide spectators with something they have never seen before. What happened on this Saturday afternoon at Met Stadium takes that dictum to a new level.

Under most circumstances, the storyline of the day would be the Twins taking advantage of a rare error by Detroit right fielder Al Kaline in the bottom of the ninth inning that led to the winning run in Minnesota's 4–3 victory. But that occurrence was overshadowed by one of the oddest events ever to take place on a diamond.

The game was humming along nicely into the seventh inning. Tony Oliva and Rich Reese had hit solo home runs for the Twins, and Mickey Stanley had hit one for Detroit. As per his custom, Jim Kaat was leaving base runners everywhere as he nursed the 2–1 lead.

Detroit pitcher Earl Wilson, a good hitter, swung and missed for what appeared to be the third out in the top of the seventh when the baseball gods intervened.

It seemed that Twins' catcher Paul Ratliff had not caught Kaat's pitch in the air. However, he rolled the ball back to the mound and headed to the dugout. Detroit third base coach Grover Resinger, however, knew his rules and told Wilson to start jogging toward first base. The rest of the Twins took no notice as Wilson rounded first base and started for second. By now, Resinger was in the middle of the field waving Wilson on.

Twins outfielder Brant Alyea, however, had figured out what was going on and ran to get the ball near the mound. But Alyea had trouble picking the ball up and Wilson kept running, rounding third base and heading for home plate. For reasons even he couldn't explain later, Minnesota shortstop Leo Cardenas suddenly ran to cover the plate. Once he got his hands on the ball, Alyea threw it in his direction.

Tigers	AB	R	H	RBI
Stanley 1b	3	1	2	1
McAuliffe 2b	4	0	0	0
Kaline rf	4	0	0	0
Horton lf	4	1	2	0
Freehan c	3	0	0	0
Northrup cf	4	1	1	1
Maddox 3b	3	0	2	0
Cash ph	0	0	0	1
Wert 3b	0	0	0	0
Gutierrez ss	3	0	0	0
Wilson p	3	0	1	0
Timmermann p	0	0	0	0
Totals	**31**	**3**	**8**	**3**

Twins	AB	R	H	RBI
Tovar cf	4	0	0	0
Cardenas ss	4	0	0	0
Oliva rf	4	2	2	1
Killebrew 3b	4	0	1	1
Reese 1b	3	1	1	1
Alyea lf	3	0	1	0
Holt lf	0	0	0	0
Ratliff c	3	1	1	0
Quilici 2b	3	0	1	0
Kaat p	2	0	0	1
Williams p	0	0	0	0
Totals	**30**	**4**	**7**	**4**

DET	0	0	0	0	0	1	0	0	2	-	3	8 1
MIN	0	0	0	2	0	0	0	1	1	-	4	7 2

Tigers	IP	H	R	ER	BB	SO
Wilson	6	3	2	2	0	2
Timmermann L(0–1)	2.1	4	2	1	0	1
Totals	**8.1**	**7**	**4**	**3**	**0**	**3**

Twins	IP	H	R	ER	BB	SO
Kaat	8.1	8	3	3	2	5
Williams W(2–0)	0.2	0	0	0	0	0
Totals	**9**	**8**	**3**	**3**	**2**	**5**

E—Detroit Kaline; Minnesota Oliva, Ratliff. DP—Minnesota 3. 2B—Detroit Wilson; Minnesota Alyea, Ratliff. 3B—Detroit Northrup. HR—Detroit Stanley (1); Minnesota Oliva (3), Reese (1). SH—Detroit—Gutierrez. SF—Detroit Cash. LOB—Detroit 5; Minnesota 2. CS—Minnesota Quilici. Attendance—11,095.

Wilson was a big man (6-foot-3, 216 pounds) and this trip around the bases had been rather exhausting. Halfway home, Wilson spotted trouble and headed back to third. But he pulled a hamstring in the process and collapsed to the ground before he could get to the bag. Cardenas tossed the ball back to Alyea, who tagged out the prone pitcher in the baseline. Officially, the play read this way: *Wilson struck out on an error by Ratliff [Wilson out at third (left to shortstop to left)]*. Afterward the umpires referred all inquisitors to Rule 6.09(b), which says that when a batter becomes a runner on a third strike not caught, he may advance to first base before he enters the bench area. Home plate ump John Rice conceded that Resinger probably shouldn't have been on the field, but since he wasn't physically assisting Wilson, he let it slide.

As it turned out, it all ended well for the Twins. Wilson couldn't stay in the game with the injury and was replaced by Tom Timmerman. Minnesota added a run in the eighth inning but Detroit knocked Kaat out of the game with two in the top of the ninth to tie the game at 3-all. In the bottom of the inning, however, Oliva singled and moved to second when Kaline, who won ten Gold Gloves in a stellar 21-year career, muffed the ball for an error. Harmon Killebrew promptly singled home Oliva, ending one of the wackiest games in team history.

It was the sort of event that, had it happened today, would be replayed for years to come. Although that particular game was televised back to Detroit, the cameras were silent during the Wilson escapade because of commercials that were airing. All that could be done was have the announcers retell the tale when they came back on the air. In this case, the words turn out to paint a pretty good picture. —⁓—

All's Well That (Eventually) Ends Well

One of the first things young managers learn is the value of patience. The events of this afternoon's game, however, may have tested Twins' manager Ron Gardenhire's composure to the extreme.

In the end, it all worked out in a 1–0, 11-inning victory over Kansas City. But it wasn't easy.

This might have the toughest 1–0 game in major league history. In the second inning, Torii Hunter's jaw collided with a Zack Greinke fastball. Hunter didn't care much for it, took a few threatening steps to discuss the matter with Greinke, and then fell into a heap near home plate. He left the game, took three stitches at the nearby hospital, and was dressed for the road trip by game's end.

In the fourth inning, catcher Mike Redmond dropped like a sack of potatoes when Tony Pena Jr. hit him in the shoulder with his backswing. He staggered to his feet and, as it turned out, fortunately stayed in the game.

Boof Bonser, the team's starter that day, had been struggling to keep the ball in the park, allowing seven home runs in his first four starts of the season. Keeping it in the park was not a problem on this afternoon. Putting it in the strike zone was.

At a Glance

WP: Rincon (1–0)

Key stat: Morneau scores in bottom of 11th on Redmond's game-winning single

In five innings, he only allowed three hits but walked seven batters (including loading the bases one inning). Thanks to some timely fielding, he managed to escape unscathed.

At that point, Gardenhire had seen enough and started sending in replacements. By game's end, the Twins had walked 10 batters but given up just five hits, stranding 14 Kansas City runners.

The only inning in which the Royals went down in order was the 11th. In the bottom of the inning, Redmond mercifully ended the game with a game-winning single. Normally, this is a cause for great celebration. Redmond was happy the game was over but had a simple request for his teammates: "Don't pound me on the back. My shoulder still hurts like hell." —⋙—

Erickson Stops Brewers Cold

There was little to suggest in advance to the 17,988 who filed into the Metrodome on this spring night that something special was about to occur. The Twins were staggering in last place in the AL Central with a 7–14 win-loss mark. Scott Erickson, the mercurial starting pitcher for that night's game with Milwaukee, had lost three games in a row and his ERA had ballooned to an unseemly 7.48.

But baseball is a game of evening up. And so it was that Erickson, who lost 19 games in 1993, reverted to his 1991 form (when he won 20 games) and retired the first 10 batters he faced. His teammates were piling up runs as well. Before anybody on the Brewers could really get a feel for things, Erickson was in his groove. When he was done, he had tossed the team's first no-hitter in 27 seasons, a 6–0 gem.

"I would never have thought a no-hitter could get tossed in this building," Twins general manager Andy MacPhail said to the media after the game. "But if anybody could do it, it would be Scott. He has that kind of stuff when he's right. But you can never predict this sort of game."

For his part, Erickson reflected back on his 1991 success, when he played a major role in the team's second World Series championship. "In the ninth inning, I pretended it was the first inning of the World Series," he told reporters.

In the first eight innings, Erickson was in such complete command that there were no close calls in the field. When he went to the mound for the final inning, he had walked just two and hit one batter. In the ninth, he retired the first two batters but then walked Bill Spiers and Turner Ward. That brought up Greg Vaughn, the powerful DH who had slugged 30 home runs the season before. With the count 2–1, Vaughn was fooled on Erickson's 129th pitch of the night but got

Scott Erickson

A fourth-round pick in 1989, he quickly made it to the big club for a short but lively run. In 1991, he won 20 games in just 32 starts. The next year, he went 13–10, his last winning season with the team. In 1994, however, he etched his name in the history books with the team's first no-hitter in 27 seasons, a 6–0 win over Milwaukee. His seven career shutouts place him tied for seventh place all-time in team history.

Scott Erickson threw the first no-hitter for the Twins in nearly 30 years on April 27, 1994, in a 6–0 win over Milwaukee.

enough of his bat on it to loft the ball down the left-field line toward what appeared to be no-man's land. Shortstop Pat Meares and left fielder Alex Cole took off at top speed in pursuit. Cole got there first, catching the ball in fair territory and then surviving a mini-collision with Meares. When he came up showing the ball, everybody—including Erickson—was able to breathe again.

"There was never any doubt I would catch it," Cole said later. "I was calling Pat off but he didn't hear me until my last yell."

Erickson, who was known for remaining calm (too calm for some people's taste), seemed relieved more than anything. "I didn't really feel that good starting the game," he told the media. "The first two guys hit bullets. But my grip on the slider felt different, a little better."

As per tradition, the Twins stayed away from Erickson for the most part during the game. Finally, Erickson wandered over to catcher Matt Walbeck for some conversation. "He started talking to me between innings to break the ice," Walbeck said. "I didn't initiate any conversations. The rhythm he was in, I thought it was best to let him just keep going."

As for offensive support, the Twins had a steady attack on Milwaukee right-hander Jaime Navarro. The top five hitters in the batting order knocked in all the runs. Kent Hrbek hit an early home run. Kirby Puckett had four hits, Chuck Knoblauch chipped in with three and DH Dave Winfield had two RBIs. They were all fine numbers, but Erickson was the story of the night.

Puckett, who was in the midst of a nine-game hitting streak that would raise his batting average 34 points, understood this perfectly. "Man, I get four hits and nobody wants to talk to me," he joked with reporters afterward. "I am very happy for Scotty. I was nervous, too. I would have been squeezing hard if any ball was hit to me in the last couple innings."

PROMISE PARTIALLY FULFILLED

The problem with being terrific early in your career is everybody expects you to do it year after year. Erickson made a big first impression on the Twins, allowing just one run on four hits in six innings in his debut with the team in June 1990. He won eight games that season and tied for the league lead in victories with 20 in the happy season of 1991. Although he would go on to a solid major league career, he would never duplicate that figure again. ―⌐∿―

Brewers	AB	R	H	RBI
Diaz cf	4	0	0	0
Spiers ss	2	0	0	0
Ward lf	3	0	0	0
Vaughn dh	4	0	0	0
Nilsson c	2	0	0	0
Seitzer 3b	3	0	0	0
Harper rf	3	0	0	0
Jaha 1b	2	0	0	0
Valentin 2b	2	0	0	0
Reed ph	1	0	0	0
Totals	26	0	0	0

Twins	AB	R	H	RBI
Cole lf	5	1	1	1
Knoblauch 2b	5	2	3	1
Puckett rf	5	0	4	1
Hrbek 1b	3	1	1	1
Winfield dh	3	0	1	2
Walbeck c	4	0	1	0
Leius 3b	5	0	0	0
Becker cf	3	1	1	0
Meares ss	4	1	1	0
Totals	37	6	13	6

```
MIL  0 0 0 0 0 0 0 0 0 - 0 0 0
MIN  1 1 1 2 0 0 0 1 x - 6 13 0
```

Brewers	IP	H	R	ER	BB	SO
Navarro L(1–2)	4	9	5	5	3	1
Henry	1.2	1	0	0	1	2
Orosco	1.1	0	0	0	1	1
Fetters	1	3	1	1	0	0
Totals	8	13	6	6	5	4

Twins	IP	H	R	ER	BB	SO
Erickson W(2–3)	9	0	0	0	4	5

DP—Minnesota 1. 2B—Minnesota Puckett 2. 3B—Minnesota Cole. HR—Minnesota Hrbek (2). HBP—Minnesota Walbeck; Milwakee Jaha. LOB— Minnesota 13, Milwaukee 4. SB—Minnesota Becker, Walbeck. Attendance—17,988.

Keeping a Streak Alive (Thankfully)

The Minnesota Twins should have been happy to see the Baltimore Orioles come to town. The defending World Series champs were off to a tepid 5–11 start, and the Birds were the only team in the league who had fewer wins.

That, however, was the problem. The Orioles had opened the season with 18 straight losses and were threatening the AL record for futility at the start of a season. The Twins didn't want to be the team that ended the streak.

The first two games had been close affairs with Minnesota holding off late rallies for victories. By the final game of the series—the one that could establish the record at 21 games—it was hard to tell who was the more anxious team.

At a Glance

WP: Anderson (1–0)

S: Portugal (1)

HR: Hrbek (4)

Key stats: Hrbek 3-for-3, 2 RBIs

As had been the case in the first two games of the series, the Orioles jumped into a lead before the Twins even got to bat. It was still 1–0 in the fourth inning when Kent Hrbek's two-run homer gave the Twins a lead. John Moses' two-run double in the sixth inning made it a seemingly safe 4–1 margin. In the seventh, starter Allan Anderson walked two batters and gave way to reliever Mike Mason, who fared no better and walked in a run. Things suddenly looked dicey. Ace reliever Jeff Reardon wasn't available. The ball was given to Mark Portugal, who had been in town less than 24 hours.

All Portugal had to do was retire veterans Fred Lynn and Cal Ripken Jr. with the potential lead run on base.

Portugal did just that as Lynn struck out and Ripken flied to left to end the threat. Portugal gave up solo hits in the next two innings, but got the outs he needed, and the Twins, 4–2 winners, happily sent the Orioles out of town.

As it turned out, it was just in time. The Orioles ended their streak the next night with a 9–0 win at Chicago. —

Did You Know?

Mark Portugal continued to have Cal Ripken's number. The Hall of Famer managed just one hit—a single—in six career at-bats against Portugal.

A Picky Way to End a Game

If any team knew how to deal with Stan Williams in 1970, one would assume it would be the Cleveland Indians. After all, he had spent the previous four seasons in their employ. Over the winter, however, he had been part of a six-player deal that would prove to be a major factor in the Twins' second consecutive Western Division title.

On this day, however, Williams turned on his old team by recording a save in a most unusual fashion.

For most of the afternoon, the starting pitchers—Cleveland's Rich Hand and Minnesota's Jim Kaat—dominated the game. The Twins had nicked Hand for a third-inning run when Tony Oliva scored on an error by third baseman Graig Nettles, an ex-Twin. After that, they did nothing offensively for the rest of the day.

As the game entered the ninth, Kaat had allowed just one runner as far as third base and was working on a five-hit shutout. He retired the first two batters easily, but Tony Horton doubled and Roy Foster walked.

Enter Williams, who had recorded 25 wins and 22 saves during his tenure in Cleveland. The Indians knew his pitches well, but they apparently forgot about one other part of Williams' bag of tricks. Vada Pinson, a dangerous hitter, was at the plate. He fouled off one pitch but never got to see another one. That's because Williams suddenly threw a nifty pickoff throw to second baseman Frank Quilici, who snapped the tag on Horton to end the game.

> ### At a Glance
> **WP:** Kaat (3–1)
>
> **S:** Williams (1)
>
> **Key stat:** Oliva scored only run

"When I was in the National League, I got Stan Musial twice and Roberto Clemente that way," Williams explained later. "I saw the opening and thought it was worth a try."

As it turned out, Williams was one of the great acquisitions of the season. He was a workhorse in the bullpen, posting a 10–1 win-loss mark with a 1.99 ERA and 15 saves. And he had a nasty pickoff move to boot. ⟞⟋

Mr. Consistency Caps a Great Month

He rarely impressed anybody with his velocity, but Brad Radke always got opponents' attention by doing things the old-fashioned way. He simply beat them. The master of the circle changeup capped off a terrific month personally (5–0, matching Geoff Zahn's 1977 start to the season) and the best April in team history with a typically efficient performance. The Twins' 2–1 victory over the Yankees gave them an 18–6 win-loss record in April, their best effort ever out of the gate.

"He can throw any pitch at any time to any batter," marveled Derek Jeter, who went 0-for-4 that night as Radke stifled the Yankees on six hits. Tino Martinez homered for the lone New York run. The rest of the night, the Yankees were held to five singles and a walk.

Meanwhile, the Twins nibbled at Andy Pettitte just enough to get a pair of runs. In the second inning, David Ortiz doubled and Doug Mientkiewicz singled him home. In the seventh inning, Mientkiewicz took things into his own hands with a solo home run that broke the tie and ended the scoring.

It was a tight margin but Radke, who had walked only four batters in his first 48 innings of work, had enough to work on. After the Martinez homer, the Yankees never got a runner past first base.

It was a typical brisk Radke performance—the type of game Twins fans got used to in a 12-year career that saw him retire after the 2006 season with 148 career victories in 377 career starts.

A NICE CLUB TO BE A MEMBER OF

Radke's first major league appearance was as a reliever against Baltimore in 1995. He moved into the starting rotation the next week and stayed there for the rest of his career. A tremendously consistent presence, he won 20 games in 1997 (for a team that went just 68–94) and finished with a 148–139 win-loss record with a 4.22 ERA. His last appearance was a four-inning start in the 2006 playoffs against Oakland. He retired that winter after deciding against surgery to repair a torn labrum.

In doing so, Radke managed to earn an unusual note. He became the first American League pitcher (and just the second one ever) to retire after a postseason appearance after starting 300 games for just one franchise. The NL pitcher who did that? Sandy Koufax. —

A Rare Quiet Sunday in Downtown Boston

Next to Yankee Stadium, the Twins' roughest place to visit historically has been Fenway Park. In the World Series year of 1987, Minnesota won just one of six games there. Things weren't off to a much better start the next season. On Minnesota's first visit, the Twins dropped the first two games of a weekend set. Then Frank Viola came along and put an end to the misery. Although the majority of the 31,124 who were on hand that afternoon might disagree, Viola seemed like "Sweet Music," indeed, throwing a nifty five-hitter in a 2–0 victory.

Rarely has there been a simpler game played in the old bandbox. In the second inning, with runners on first and third and nobody out, Tim Laudner bounced into a double play that scored the only run the Twins would need. Gary Gaetti added a solo home run two innings later and the scoring was done for the day. Kirby Puckett had a single to extend his hitting streak to 14 games. But that was about it for offense. It was a rare peaceful Sunday afternoon at Fenway . . . and Viola was the main reason why. The normally raucous Fenway fans could only watch in disbelief. Never did silence sound so nice.

In tossing the first complete game by a visiting lefty at Fenway in four years, Viola threw just 29 balls out of 111 pitches. The Red Sox advanced only one runner as far as third base all afternoon. Suddenly, all the worries about the team's starting rotation seemed much ado about nothing. Still, the lefty told the media afterward that it wasn't as easy as it appeared to be. "In this ballpark, you never feel comfortable," he said. Looks can be deceiving.

Frank Viola

He was, indeed, "Sweet Music" for most of his tenure with the Twins. A former No. 2 draft choice, he fast-tracked his way to the bigs in one year and was a key member of the 1987 World Series champs, earning MVP honors for winning two games. The next year, he won 24 games (second most in team history) and took home the Cy Young Award as the top pitcher in the AL. A workhorse, he ranks fifth all-time on the team's list for innings pitched and strikeouts.

On May 1, 1988, Frank Viola turned up the "Sweet Music" for Twins fans by throwing a complete-game five-hitter against the Red Sox. Viola threw 29 balls out of 111 pitches.

A MEMORABLE MAY

As it turned out, Viola's gem was the start of some very good things to come. Although the Twins lost their next three games after Viola's shutout, the club went 17–10 for the month, moving from sixth to second place. Viola's May numbers are among the best one-month totals in team history. The southpaw won all six of his starts with a 1.53 ERA, including a pair of shutouts against the Red Sox and two wins against a free-swinging Detroit team. In 47 innings, he walked only six batters and struck out 39. Viola was named to the All-Star team at midseason and, by year's end, ended up with career highs in victories with 24 (three better than Oakland's Dave Stewart) and a 2.64 ERA. His season was capped by winning his only Cy Young Award. Unfortunately, his time in Minnesota ended the next season when he was traded to the New York Mets. ⟿

Did You Know?

Frank Viola was a key player in both of the Twins' championships, even though he only played in one World Series. Two seasons after helping the Twins win the 1987 World Series, Viola was traded to the New York Mets in a deal that helped set the stage for the 1991 triumph.

On July 31, 1989, the Twins traded Viola to the New York Mets in exchange for five pitchers. Two of those—starter Kevin Tapani and reliever Rick Aguilera—went on to play prominent roles for the 1991 Twins. Tapani was a key member of the team's starting rotation, and Aguilera was its closer.

As for Viola, he went on to have some success in New York (he won 20 games and threw nearly 250 innings in 1990) and later recorded 24 victories in two full seasons for the Red Sox. But he never quite got the form back he showed in Minnesota.

On May 23, 1996, he was pitching for the Toronto Blue Jays when he faced the Twins at SkyDome. He gave up four runs in 5 1/3 innings, including surrendering a two-run homer to Roberto Kelly. He pitched just one more game for the Blue Jays before retiring from the game for good.

A Record-Setting Power Performance for Twins

This wasn't exactly what Kansas City owner Charlie Finley had in mind. In an attempt to poke fun at Yankee Stadium's short right-field porch, he built a "One-Half Pennant Porch" that was supposed to help the A's. The move achieved one goal: the 239 home runs hit at Municipal Stadium in 1964 led the league by a wide margin. (Met Stadium was second with 203.) But the overall results seemed to benefit the visiting teams.

On this night, for example, the Twins tied a pair of home run records in a weird, wild 7–3, 11-inning victory. Tony Oliva and Harmon Killebrew hit two each with Bob Allison and Jimmie Hall contributing one apiece. That foursome went back-to-back-to-back-to-back in the 11th inning, just the third time in MLB history that had occurred.

At a Glance

WP: Arrigo (1–0)

HR: Oliva 2 (4), Killebrew 2 (4), Allison (4), Hall (3)

Key stat: Twins hit 6 HR in game, including 4 in a row in top of 11th inning

Early on, it appeared like this would be a quiet Saturday night. Oliva's two-run shot in the third inning off the wonderfully named Aurelio Monteagudo gave the Twins a 2–0 lead. That score lasted until the seventh inning when Charlie Lau, who would later gain considerable fame as a hitting coach, tripled home a pair of runs to tie the game off Minnesota starter Lee Stange.

In the ninth, Killebrew, who had been battling a 1-for-17 slump, homered off reliever John Wyatt for a 3–2 lead. However, Rocky Colavito singled home a run off ace reliever Bill Dailey in the bottom of the inning to send the game into overtime.

The A's Dan Pfister, working in just his second game of the season, had an uneventful 10th inning and a nightmarish 11th frame. It started when Oliva hit a 3–2 pitch into Finley's mini-porch in right for his second homer of the night. Allison worked the count to 3–2 and then followed suit with a shot to left. Pfister was now a bundle of nerves as he threw three straight balls to Hall. The fourth pitch was in the strike zone and Hall quickly slapped it over the right-field fence for a 6–3 lead. That brought in rookie Vern Handrahan, who had never faced Killebrew before. Their meeting was brief—just one pitch that went far over the left-field fence. In a matter of minutes, the Twins had broken a tight game apart and had earned an unusual niche in the MLB record book. —᠕᠊

A Bright Memory in a Dark Season

The 1995 season didn't have many fond memories attached to it. The remnants of the 1994 strike that ended the season prematurely lingered, and the new campaign didn't start until the last week of April. The Twins lost their season opener 9–0 at Boston and struggled all the way, finishing up with a 56–88 win-loss mark and a horrid 44 games out of first place.

But one of the moments of pure joy came on an early May night at the Metrodome. A game that started out like it would be a disaster ended up as a thrilling come-from-behind 10–9 victory over Kansas City.

Marty Cordova's solo home run in the second inning, his first MLB long-ball, had given the Twins an early 1–0 lead. In the next inning, seven of the eight batters Pat Mahomes faced reached base and all of them scored. It looked like another losing night was about to unfold. Minnesota, however, began to peck away in the bottom of the third inning. With a man on base, Chuck Knoblauch lined a ball that center fielder Tom Goodwin misplayed into a four-base error and two runs. A walk and two singles made it 7–4 before the inning was over.

Kevin Maas and Cordova opened the fifth inning with singles, sending Kansas City starter Tom Gordon to the showers for the night. After a fly out, Scott Leius' two-run single cut the deficit to a workable 7–6. In the sixth, an error by ex-Twin Greg Gagne opened the door for the tying run to score. Cordova, who was en route to a terrific season that culminated in being named American League Rookie of the Year, doubled home a pair of runs for a 9–7 lead.

> ## At a Glance
> **WP:** Stevens (2–0)
>
> **S:** Aguilera (3)
>
> **HR:** Cordova (1)
>
> **Key stats:** Cordova 3-for-5, 3 RBIs

But the Royals came right back, roughing up reliever Carl Willis for a walk and a pair of hits to make it 9–8. Mark Guthrie was called on to stem the tide but only complicated matters by heaving a wild pitch that re-tied the game at 9-all. Guthrie walked one batter but retired the next two before Dave Stevens got the final out of the inning. Stevens then worked a perfect eighth, setting up the winning rally.

It happened suddenly. Rusty Meacham was on the mound to start the inning. Chuck Knoblauch greeted him with a drive over right fielder Felix Jose's head for a triple. Alex Cole followed with a ringing shot past Jose for a double that gave the Twins their third—and final—lead of the night.

A game this chaotic just couldn't have a routine finish. And it didn't. Rick Aguilera started the ninth inning well, retiring the first two batters easily. Pinch-hitter Pat Borders, however, tightened things with a double to right. Phil Hiatt then walked and, suddenly, the potential lead run was on base (again). Wally Joyner, who had two hits and a RBI in the game and was 2-for-2 in his career against Aguilera, was next.

This time, the veteran reliever won the battle, striking out Joyner to end the game. Thus, manager Tom Kelly was able to smile after a game . . . even if it took six pitchers and more than three and a half hours to do so.

THE CURIOUS CASE OF MARTY CORDOVA

It is not fair to call Marty Cordova a flash in the pan. After all, his second season produced better numbers than his first and he did play in the major leagues for nine seasons and for four teams, finishing with a career batting average of .274 with 122 home runs. But few players' fortunes seemed to fall faster than the Las Vegas native. A 10th-round draft choice of the Twins in 1989, it took Cordova six seasons to move up to the big team. When he did, he made a big impression in left field. A week after helping the Twins to that comeback win over the Royals, he had four hits in a 17-inning game at Cleveland. Cordova hit a solid .277 with 20 stolen bases and played excellent defense. He followed up his Rookie of the Year campaign with a .309 batting average the next year and 111 RBIs. In 1997, however, he began to have back problems, something that would plague him for the rest of his career. He still put up decent numbers, hitting .285 with 70 RBIs in 124 games. But the risks outweighed a potential big contact and nobody *seemed* upset when Cordova was allowed to leave as a free agent. He kicked around with three teams in four seasons (including a very good season in Cleveland in 2001), but he was never the same player. The final straw was an elbow injury that limited him to just nine games with Baltimore in 2003. As good as his career was, there will always be this question: "Did Marty Cordova achieve his potential as a big leaguer?" —⌇—

Gravity Be Damned

Had Sir Isaac Newton been able to look ahead roughly 300 years, he might have revised his well-known "Rules of Gravity" slightly to read as follows: "What goes up must come down . . . except at the Metrodome." Of all the odd happenings in Metrodome, few have been stranger than was occurred during Minnesota's 3–1 win over Oakland on this night in early May, when Dave Kingman hit a pop fly ground-rule double that never landed on the field.

Frank Viola and Ray Burris zipped through the first three innings of this game uneventfully. Each pitcher allowed one hit, one other base runner, and no runs. In the top of the fourth inning, Oakland's Mike Heath and Davey Lopes grounded out. That brought up Kingman, best known for his gargantuan home runs and strikeout totals. Viola gave Kingman a changeup that went straight up over the pitcher's mound. A committee of infielders waited for the ball to come down . . . but it never did.

> ## At a Glance
>
> **WP:** Viola (2–3)
>
> **S:** Davis (5)
>
> **Key stats:** Viola allows 4 hits in 7 2/3 IP; 5 of Twins' 7 hits are doubles

That's because the ball (3.5 inches in diameter) found one of the seven-inch air ducts that are part of the Metrodome roof, and stayed put. Many in the crowd of 10,155 never saw the ball go in. When it was figured out what had occurred, many wondered what the ruling would be.

As it turned out, home plate umpire Jim Evans knew exactly what to do. It was baseball's version of an unplayable lie. Based on a similar play in Seattle (where a ball got stuck in a speaker), Kingman was awarded a ground-rule double. There was little argument from the Twins and play resumed.

The unusual play, however, may have unnerved Kingman more than anybody. Carney Lansford, the next hitter, hit a sharp grounder to third baseman John Castino, who looked up in surprise to see Kingman running right at him. Castino tagged him out easily to end the threat.

It took the Twins a while but they finally roughed up Burris for two runs in the sixth inning. With runners on first and second and two out, Tim Laudner doubled to left to break the scoreless tie. Burris then wild pitched a second run home for a 2–0 lead. That looked like plenty for Viola, who was cruising along with a three-hit shutout with two outs in the eighth. That's when trouble began. Tony Phillips singled and Rickey Henderson walked. Manager Billy Gardner, fearful the game was getting away from his young lefty, turned to closer Ron Davis, who retired Mike Heath on a grounder to end the threat.

In the bottom of the inning, Mickey Hatcher doubled and Castino singled him home for what looked like the icing on the cake. But things were frequently not this easy with Davis on the mound. With one out in the ninth, Kingman did what he was known for—hit a long homer to left field. Lansford, no slouch at the plate either, followed with a sharp single, and the crowd became uneasy. Davis got a second out, but now faced another tough out. Joe Morgan was 40 years old and in the final season of his 22-year Hall of Fame career. But he could still swing the bat with the best of them. Davis tried a fastball that didn't fool Morgan for a second. The result was a scorching line drive . . . that went straight into the glove of second baseman Tim Teufel to end the game. It was a quick ending to one of the oddest games ever played in the stadium's history. —⁓—

Did You Know?

Joe Mauer entered the 2010 season with the second highest career batting average of any Twins' player with 1,500 or more career at-bats (.327). Rod Carew is the all-time leader at .334. The only players who hit over .300 during their Twins tenure are Kirby Puckett (.318), Paul Molitor (.312), Shane Mack (.309), Brian Harper (.306), Chuck Knoblauch (.304) and Tony Oliva (.304).

Tiant's Chilly Walk in the Park Ends Well

There was nothing routine about Luis Tiant. In his 19-year MLB career with six different teams, he delivered pitches from nearly every conceivable angle on the mound. He didn't throw all that hard. But he made up for it with a great pickoff move and an arm that never seemed to get tired. His start on this chilly night at Tiger Stadium wasn't one of his best efforts. But he somehow managed to end up on the right side of an 8–5 decision—despite setting a team record for walks in a game.

Tiant gave up just two hits in 5 2/3 innings, a good number against a potent Detroit offense. But he walked nine batters (none of whom scored), and it took considerable work by a trio of relievers to allow the Twins to escape with the win.

"It was a bad night to pitch. It was a bad night to hit," Tiant told reporters later. "I couldn't get loose no matter what I did. When I sat in the dugout, my arm would stiffen up quickly."

Fortunately for Tiant, fellow Cuba native Tony Oliva warmed up to his task, driving in six runs to lead Minnesota to the win.

Oliva, who always seemed to hit well at Tiger Stadium, got things off to a good start by drilling a two-run home run in the top of the first inning off Detroit lefty Mickey Lolich. In the third inning, he singled home another run to make it 3–0. Dick McAuliffe's two-run longball in the fourth cut the Twins' lead to 3–2, but Oliva widened the gap to 6–2 with a bases-loaded triple in the next inning.

Tiant plugged along into the sixth inning until he walked McAuliffe for his ninth free pass of the night. Manager Bill Rigney had seen enough and waved in Tom Hall to end the inning. Before it was over, Hall, Stan Williams, and Ron Perranoski walked four more batters. Harmon Killebrew added a home run and both teams eventually trooped off to take some very warm showers.

Rigney didn't know what to make of Tiant's wild night, but he had a definite view about Oliva. "You're the best hitter I have ever seen," he said after the game.

At a Glance

WP: Tiant (5–0)

S: Perranoski (7)

HR: Oliva (4), Killebrew (6)

Key stats: Oliva 3-for-4, 6 RBIs

TIANT'S MERCURIAL RIDE THROUGH MINNESOTA

Tiant first drew the Twins' attention when he pitched a 19-strikeout, 10-inning game against them while with Cleveland in 1968. Desperate to improve their pitching after being blown out by Baltimore in the 1969 playoffs, the Twins traded four players (including veteran Dean Chance and promising third baseman Graig Nettles) for Tiant and Stan Williams during the winter. The latter was a big hit, recording 10 wins and 15 saves out of the bullpen. Tiant got off to a great start. But he hurt his scapula in a game at Milwaukee that saw him improve his record to 6–0. He didn't pitch again for two months. When he returned, he struggled, winning only one more game. The Twins released him near the end of spring training the next year, thinking his career was over. But Tiant rehabbed himself and signed with Boston in May. He went on to pitch 12 more seasons, finishing with career totals of 229 wins and a 3.30 ERA. In the 1975 World Series, he won two games—a shutout and a 163-pitch complete game. —⁓—

Did You Know?

Although Dean Chance is considered one of the worst hitting pitchers ever (his lifetime batting average is .066), he fared surprisingly well against some very good pitchers. He got a pair of hits (including his only career double) off Yankee Hall of Famer Whitey Ford. He also went 2-for-5 against Detroit's Frank Lary, who won 117 games in a seven-year period in the late 1950s and early '60s.

Mauch Finally Gets a Good Night's Sleep

Things were not going very well for the Twins when they arrived for this game at Baltimore's Memorial Stadium. The night before, Geoff Zahn tossed a complete-game six-hitter, but Mike Flanagan threw a complete-game four-hitter and emerged a 2–1 winner, the Twins' 14th loss in their last 16 games. With Dennis Martinez and Jim Palmer waiting in the wings to take their starts, manager Gene Mauch was understandably grumpier than usual.

For eight innings, the Twins did little to change Mauch's mood. The Orioles blitzed Roger Erickson for five runs in the third inning. Mauch gave the ball to St. Cloud, Minnesota, native Greg Thayer, whose threw 5 2/3 innings of scoreless, four-hit relief in a seemingly lost cause. Baltimore led 5–1 when Minnesota then turned on Martinez and a trio of relievers for seven ninth-inning runs and a highly improbable 8–7 win.

The rally started innocently enough when Danny Ford and Glenn Adams led off the inning with singles. Enter Don Stanhouse, who had five saves and an ERA of 0.67 at the time. Rich Chiles walked to load the bases. Butch Wynegar hit what looked like a double-play grounder, but shortstop Kiko Garcia booted it, and two runs scored. After pinch-hitter Jose Morales fanned, Hosken Powell singled home Chiles and, suddenly, it was a 5–4 game. Stanhouse walked Roy Smalley to load the bases for the second time in the inning, causing manager Earl Weaver to send in veteran Tippy Martinez to face Rod Carew and put an end to the nonsense.

> ## At a Glance
>
> **W:** Thayer (1–1)
>
> **S:** T. Johnson (2)
>
> **Key stats:** Carew 4-for-5, 3 RBIs; Twins score 7 in top of ninth

Carew, however, was having none of that. He tripled to deep center field to clear the bases and give the Twins a 7–5 lead. Mike Cubbage singled to score Carew, and Weaver called on rookie John Flinn to make his major league debut.

The Twins knocked three veterans all over the ballpark in the ninth inning. Flinn got his major league career off to a solid start, however, by getting Ford to ground into an inning-ending double play.

When a team has lost 14 of its last 16 games, nothing is easy. Four of the first five batters who faced Tom Johnson reached base. Two scored. It was now 8–7 with runners on first and second and one out. Johnson breathed hard and whiffed Larry Harlow. That brought up powerful Lee May, who had already hit three career home runs off Johnson. This time, however, was different. Johnson gritted his teeth and struck out May as well to end the game. —⟋⟋—

Late Start No Problem for Gomez

The night before, Chicago's Gavin Floyd had taken a no-hitter into the ninth inning only to see Joe Mauer ruin it with a double. Carlos Gomez, whose average had dropped 72 points in his previous 20 games, was determined not to see history repeat itself the next night at U.S. Cellular Field. Shaking off a 104-minute rain delay, Gomez hit Mark Buehrle's third pitch for a home run and sprinted around the bases, explaining later, "The game started too late. And I said, 'Let me run the bases quickly so the game go fast.'"

As it turned out, he kept running all night. By the time he was done, Gomez became the first Twin to hit for the cycle in 20 years during a 13–1 romp.

The final score was a little deceptive. It was still 1–0 in the fifth inning when Gomez tripled home a run. Livan Hernandez had been keeping the White Sox in check all night. Buehrle, who normally does very well against the Twins, was chased in a five-run sixth inning that was capped by Gomez's double.

By the ninth inning, the Twins had a comfortable 7–0 lead and the only drama left for the night was to see if Gomez could get a single to cap his big night. He sealed matters with a shot off the glove of pitcher Ehren Wassermann, thus becoming the first Minnesota player since Kirby Puckett in 1988 to hit for the cycle. For the night, Gomez had the first four-hit game of his major league career with two runs scored and three RBIs. He remained a thorn in the White Sox's side for the rest of the season, batting .373 against them, including two of his seven home runs.

At a Glance

W: Hernandez (5–1)

HR: Gomez (2)

Key stats: Hernandez 9-hitter; Gomez 4-for-6, 3 RBIs

Did You Know?

Minnesota has beaten the Chicago White Sox more than any other opponent. Through the end of the 2009 season, the Twins had 394 wins over the White Sox. Detroit was second on the list with 370.

Puckett's Memorable Entrance

It wasn't exactly the way to make a good impression on your new boss. Two hours before his team was scheduled to take the field to start a series with the California Angels at Anaheim Stadium, Minnesota manager Billy Gardner was prowling around the clubhouse in search of his newest player. "Where's Punkett?" he asked repeatedly. "He didn't go to Dodger Stadium, did he?"

It turned out that then 24-year-old Kirby Puckett, late of the AAA Toledo Mud Hens, hadn't done that. But he learned a valuable, expensive lesson about taxicabs and California freeways on his first day in the bigs. By the time he had gotten his bags at the airport and hit the road in a cab, it was too late to get to the team's hotel. So, he had the cabbie take him directly to Anaheim Stadium where he asked traveling secretary Mike Robertson for a quick loan.

Seems the bill for the ride was $83.

Gardner decided this was enough of an adventure for one night and decided to wait for the next day to check out the rookie, who was built along the lines of former Houston star Jimmy Wynn, known as the Toy Cannon. Eddie Hodge, who had been a teammate of Puckett's in the minors, had an even better description. "He looks he's a star of the football team and probably the wrestling team, too," Hodge said.

At a Glance
W: Viola (3–3)
HR: Brunansky (4), Laudner (4)
Key stats: Puckett 4-for-5; Viola 4-hitter

When Puckett made his major league debut the next night, there were several more words added. The Twins had nice things to say while the Angels' thoughts weren't quite as heavenly. All Puckett did was go 4-for-5 with a stolen base and a run scored. He was just the ninth player in major league history to open with a four-hit performance. Tom Brunansky and Tim Laudner hit home runs and Frank Viola was in control on the mound all night, allowing four scattered singles in a 5–0 victory.

It was a start of a beautiful 12-year career for the fireplug outfielder. Although he had batted just .263 at Toledo before being called up to replace ailing outfielder Jim Eisenreich, Puckett quickly adapted to AL pitching in 1984, getting hits in the first seven games of his career. By the end of the season, he led the club in multi-hit games with 46, finishing with a .296 batting average in 128 games. In the field, his 16 assists led the league and helped the Twins stay in contention in the AL West until the last weekend of the season.—∽—

Kirby Puckett batted in the leadoff spot in his first game with the Twins, but he soon developed into the Twins' everyday No. 3 hitter.

A Stand-In Stands Out

Looking back at it now, it seems like a made-for-TV pitching matchup. Boston's Pedro Martinez, who had won 20 games the year before and had held the Twins to one run on five hits in his previous start, was facing Johan Santana, he of the nasty change-up and propensity to strike out batters in bunches.

Only it really wasn't that way. On this night, Santana was making his first start of the season . . . and the only reason was because Rick Reed was injured.

By the time the Twins' 5–0 victory at the Metrodome was complete, however, there were people in the organization convinced the time had indeed come to make the left-hander a permanent member of the starting rotation.

In his previous start, Martinez had stifled the Twins completely, recording 12 strikeouts. This game, however, was different from the beginning. Jacque Jones and Cristian Guzman opened the first inning with singles. One out later, DH Todd Sears singled home a run. In the next inning, Sears hit his first major league home run—a three-run shot—and a tight game was suddenly a rout.

Although he only walked one batter and allowed four hits, Santana labored at times, throwing 76 pitches in five innings. That was enough for manager Ron Gardenhire, who turned the game over to the bullpen. LaTroy Hawkins, J. C. Romero, and Eddie Guardado came

> ### At a Glance
>
> **WP:** Santana (2–0)
>
> **HR:** Sears (1)
>
> **Key stats:** Sears 2-for-4, 4 RBIs

through big, facing just one batter over the limit. As a result, the Twins had back-to-back shutouts (they had blanked Tampa Bay the night before) for the first time in 11 seasons.

PERSEVERANCE PAYS OFF

Despite that excellent fill-in start, Santana didn't become a regular in the starting rotation for another two months. Reed, a veteran in his third season with the team, returned to his accustomed spot and Santana returned to the bullpen in various short-inning roles, ranging from finishing up games to setting up Guardado, the team's closer. He came back to the rotation for a pair of games against National League teams. Filling in at San Diego, he gave up just one run on three hits in six innings. Six days later, he went one better, allowing a run on two hits in seven innings. Still, he stayed in the pen until getting the ball July 11 at Anaheim. He lost that night but was beaten just once more the rest of the season, winning eight games in a row, finishing with a club record .800 won-lost percentage (12–3).

For the remainder of his Twins career (until he was traded to the Mets prior to spring training in 2008), Santana never worked in relief again. —⁓—

A Rally for the Ages

One of baseball's most endearing traits is that rallies can appear from no-where—sometimes with the most unlikely participants. Such was the case with the biggest comeback in team history. That the Twins rallied from a seven-run seventh inning deficit for a 10–9 victory over Cleveland was surprising in itself. That the team did so with a game-winning home run from a player who hit 22 homers total in an 11-season major league career is absolutely astounding.

But we digress.

This tale was slow in getting underway. For four innings, Minnesota starter Sean Bergman matched the Tribe's Charles Nagy in a 1-all tie. Jim Thome, a longtime Twins' nemesis who had homered earlier, doubled to open the fifth inning and kickstarted a three-run outburst. Bergman labored into the seventh when the Tribe broke loose again and chased him from the game. His replacements, Hector Carrasco and Travis Miller, didn't fare much better, and it was 8–1 when the Twins came to bat in the bottom of the inning.

Before the frame began, Nagy had allowed just three hits for the night. Then he faced four batters—and all of them recorded hits. David Ortiz singled and Marcus Jensen, the Twins' catcher signed as a free agent in January, hit one of his six career home runs to make it 8–3. Jacque Jones doubled. Torii Hunter moved him up with a single.

Exit Nagy. Enter lefty Tom Martin. A ground out produced a run. Denny Hocking walked. Matt Lawton sharply singled to make it 8–5.

Exit Martin. Righty Sean DePaula was called upon to tackle Ron Coomer. Hocking and Lawton startled the Indians with a successful double steal. Coomer grounded out, but Hocking scored and it was now 8–6. Some in the crowd of 9,505 returned to their seats. This was getting interesting.

Exit DePaula. Enter Ricardo Rincon, another lefty. Butch Huskey was inserted to pinch-hit for the left-handed swinging Corey Koskie. Huskey didn't hit much for average, but he was quite capable

Indians	AB	R	H	RBI
R. Alomar 2b	5	1	2	0
Wilson ss	5	1	2	2
Justice dh	5	1	1	1
M. Ramirez rf	5	0	1	2
Thome 1b	4	2	3	1
Sexson lf	4	1	1	1
Fryman 3b	4	1	1	2
S. Alomar c	4	0	0	0
Cabrera cf	4	2	3	0
Totals	40	9	14	9

Twins	AB	R	H	RBI
Guzman ss	5	0	1	1
Hocking 2b	4	1	0	0
Lawton rf	5	3	3	1
Coomer 1b-3b	5	0	1	2
Canizaro pr	0	1	0	0
Koskie 3b	2	0	0	0
Huskey ph-1b	1	0	0	0
Ortiz dh	3	1	2	1
LeCroy ph-dh	0	0	0	0
Cummings ph-dh	2	1	2	3
Jensen c	3	1	1	2
Jones lf	4	1	1	0
Hunter cf	4	1	2	0
Totals	38	10	13	10

CLE	0 1 0 0 3 0 4 0 1 -	9	14	1
MIN	0 0 0 1 0 0 6 0 3 -	10	13	1

Indians	IP	H	R	ER	BB	SO
Nagy	6	7	5	5	2	6
Martin	0.1	1	2	2	1	0
DePaula	0.1	0	0	0	0	0
Rincon	0	0	0	0	1	0
Shuey	1.1	2	0	0	0	0
Karsay L(0–2)	0.2	3	3	3	0	0
Totals	8.2	13	10	10	4	6

Twins	IP	H	R	ER	BB	SO
Bergman	6.1	10	8	8	0	2
Carrasco	0.1	1	0	0	0	1
Miller	0.1	1	0	0	0	0
Wells	1	1	0	0	0	1
Guardado W(3–1)	1	1	1	1	0	0
Totals	9	14	9	9	0	4

E—Cleveland S. Alomar. Minnesota Koskie. DP—Minnesota 1. 2B—Cleveland Thome, Sexson. Minnesota Lawton 2, Jones. HR—Cleveland Thome (9), Fryman (5), Justice (5). Minnesota Jensen (3), Cummings (1). LOB—Cleveland 4. Minnesota 6. SB—Cleveland Cabrera, Wilson. Minnesota Hocking, Lawton, Guzman. Attendance—9,505.

of swatting the ball into the seats. The Indians thought better of taking their chances with Huskey and intentionally walked him.

Instead of sending left-handed swinging David Ortiz to the plate, Matthew LeCroy walked to the plate as another pinch-hitter.

Exit Rincon. Enter Paul Shuey, a mainstay of the Indians' pen for several seasons. Twins manager Tom Kelly was anticipating this move and offered up Midre Cummings as a pinch-hitter. Cummings had been signed as a free agent in 1999. He didn't play much that season but he was hitting well in 2000. He singled to center field to make it 8–7.

Getting this close was commendable, but the Twins' bullpen needed to keep it that way to give the offense another crack at things. The Twins nearly tied it in the last of the eighth. With two out and nobody on, Cristian Guzman singled. Looking to make things happen, Guzman headed for second base on a steal attempt. Sandy Alomar's throw sailed into center field. Guzman got up and started running. He went past third base and headed home. Unfortunately for him, center fielder Jolbert Cabrera chased the ball down and gunned Guzman out at the plate. "It's a great play if he makes it," Kelly sighed after the game. "Unfortunately, he didn't."

Eddie Guardado, called on in a rare non-save role, coughed up a two-out solo homer to David Justice in the ninth inning. Minnesota now needed two runs to tie the game.

Steve Karsay, who had been given the job of closer for the Indians at the start of the season, took over. After getting Hocking on a grounder, Matt Lawton smoked a double. Coomer singled him home to make it 9–8. Again, folks headed to the exits sat down. Huskey flied to right for the second out, leaving Cummings as the last hope. He was a fellow with a simple approach to hitting. "I just try to get good wood on the ball and hope it goes somewhere," he said.

Karsay was careful, throwing two pitches wide. The next pitch was a strike and Cummings was ready for it, drilling a liner into the left field seats. Those who had stayed roared in appreciation. It marked the second time the Twins had won a game in 2000 when behind after eight innings—one more than their total for the 1999 season. —⁓—

Mr. Aguilera Signs Off

Roger Angell, the longtime baseball writer of "The New Yorker" once observed that great baseball stats come when we least expect them. In a way, such was the case when the Twins ended a lengthy losing streak with a 2–1 win over Tampa Bay at Tropicana Field.

At the time, the crux of the story was about Minnesota starter Brad Radke and outfielder Chad Allen. Radke, who lived in nearby Largo and attended high school in Tampa, threw eight solid innings to gain the victory. Allen provided the margin of victory with an RBI single off Devil Rays starter Ryan Rupe, who had been his college roommate at Texas A & M for three years.

At a Glance

WP: Radke (4–2)

S: Aguilera (6)

Key stat: Twins use 3 of their 5 hits to score 2 runs in 5th inning

But the real story of this game drew little mention at the time. As he has done so often, Rick Aguilera tossed a 1–2–3 ninth inning to get the save. It was his sixth save of 1999, and his 254th as a member of the Twins. As it developed, it was also his last one as a member of the Twins. Aguilera was traded a week later to the Chicago Cubs.

Aguilera had turned out to be the best acquisition in the five-player deal that sent ace lefty Frank Viola to the Mets a decade earlier. In 1990, he took over the closer's role for the team. For most of the next decade (he spent three months with the Red Sox in 1995), he was the guy Tom Kelly turned to with the game on the line. In the World Series season of 1991, he saved a career-high 42 games in the regular season, three ALCS wins against Toronto, and two more in the World Series against Atlanta.

He stayed in that role until, with the Twins well out of the pennant race, he was traded to Boston in July 1995. He saved 20 games for the Red Sox but, like many of his teammates, stumbled in a playoff series with Cleveland. The Red Sox let him go, and the Twins gladly took him back.

The 1999 Twins were rebuilding and weren't expected to contend for anything. There were 10 rookies on the team and the word was that owner Carl Pohlad had ordered

He was an established pitcher when the Twins picked him up as part of the Frank Viola trade with the Mets. He quickly became a premier closer and is the current franchise record-holder in saves with 254 and second in appearances with 490. In 1991, his star shone brightly as he recorded 42 regular-season saves. He added three more saves in the ALCS rout of Toronto and a win and two saves against Atlanta in the World Series.

Rick Aguilera

more salaries cut. Aguilera, making more than $4 million, was a logical choice for a trade.

But it wasn't that easy. For one thing, he had a no-trade clause. For another, Kelly liked him a lot. Aguilera, however, understood the inner workings of the game and told writers, "Instead of quickly saying no, I'll look at the whole situation."

The Cubs, who had lost closer Rod Beck to an injury, proved to be the suitor with the best offer. On May 21, Aguilera was part of a four-player deal. Kyle Lohse, a pitcher who ended up doing very well *after* he left Minnesota, was the most notable player the team received in return.

Aguilera left the team the way he left many games—quietly and efficiently. —

Did You Know?

There have been four Twins who homered in their first at-bat in the major leagues. Rick Renick was the first to do it on July 11, 1968, connecting off Detroit's Mickey Lolich. Dave McKay (1975), Gary Gaetti (1981) and Andre David (1984, off Jack Morris) are the others. Four other players did it in their first game. Hal Haydel did it in 1970 and Eric Soderholm followed suit nearly a year later. In 1981, Kent Hrbek and Tim Laudner, who would be teammates on the 1987 World Series championship team, achieved it four days apart.

A week after he recorded his 254th save with the Twins, Rick Aguilera was traded to the Cubs. Aggie chalked up a career-best 42 saves during the Twins' run to the 1991 World Series title.

The Few Who Saw It Will Never Forget It

There were several very good reasons why only 3,572 fans visited Met Stadium for this Tuesday night game. For one thing, the Twins were already 11 games out of first place and the Red Sox were under .500 as well. For another, the NHL's Minnesota North Stars were opening the Stanley Cup Finals that night on television.

But the folks who were there saw a remarkable turnaround. Down to their last out and trailing by a run, the Twins rallied for a 4–3, 10-inning victory on back-to-back home runs by Mickey Hatcher and Roy Smalley off Tom Burgmeier, the Red Sox closer. Where was Al Michaels to say, "Do you believe in miracles? Yes!" when you needed him?

Ron Jackson's two-run homer in the seventh inning erased an early deficit and forged a 2-all tie. It was still that way in the 10th when Carl Yastrzemski, who started his pro career at Met Stadium as a minor leaguer, hit a sacrifice fly to break the tie. Burgmeier, an ex-Twin, recorded two routine outs. Hatcher, not known for his power, was bothered with a virus and had thrown up in the dugout earlier in the game.

> ### At a Glance
>
> **WP:** Corbett (2–1)
>
> **HR:** R. Jackson (3), Hatcher (2), Smalley (7)
>
> **Key stat:** Hatcher and Smalley solo HRs in bottom of 10th

Now he made Burgmeier ill by hitting a hanging curve ball into the left-field seats to tie the game. Smalley served as the DH because of a bad shoulder. "No one, in his right mind, would have dreamed I would hit a home run after Mickey hit his," Smalley said later. "It's one of the most unbelievable experiences I have ever been a part of." —⁓—

Did You Know?

Mickey Hatcher was one Twin sad to see Met Stadium go. In his only year at the Met, he batted .280 there (as opposed to a .229 mark on the road) and hit all three of his home runs. He would go on to play six seasons for the Twins before returning to the Dodgers for the final four seasons of his career.

Puckett Adds Another Mark to the Record Book

By 1989, Kirby Puckett no longer surprised people with remarkable performances. On this afternoon, he gave a national TV audience another reason to marvel at his overall game. Puckett tied an AL record when he recorded four doubles in a closer-than-it-should-have-been 10–8 victory.

It looked like a pitching mismatch. The Blue Jays were starting ace Dave Stieb against lefty Shane Rawley, who had gone 8–16 for the Phillies the year before. But Minnesota got off to a good start when center fielder Lloyd Moseby broke late on Puckett's short fly, which fell for his first double and an RBI. It was 1–1 in the fifth inning when Stieb suddenly fell apart, giving up five hits to the first six batters he faced. The last of those was Puckett's second two-bagger, a laser to left field. Reliever Tony Castillo struggled as well, and it was 7–1 by the end of the inning.

At this point, the security guard near the bullpen suggested to Jeff Reardon, who had saved three games in a row, he would finally get a day off. The reliever sighed, saying that in baseball, you never really know.

Double No. 3 came in Puckett's next at-bat (in the sixth) and produced another RBI. By the end of the inning, the Twins led by a seemingly comfortable 9–1 margin.

At a Glance

WP: Rawley (3–4)

S: Reardon (7)

Key stats: Puckett 4-for-5, 3 RBIs; Gagne 3-for-4, 3 RBIs

Turned out Reardon knew what he was talking about. Tired, Rawley gave up a series of hits the next inning and left in favor of reliever Steve Shields. It took a while to end the inning because Shields coughed up two hits and a wild pitch before finally getting the third out. Toronto now trailed 9–6.

Reardon suddenly looked like one smart guy.

Puckett finished his quartet of two-baggers with a drive down the right field line. By that time, the Twins had another run and Reardon appeared to be headed for his day off.

Guess again.

German Gonzalez, who had pitched a scoreless eighth, started the final inning by walking Nelson Liriano. Reardon got up and started throwing. Rob Ducey was retired but Gonzalez plunked Junior Felix with a pitch.

That did it. Reardon entered the game but was hardly loose. He promptly threw a wild pitch. Kelly Gruber singled home a run. Tony Fernandez's sacrifice fly brought in another. Now it was 10–8 and George Bell, the league MVP in 1987, was waiting. But Reardon had always fared well against Bell, and this game was no exception. Bell flied to right to preserve Puckett's big day. Puckett now led the league and was on a pace to get 78 doubles for the season, which would have shattered Earl Webb's AL record by 11. That didn't happen, but Puckett did end with a career-best 45 in that department.

LATE POWER BLOOMER

Despite his physique, Kirby Puckett showed little power in the early part of his career. Although he finished with 207 career home runs, Puckett didn't go deep until April 22, 1985, off Seattle's Matt Young . . . in his 141st game. Ironically, perhaps his best-known hit—his 11th-inning shot off Charlie Leibrandt in Game 6 of the 1991 World Series—was a home run. —∞—

Did You Know?

There have been just five players in team history to record more than 200 hits in a season for the Twins through the 2009 season. Kirby Puckett did it five times (1986–89, 1992), one better than Rod Carew (1973–74, 1976–77). Tony Oliva turned the trick in 1964 and 1970. Cesar Tovar achieved it in 1971 and Paul Molitor did it in 1996.

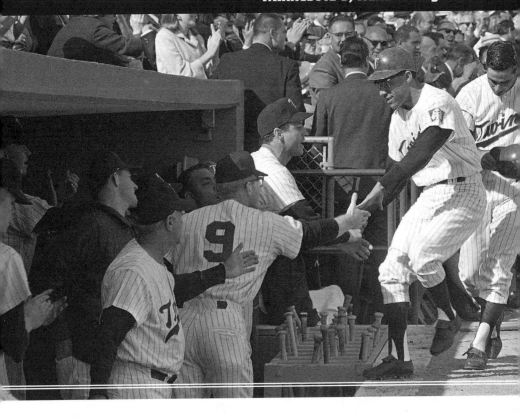

Versalles Shows Why He Was the MVP Choice

To an outsider, Zoilo Versalles' selection as the American League's Most Valuable Player of the 1965 season may have seemed like an odd choice. True, he led the league in runs scored and was tied for the top in doubles and triples. But he didn't even crack the top 10 in the league in batting average and actually ranked fourth on his own team among regulars in that department.

But the little shortstop from Havana seemed to get the big hits when they were needed . . . even if that wasn't the original plan.

On this night at Municipal Stadium, the Twins spent seven innings kicking the ball around against the lowly A's, committing four errors (including one by

On his way to the 1965 AL MVP Award, Zoilo Versalles had a hand in plenty of Twins victories. On May 14, his single after two failed bunt attempts brought in the game-winning run.

Versalles). As a result, they trailed 3–0. Things changed quickly in the eighth inning when Bob Allison unloaded a three-run home run to tie the game.

In the top of the ninth, a strange turn of events—and a key hit by Versalles—decided the game. Jerry Kindall opened the frame with a single. Jerry Zimmerman pinch-hit and dropped an unsurprising bunt down. As A's catcher Rene Lachemann chased the ball up the basepath, he collided with Zimmerman. Home plate umpire Al Salerno awarded Zimmerman first base on interference and sent Kindall to second.

At a Glance

WP: Fosnow (2–2)

S: Pleis (1)

HR: Allison (4)

Key stat: Allison's 3-run HR ties game in eighth

Versalles was ordered to bunt as well. He tried twice to bunt but fouled off each pitch. So he swung away instead . . . and singled to center field to score Kindall with the tiebreaking run. A wild pitch added an insurance run, and the Twins were in for the night.

It was typical of how 1965—and Versalles' season—went for the Twins. —∾—

Pete Redfern's Memorable Debut

As major league debuts go, this one was pretty darn good. The problem was that not a lot of people back home knew about it until the next day.

The Twins were in Anaheim playing a rare twi-night doubleheader against the Angels. That meant a late start—and an even later finish for local fans. When you consider this was also a Saturday night, it is understandable that many folks were unaware of the happenings of this remarkable second game of the twin bill.

Larry Hisle, Dan Ford, and a rookie pitcher named Pete Redfern turned in efforts that should have been talked about for days.

At a Glance

WP: Redfern (1–0)

S: Campbell (3)

HR: Ford (5)

Key stat: Ford 3-for-4, 6 RBIs; Roof 3-for-5, 4 RBIs

Bert Blyleven had gotten the evening off to a good start with an eight-hit, 12-strikeout complete game in a 5–2 win.

For the second game, Redfern, the Twins' top draft pick in January's secondary draft and a native of nearby Glendale, made quite an impression in his first major league appearance.

The strapping right-hander was so dominant that it took the Angels 19 batters before they managed a base hit. By the time Jerry Remy singled to right field, the game was already in the sixth inning and the Twins had a 13–0 lead.

Unfortunately for Redfern, major league reality set in shortly thereafter. Before the inning was over, Bobby Bonds hit a grand slam home run to end the rookie pitcher's night. Fortunately, Bill Campbell came on for a four-inning save and the Twins' bats picked up the pace for a 15–5 win.

Although he had just one hit in the game, a double, Hisle scored a career-high four runs. Ford, a Los Angeles native, went 3-for-4 with a double, a home run and a career-best six RBIs. For good measure, Rod Carew, Phil Roof, and Danny Thompson also had three hits apiece. There probably weren't many people back home paying attention at the end, but the Twins didn't care. They had a terrific night at Anaheim Stadium.

Later, Redfern was the topic on everybody's mind. He had dropped out of the University of Southern California to sign with the Twins. He spent spring training with the team and was told he would be an early call up.

The can't-miss prospect had lived up to his advance billing. As his catcher that night, Roof, put it, "He has so much potential it is terrible for hitters to think about. And he was easy to work with. He'll throw a breaking ball for a strike when he's behind the count. It doesn't faze him at all."

Unfortunately, fate wasn't very kind to Redfern. He did toss a shutout late in the season on the road against the Chicago White Sox, but that was the only one of his major league career. Although he stayed with the team for six more seasons, he was hampered often by injuries, posting a 42–48 win-loss mark in seven seasons. He was the team's starter in their first regular-season game at the Metrodome in 1982. But he only went 5–11 on the season and was released in spring training the next year. But his debut effort remains one of the best first-game efforts in team history.

REDFERN'S ROUGH POST-BASEBALL CAREER

After being released by the Twins in March 1983, Redfern returned to his southern California roots. He didn't get picked up by a major league team, but that wasn't his biggest hurdle that year. In October, he was paralyzed in a diving accident in Newport Beach. To this day, he remains in a wheelchair.

Redfern didn't totally stay away from baseball, however. He served as an assistant coach at a local high school and at The Master's College in Santa Clarita, California, before retiring to watch his son, Chad, play. An outfielder by trade, Chad played for San Diego State University in the spring and spent the summer with the amateur Alaska Goldpanners in Fairbanks, Alaska. While in Alaska, his strong arm drew the attention of the Atlanta Braves, who signed him to a free-agent contract, hoping to convert him to his dad's old spot on the mound. He spent two seasons in the minors but never got higher than the rookie-level Appalachian League. —⁓—

No Chance to Beat this Guy in a 1–0 Game

When they arrived at Comiskey Park, the Twins were in eighth place, trailing the surprising White Sox by 7½ games just 26 games into the season. To make matters worse, the Sox were getting great pitching, having held opponents to just 13 runs total during a 10-game winning streak.

When the Twins grabbed a 1–0 lead in the second inning on back-to-back doubles by Bob Allison and Zoilo Versalles, it seemed like the team would need a dominating pitching effort to get a win.

At a Glance

WP: Chance (6–1)

Key stats: Chance 5-hitter; Allison, Versalles doubles in second inning

As it turned out, Wilmer Dean Chance was up to the task. The right-hander retired the last 11 batters in a row, allowed no runner past second and stuffed the Sox on five singles for a 1–0 win. It was the 12th time in Chance's career he had won by such a score, moving him into third place behind Walter Johnson (38) and Grover Cleveland Alexander (17) in that department. It improved his record at the time to 6–1. No one seemed less surprised than Chance himself, who told reporters, "I feel so good this year I think I can win more games than I did in 1964 [when he won 20 for the Angels and claimed the Cy Young Award]."

As it developed, Chance matched his 1964 win total, leading the AL in complete games with 18. Chicago manager Eddie Stanky, a man not known for gushing over opponents, was suitably impressed with Chance, saying, "When he had that 1–0 lead the last three innings, there was no touching him."

To a pitcher like Dean Chance, there could hardly be higher praise. ⟶⟋⟍⟋

Big Bob Bops the Tribe

It didn't start out as one of the better games of the 1,541 in Bob Allison's major league career. Cleveland pitcher Gary Bell had retired him on a pop foul and a strikeout in his first two trips to the plate. "I had been lunging at the ball and jerking my head all over the park," Allison recalled later.

Minnesota had rallied from an early deficit for a 4–3 lead and a different pitcher—future teammate Jim "Mudcat" Grant—was on the mound when Allison came to the plate in the fifth inning with two runners on and two out. This time, Allison kept everything straight and drilled a home run to left field.

Suddenly, a sour night at the plate turned into one of the best nights of Allison's career. He followed up his first four-bagger with a 450-foot plus drive to dead center in the seventh inning and an opposite-field blast the next inning.

By the time the night was done, Minnesota had an 11–4 win. Allison, who had started at the plate 0-for-2 ended with a 3-for-5 night and six RBIs, which propelled him into the league lead with 29 overall. It was the first time a Minnesota player had ever hit three home runs in a game. The man who used one of the biggest bats in the league (36 inches, 36 ounces) is one of just four players in team history to record baseball's version of a hat trick. Only Harmon Killebrew, Tony Oliva, and Justin Morneau have done it since.

> ## At a Glance
>
> **WP:** Perry (1–2)
>
> **S:** Moore (2)
>
> **HR:** Killebrew (2), Versalles (1), Allison 3 (9)
>
> **Key stats:** Allison 3-for-5, 3 HRs, 6 RBIs

A TRADE THAT DIDN'T WORK OUT

Although Allison had been on a tear (he was hitting .330 on the night of his three-home run game), the Twins were still looking for more offense. Center fielder Lenny Green's average had fallen into the .240s. Accordingly, outfielder Wally Post was acquired from nearby Cincinnati just prior to the game in Cleveland. He was near the end of his career by now, but manager Sam Mele, a former teammate, was hoping he could add a little more sock to his attack.

The next night, Allison started in center field for the first time in three seasons. Post played right field and performed as hoped, going 2-for-4 with a home run and three RBIs as the Twins tore up Sam McDowell for an 8–1 win. Mele looked like a genius.

But looks were deceiving. Post managed just seven more hits and one more home run the rest of the season, finishing with a .191 batting average. Meanwhile, Allison started just eight more games in center field. Although his average fell to .271 by the end of the season, he led the league in runs scored with 99 and had a personal best in home runs with 35. —m—

A Big Step Forward

The dismal 1982 season had been forgotten by most of the Twins. In theory, a 15–21 win-loss mark doesn't sound impressive. But when you consider the team didn't get its 15th win the year before until June 16, things didn't look so bad.

There was one exception to the overall better mood around the Metrodome. Frank Viola had a 0–2 record and an ERA of 5.26 when the Twins took on the A's in a matinee. Although the ERA actually went up a few points (to 5.44), Viola finally left the Dome in a good mood. That's because his teammates rapped out a season-high 20 hits, rolling to a 16–5 win that was as much fun as it sounds.

Gary Ward had three hits and five RBIs and Gary Gaetti had four hits. The Twins unloaded six doubles and a home run off starter Bill Krueger and two successors in the first six innings of the game. At that point, A's manager Steve Boros had seen enough and called upon Wayne Gross, normally the team's third baseman, to take the mound. Gross, who said he hadn't pitched since Little League, gave up two hits and a walk but no runs in his 2 1/3-inning effort. "I put a joke pitcher into a joke ballpark," Boros growled later.

At a Glance

WP: Viola (1–2)

S: Ward (6)

Key stats: Ward 3-for-5, 5 RBIs; Gaetti 4-for-6

Viola, who pitched into the eighth inning, was in a much better mood, quipping after the game, "I could have gotten married and had a baby since my last win [August 24, 1982 at New York]."

After the growing pains of 1982, the lefty was happy to be . . . happy again. ―〰―

Rigney Gets His Revenge from an Unexpected Source

A movie entitled "The California Angels . . . the First Ten Years" was scheduled for a local television broadcast when the Twins came calling for a series. Bill Rigney, the original Angels manager who was now running the Twins, claimed not to be bothered by the fact he had just a cameo role in this film, appearing for less than three minutes in a 60-minute show.

Instead, Rigney looked to get his revenge the night of the first showing of the movie by sending 1970 Cy Young winner Jim Perry to the mound. Unfortunately, this didn't work out as well as planned. Perry had a rough night, getting tagged for six runs and seven hits in just 2 2/3 innings of work. However, thanks to some stellar bullpen work and some timely hitting, Rigney came away happy with a 12–6 victory.

Fortunately for Perry and Rigney, Jim Strickland and Tommy Hall had their backs. Strickland was a rookie lefty who had an unusual diet plan. "I could eat a three-ounce candy bar and gain five pounds," he told Dan Stoneking of the *Minneapolis Star* when he was called up. "Instead, I chew tobacco." On this night, he bailed Perry out of a third-inning mess and then worked two more scoreless innings, whiffing two pretty good hitters—Alex Johnson and Tony Conigliaro—to earn the victory in his first major league appearance. Hall followed with four perfect innings of relief, fanning six batters. Meanwhile, two old reliables—Tony Oliva and Harmon Killebrew—had three RBIs each and the Twins romped home from there.

At a Glance

WP: Strickland (1–0)

S: Hall (2)

HR: Oliva (10)

Key stats: Hall 4 perfect innings; Cardenas 3-for-5, 2 RBIs

Rigney, an honest guy, admitted he enjoyed the evening very much. "I don't like losing any game, but especially to the Angels," he said, referring to the team he nurtured from scratch in 1961 before being let go in May 1969. —⁓—

The Hits Kept on Coming... and Coming... and Coming

In the course of a long baseball season, the best (and worst) of teams are going to have periods where everything goes right. The Twins were in one of those wonderful periods when the Red Sox came to town. Earlier in the homestand, the Orioles stopped in leading the AL East—and left with heads hanging after a sweep that saw Minnesota outscore them 17–8. The Yankees had replaced the O's in first place, but they were treated just as rudely in a two-game series. Boston, off to its best start in 23 seasons with a 26–13 win-loss mark, figured to be a tough test.

Over the years, Boston had become known for bashing teams all around their little bandbox home park. On this night, the Twins returned the favor and then some, setting four team records in a 21–2 thumping at the Metrodome that was not as close as it looked.

Minnesota led 10–0 after three innings, took an inning off, and then sent 16 batters to the plate in an 11-run fifth inning that caused Sox manager Butch Hobson to consider rearranging his spring training schedule for the future. Since both teams do spring training in Fort Myers, Florida, they naturally play each other several times. After absorbing this pounding, Hobson said, "We ain't going to play them but twice next year. [Bleep] this [bleep]."

Ironically, the night didn't start well. Scott Erickson, the Twins' scheduled starting pitcher, had been on a good run since his no-hitter against Milwaukee the month before. Minnesota had won 12 of 17 games since then, causing Erickson to observe, "Weird things make weird things happen. The atmosphere around here has certainly changed."

The atmosphere was a little darker, however, five

Red Sox	AB	R	H	RBI
Nixon cf	2	0	0	0
Tinsley ph-cf	2	0	0	0
Hatcher rf	4	0	1	0
Vaughn 1b	2	0	0	0
Rowland 1b	2	0	1	1
Dawson dh	3	1	2	1
Fletcher pr-dh	1	0	1	0
Greenwell lf	3	0	1	0
Berryhill ph	1	0	0	0
Naehring 2b	3	0	0	0
Cooper 3b	3	0	0	0
Valle c	3	0	0	0
Rodriguez ss	2	1	0	0
Totals	**31**	**2**	**6**	**2**

Twins	AB	R	H	RBI
Knoblauch 2b	2	3	2	2
Reboulet ph-2b	2	1	1	2
Leius 3b	4	4	2	1
Puckett rf	3	1	3	7
Dunn ph-1b	1	1	1	1
Mack cf	4	1	2	3
Winfield lf	3	1	0	0
Hale ph-dh	2	0	1	0
Munoz lf	2	1	1	0
Cole ph-cf	4	0	1	0
McCarty 1b-rf	6	2	2	1
Walbeck c	4	3	3	2
Parks c	2	0	1	0
Meares ss	5	3	2	2
Totals	**44**	**21**	**22**	**21**

```
BOS  0 0 0 1 0 0 0 0 1 - 2 6 1
MIN  1 5 4 0 11 0 0 0 x - 21 22 0
```

Red Sox	IP	H	R	ER	BB	SO
Hesketh	1	3	4	4	2	0
Quantrill	0.1	4	2	2	0	0
Frohwirth	3	5	9	9	4	1
Harris L(2-2)	0.1	7	6	6	0	1
Ryan	1.1	2	0	0	0	3
Tomberlin	2	1	0	0	1	1
Totals	**8**	**22**	**21**	**21**	**7**	**6**

Twins	IP	H	R	ER	BB	SO
Pulido W(2-3)	7	3	1	1	0	0
Stevens	1	0	0	0	0	1
Merriman	1	3	1	1	1	0
Totals	**9**	**6**	**2**	**2**	**1**	**1**

E—Boston Valle. DP—Minnesota 2. 2B—Boston Greenwell. Minnesota Walbeck 2, Knoblauch, Dunn, Parks. HR—Boston Dawson (9). Minnesota Puckett (6). SF—Minnesota Puckett, Knoblauch. HBP—Minnesota Leius. LOB—Boston 3. Minnesota 9. SB—Minnesota Knoblauch. Attendance—20,766.

minutes before game time when Erickson reported back pains as he warmed up. Manager Tom Kelly turned to rookie lefty Carlos Pulido, who hadn't pitched in 10 days. When things are going well, however, a rookie with a 5.40 ERA can look like Sandy Koufax. Pulido retired nine of the first 10 batters he faced with little dissent.

Meanwhile, his teammates were offering considerable support, chasing Red Sox starter Joe Hesketh out of the game after just eight batters. It took two more pitchers before the Twins' five-run second inning ended. In the third inning, four more runs came home. Todd Frohwirth, the victim of that uprising, labored into the fifth when the bats really went to work. After Pat Meares grounded out, Chuck Knoblauch singled and Scott Leius was hit by a pitch. Kirby Puckett's three-run homer made it 13–1, leaving Greg Harris to stem the tide.

Alex Cole struck out, but the next seven Twins torched Harris for hits. Ken Ryan replaced Harris and surrendered an eighth consecutive hit before Cole fanned again to finally end the inning.

Final total for the fun-filled fifth inning: 16 batters, 11 runs, 10 hits, a walk, a hit by pitch, a wild pitch, two runners left on base, and a scorecard that looked like it had lines for every lake in the state of Minnesota. While this carnage was going on, Kelly could hardly be accused of pouring it on. Indeed, he may have set an unofficial modern AL record when he sent up three pinch-hitters in the inning, and all of them recorded hits. Puckett, who had a career-high seven RBIs in just three at-bats, was one of the players taken out early.

Give this kind of cushion, Pulido and his mound successors—Dave Stevens and Brett Merriman—had little problem the rest of the way. Ironically, on a night when the Twins ended with 22 hits, Dave Winfield was the only one of the 14 different batters who came to the plate who did not record a hit.

Cole, who had entered the game in the fourth inning and ended up with four at-bats, understood that this type of rockslide happens from to time. "When I was with California and Cleveland, we used to get bashed like this all the time," he said after the game. "This was more fun."

A VERY DIFFERENT ENCORE

Scott Erickson's observation about the intricacies of baseball was proven true the next night. The Red Sox started a rookie righty with the unlikely name of Anders Gar Finnvold. Finnvold was making his second big league appearance against Minnesota's Kevin Tapani, who was coming off a five-hit complete-game win over the Orioles. The only offense the Twins could muster came in the fifth inning, when David McCarty doubled and Chuck Knoblauch's run-scoring single drove him home. But that turned out to be enough when Tapani and Rick Aguilera combined on an eight-hit shutout. That's right. One night after they won 21–2, Minnesota beat Boston 1–0. —⁓—

A Week's Worth of Frustrations Exorcised in a Span of Three Hours

It had been one of the most miserable road trips in team history. The Twins had dropped four straight games at the new Yankee Stadium, two in extra innings. Things didn't go any better in Chicago with two more losses against the White Sox. By the time the team reached U.S. Cellular Field for the final game of the trip, the team could hardly be blamed for wanting to go home.

Minnesota manager Ron Gardenhire was willing to try almost anything to get his offense moving. So he moved Joe Mauer to the No. 2 spot in the batting order and hoped for the best. The result—a 20–1 victory—was more than anybody could have imagined.

> **At a Glance**
>
> **WP:** Blackburn (3–2)
>
> **HR:** Cuddyer (6), Crede (6), Mauer (8), Tolbert (11)
>
> **Key stats:** Mauer 3-for-4, grand slam, 6 RBIs; Tolbert 3-for-6, 3-run HR, 4 RBIs; Cuddyer 4-for-6, 3-run HR; Twins 20 hits

"Things haven't been going our way, and sometimes you have to make them go your way," Gardenhire said later. "Today, I thought we pushed the issue and put some good swings on the ball."

Here is what happened with those good swings:

- The Twins scored runs in six of the nine innings, including seven in the second inning, six in the sixth inning, and four in the seventh inning.

- Michael Cuddyer and Joe Crede hit back-to-back home runs in that seven-run second frame.

- Jose Morales, the third-string catcher, went 3-for-4, walked twice, and scored three runs.

- Not to be outdone, Mauer, serving as the DH, also went 3-for-4. His six RBIs (fueled in great part by a grand slam home run) were a career high.

- The margin of defeat tied the worst ever for the White Sox, who have been in the major league baseball business since 1901.

All in all, it was quite an afternoon. Mauer, never one to get too excited about things, tried to take the afternoon in stride. Asked after the game about the new lineup, he said, "I like scoring 20 runs. I don't know, I think it worked today. If we keep scoring runs, I guess we'll just have to see how it goes." —

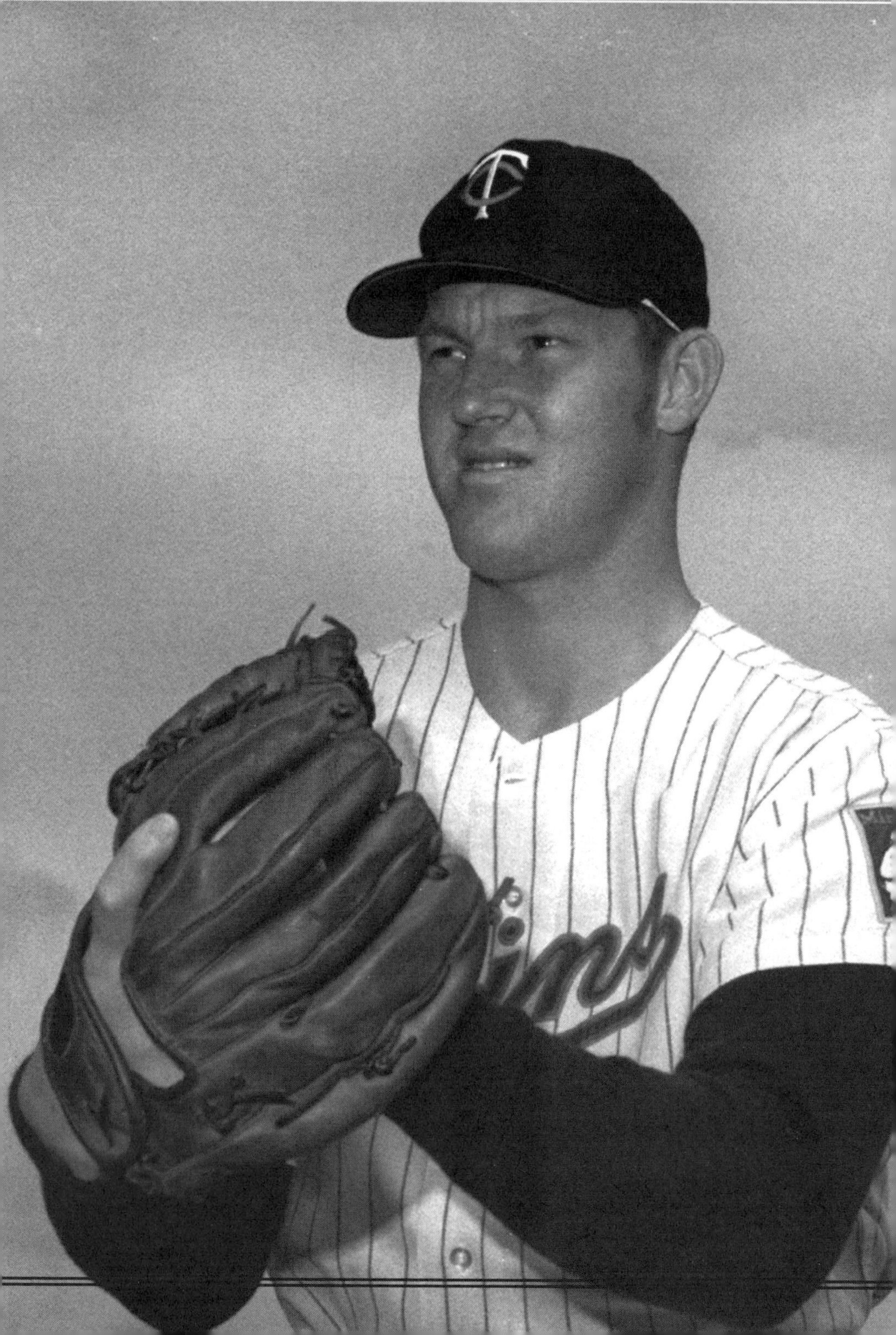

Marathon Man Kaat Hangs in Long Enough to Get the Win

It is a common refrain that has been uttered in baseball since the days of Cy Young: "They don't make pitchers like they used to." In the case of Jim Kaat, it is undeniably true. In his 25-year big league career that encompassed nearly 900 appearances, Kaat pitched more than nine innings on 18 occasions. Amazingly, he was the winning pitcher in 10 of those games.

But this effort at Kansas City's Municipal Stadium may have been his finest achievement. For 11 innings, Kaat and the Royals' Dick Drago tossed goose eggs at each other. Eventually, Drago gave an inch and Minnesota took advantage for a 12-inning, 1–0 victory.

Kaat faced 40 batters and allowed just five hits and three walks. The Royals didn't even get a runner to third base until there was one out in the 10th inning. Kaat wiggled his way out of that problem. In the next inning, he was in more trouble when the Royals put runners on first and second and one out. Manager Bill Rigney went out to visit the pitcher but went away after Kaat said, "I didn't pitch this long for a tie." He promptly induced Lou Piniella to hit into a double play and the game went on.

The Twins weren't faring much better against the veteran Drago. They managed just four hits and had moved just one runner as far as second base in the first 11 innings of the game. But that changed quickly in the 12th. Danny Thompson led off with a looping drive to center field and hustled to second base before center fielder Amos Otis could get the ball to the infield. Rod Carew was next up and everybody still remaining in the park figured the bunt was on. That included Drago, who threw two high pitches that Carew fouled

Jim Kaat pitched 11 innings in a 1–0 win over the Royals in Kansas City. Kaat allowed five hits and three walks.

off. With the count 0–2, Carew swung away and singled to center to score Thompson and break the tie.

When Harmon Killebrew was safe on an error, it appeared Minnesota was ready to break the game wide open. But Drago, who struck out 13 batters in the game, settled down and got out of the inning with no more harm done.

Kaat, who had only gone to one full count in the entire game, had pitched 12 innings once before. But this is what bullpens are for. Wayne Granger, who was slowly evolving into becoming the team's closer, came on to work a perfect inning and bring the marathon to a happy end.

Drago had outdueled Kaat in innings and strikeouts, fanning 13 to the southpaw's seven. But that mattered little to Kaat. "He can have all the strikeouts he wants," Kaat told reporters afterward. "I'll take the victories." —⁓—

> ## At a Glance
>
> **WP:** Kaat (5–1)
>
> **S:** Granger (7)
>
> **Key stat:** Kaat allows 5 hits in 11 IP; Thompson scores game winner on Carew single

No Ill Wind at Fenway

It was a couple hours before game time and the wind was blowing out at Fenway Park. The schedule had landed the Twins in Boston for a twi-night doubleheader in their first trip to Fenway that season. Such a concept might seem scary to some folks. But to a club that was leading the league in batting average and runs scored, it was perfect baseball weather. "This is the way we like it," said manager Gene Mauch before his team went out and dismantled the Red Sox 13–5.

At a Glance

WP: Goltz (3–3)

S: Burgmeier (5)

HR: Hisle (11), Ford (3)

Key stats: Hisle 3-for-6, 5 RBIs; Twins 24 hits

Twelve different players had at least one of the season-high 24 hits Minnesota inflicted on five fairly helpless pitchers. Some players, like Rod Carew (who had the last of his five five-hit games here), had more. Larry Hisle had a productive night for a leadoff guy—three hits and five RBIs. The one guy who didn't get a hit was second baseman Rob Wilfong, who went 0-for-3. His replacements in that spot in the batting order—Willie Norwood and Bobby Randall—made up for it with a hit apiece.

The Twins ended the game with a .500 batting average (24-for-48), a fact that amazed even the normally stoic Carew. "Some days, it doesn't make any difference what pitchers we face," Carew said. "We're just gonna hit."

Boston manager Don Zimmer couldn't have agreed more. "Everybody on that team looks like they are fighting for the batting title," he sighed. —⁓—

Bostock Catches a Spot in the Record Book

Lyman Bostock had already had an eventful night. He went 2-for-6 and flagged down five balls in spacious center field in the Twins' romp to victory in the first game of the doubleheader. As it developed, that was merely a preview of coming attractions.

Minnesota completed a sweep with a 9–4 victory. Bostock had another productive game at the plate, going 2-for-3, scoring twice and knocking in a run. But he made a bigger presence in the outfield, tying the American League record for outfielders with 12 putouts. (His 17 for the twin bill is also a major league record.)

Bostock started slow, recording just three outs in the first four innings. But he picked up the pace, chasing down three fly balls in the fifth inning. From there, it was a steady stream of action that ended, appropriately enough, when he caught Fred Lynn's effort to end the game.

At the plate, the Twins worked their way to nine runs on 11 hits. Boston's Mike Paxton got his big league career off to a good start when he fanned Larry Hisle to start the game. In short order, however, Roy Smalley doubled, Rod Carew singled and went to second on an unsuccessful throw to the plate, and Bostock singled to make it 2–0. Minnesota kept pecking away at Paxton and his successors until the game ended at nearly 1 a.m.

> ## At a Glance
>
> **WP:** Thormodsgard (3–2)
>
> **Key stats:** Adams 2-for-4, 3 RBIs; Top four Boston hitters 2-for-16

Bostock may have earned a place in the record book, but he was quick to say he wasn't the only busy guy on this long night. "I may have lost some weight running down those fly balls but I didn't lose as much as Lynn did chasing all those balls we hit over his head. He ran the Boston Marathon out there tonight." —⁓—

Rough Day for Closers Ends Well for Twins

There are some games that just don't make sense. Imagine a game in which a Hall of Fame closer—and another guy who might make it there someday—each blow a chance to get a save. Imagine further the guy who gets the win is a fellow who was scheduled to go back to the minors later in the day. Instead, he ended with his first (and, as it turned out, only) major league win and then finished the day in the hospital with a stomach ailment of some sort.

Such was the case in the Twins' 12–11 victory at the Oakland-Alameda Coliseum on this Wednesday afternoon.

Neither starting pitcher—Minnesota's Kevin Tapani nor Oakland's Ron Darling—fared well. Tapani went a bit longer, going 4 2/3 innings as opposed to Darling's 2, but the result was the same: each guy gave up five runs.

Unfortunately for the Twins, Tapani's successor, Mike Trombley, gave up three runs in the sixth inning. Thus the Twins trailed 8–5 entering the eighth inning, when the fun really began.

Rich Gossage was on the down side of his 22-year career, but he could still throw hard. He had zipped through the seventh inning and seemed in control the next inning with one runner on second and two out. Although Gossage was always a fireballer, he generally had good control. This time, however, he uncorked a wild pitch (one of just 63 he threw in an 1,800-plus inning career). Kirby Puckett followed with an RBI single to make it 8–6, causing Gossage to leave for southpaw Rick Honeycutt.

Honeycutt was in the game for one reason: to retire fellow lefty Kent Hrbek, who had fanned seven times in 16 trips against him. But Hrbek was always at his best when the game was afoot. He promptly singled to center to bring the tying run to the plate. The game was starting to get away from

Twins	AB	R	H	RBI
Knoblauch 2b	3	3	2	0
McCarty rf-lf	6	1	1	1
Puckett cf	6	2	4	4
Hrbek 1b	5	2	2	2
Harper c	4	1	2	1
Larkin dh	3	0	2	2
Munoz lf	4	0	1	0
Bush ph	1	0	0	0
Winfield rf	0	0	0	0
Pagliarulo 3b	5	1	1	0
Meares ss	5	2	2	1
Totals	**42**	**12**	**17**	**11**

Athletics	AB	R	H	RBI
R. Henderson lf	5	3	1	0
Gates 2b	5	3	3	1
Sierra rf	5	1	2	4
D. Henderson cf	4	1	1	0
Blankenship cf	0	0	0	0
Steinbach c	4	0	3	2
Neel dh	4	0	0	1
Sveum 3b	2	1	0	0
Seitzer ph-3b	1	0	0	0
Armas 1b	5	2	2	1
Bordick ss	5	0	2	0
Totals	**40**	**11**	**14**	**9**

MIN	0	0	5	0	0	0	0	4	3	-	12	17 2
OAK	0	1	2	1	1	3	0	2	1	-	11	14 2

Twins	IP	H	R	ER	BB	SO
Tapani	4.2	8	5	3	1	2
Trombley	2.1	2	3	3	3	4
Willis	0.1	1	1	0	0	0
Guthrie	0.1	0	1	1	1	0
Aguilera	0	0	0	0	3	0
Tsamis W(1–0)	1.1	3	1	1	0	1
Totals	**9**	**14**	**11**	**9**	**8**	**7**

Athletics	IP	H	R	ER	BB	SO
Darling	2	5	5	5	2	1
Downs	4	4	0	0	2	3
Gossage	1.2	2	2	2	1	2
Honeycutt	0	1	1	1	0	0
Eckersley	0.1	2	1	1	0	0
Boever L(1–1)	0	3	3	3	1	0
Mohler	1	0	0	1	0	0
Totals	**9**	**17**	**12**	**12**	**7**	**6**

E—Minnesota McCarty, Meares 2. Oakland Steinbach, Seitzer. DP—Minnesota 2. Oakland 2. 2B—Minnesota Knoblauch, Larkin, Pagliarulo. Oakland D. Henderson, Armas, Steinbach 2, Sierra, R. Henderson. 3B—Minnesota Meares. HR—Minnesota Hrbek (7). Oakland Gates (2), Armas (1) SH—Minnesota Hrbek. HBP—Minnesota Harper. LOB—Minnesota 12. Oakland 10. SB—Oakland Sierra. Attendance—18,276.

the A's. When that looked like it might happen, there was only one guy the A's trusted to stem the flow: Hall of Fame closer Dennis Eckersley.

The Twins, however, were not awed. Brian Harper doubled to score Puckett. Gene Larkin followed with another double, scoring Hrbek and Harper. Minnesota now led 9–8.

But no lead was safe for long on this day. Carl Willis and Mark Guthrie made cameo appearances on the mound in the bottom of the inning. By the time Rick Aguilera was summoned, runners were on first and third base with two outs. Aguilera was a great closer for the Twins, but he did have occasional bouts of wildness.

This was one of those bouts.

Lance Blankenship walked to load the bases. Terry Steinbach also walked, forcing in the tying run. So did Troy Neel, and the game was untied again.

Tom Kelly didn't have a lot of options left. He turned to rookie George Tsamis, a lefty who had appeared in just seven games. The rookie did what the veteran Aguilera hadn't been able to do. He threw a called third strike past Kevin Seitzer.

It didn't take long for the Twins to start another rally. Mike Pagliarulo doubled off the new pitcher, Joe Boever, and Pat Meares tripled. The game was now 10–10, the fourth tie of the afternoon. A walk and an error loaded the bases. Puckett, who had three hits and two RBIs already, came through big with a two-run single to make it 12–10.

But hardly anyone thought that might be enough to decide this game. This notion was given more credence when Marcos Armas greeted Tsamis with a home run to make it 12–11. Mike Bordick singled and Rickey Henderson came to the plate. In his 25-year major league career, Henderson hit into just 172 double plays in 10,961 official at-bats.

Naturally, this was one of those times. But that didn't settle the issue. Brent Gates singled, bringing up Ruben Sierra, who had two hits and four RBIs in the game. Tsamis sighed and induced Sierra to pop out to second to end the game.

In the end, there had been five lead changes, 30 hits, 15 walks off 13 pitchers, and 22 runners left on base. Both teams' closers had blown a save opportunity, and a rookie who had given up three hits to six batters ended up with the win.

Tsamis didn't get to celebrate his win for long. That night, he ended up in an Oakland hospital with a stomach ailment. —∾—

A Memorable Monroe Moment

The Twins had picked up Craig Monroe for basically nothing (future consid-erations) from the Cubs the previous November. They remembered when he used to rope a lot of long home runs for Detroit, particularly in that team's re-markable run to the 2006 World Series. He may not have had a big average, but if he bopped a few long bombs, the Twins would be satisfied. By the end of May, however, Monroe wasn't playing much, and his average had dropped to .226.

The Royals had cuffed Livan Hernandez for eight runs (six earned) on 13 hits in six innings. Kansas City led 8–3 with two outs and one runner on base in the ninth inning, when the game quickly changed. There were two singles fol-lowed by a Carlos Gomez single that scored two runs to make it 8–5. The locals were starting to mutter as right-hander Joel Peralta entered the game.

On the Twins bench, manager Ron Gardenhire was considering hitting for Alexi Casilla, a decent hitter with little power. But if Casilla left the game and the Twins rallied, the result would be that Matt Macri, who had been with the team for just four days, would have to play second base.

At a Glance

WP: Crain (3–2)

S: Nathan (14)

HR: Monroe (5), Morneau (9)

Key stats: Lamb 3-for-4, 2 RBIs; Monroe 3-run HR in ninth

No matter. Gardenhire sent up Monroe to pinch-hit. Six pitches later, Monroe justified the decision by drilling a line drive well into the left-field seats for a three-run homer that tied the game at 8-all. Silence never sounded so good.

One inning later, Justin Morneau untied it with a rocket of his own to right. Joe Nathan quickly quieted the Royals in the bottom of the inning, and the Twins escaped with the type of victory that exhilarates the winners and devastates the losers.

IT SEEMED LIKE A GOOD IDEA AT THE TIME

Monroe's big blow to turn around the game in Kansas City turned out to be one of the few highlights of his brief tenure with the team. In early May, he had hit a pair of home runs in another 9–8 win, this one over the Red Sox. Never known as a great outfielder, he saw most of his playing time as a designated hitter or pinch-hitter. In the latter role, he hit another home run (at San Diego). He helped to burn his old team with a home run in a July 1 victory, but his batting average was only .218. A month later, the average was down to .202 and the team gave up the ghost, released him and brought up Randy Ruiz, a 6-foot-3, free-swinging DH. —m—

Molitor, Selig, and Milwaukee Make Up

Paul Molitor had been to Milwaukee several times as a visiting player. The guy who had been such an important part of the Brewers for 15 seasons (including the team's only World Series trip in 1982) had signed as a free agent with Toronto in 1993. Folks in town didn't like it, but they understood that free agency was now an integral part of the game.

But things were different when the Twins came for their first visit in 1996. After three years in Toronto, Molitor was a free agent again. There had been considerable talk that he wanted to go home to finish his career. The good people of Milwaukee presumed that meant he was returning to County Stadium to finish out his career.

But Molitor had a different home in mind. In December 1995, the St. Paul, Minnesota, native signed a deal with the team of his youth. Milwaukee president Bud Selig was reportedly so incensed that he refused to take his calls afterward. It didn't help that Molitor got off to a great start with his new team and was hitting .332 when the Twins arrived for a two-game series. Molitor was booed when he came to bat and went 0-for-4 in a 7–3 loss that ended Milwaukee's four-game losing streak.

> ## At a Glance
>
> **WP:** Hansell (3–0)
>
> **HR:** Myers (3)
>
> **Key stat:** Hollins bunt single in 12th inning leads to GW run

The next morning, Molitor decided he would make another attempt at peace. From the Twins' clubhouse, he called to the Brewers' front office and talked to Selig. Ten minutes later, the pair who had helped bring Milwaukee back as a baseball town seemed on good terms again. "I told him it wasn't personal," Molitor told reporters later. "People have a tendency to look for negatives. But you have to look forward in this game. I thought this [signing with the Twins] was the best thing for me and my family."

Whether the phone call had anything to do what transpired a few hours later can never be proven. But Molitor shook off his tough previous game with three singles, a walk, a run scored, and a RBI. By the end of the afternoon, the boos seemed more muted and the crowd a little more accepting of the prodigal son. His teammates picked up the pace as well, slapping out a dozen hits. Finally, in the 12th inning, Dave Hollins led off with a bunt single, was sacrificed to second and raced home with the winning run on Jeff Reboulet's single for an 8–7 win. It hadn't been a storybook return. For Paul Molitor, however, it was good enough. —⁓—

A Very Good Night at The Ballpark in Arlington

The first pitch hadn't been thrown, but it had already been an encouraging day for the Twins. The later events of the evening—a five-hit game by Chuck Knoblauch plus a dramatic six-run ninth inning rally that resulted in a 9–5 victory at The Ballpark in Arlington—nearly took a back seat to the following events:

First, the team had received encouraging news from Florida: injured reliever Rick Aguilera reported no ill effects from working six solid innings in a game in Fort Myers. (He would return to the team ten days later.)

Then, Kirby Puckett took batting practice for the first time since waking up one morning late in spring training with blurry vision. Just seeing Puckett on the field again seemed to perk up a team that was staggering along with a 23–28 record, 11½ games out of first place. (Sadly, however, Puckett never returned to action.)

For seven innings on this steamy night, the game was a mixture of pitching and hitting: Brad Radke stifled the potent Ranger attack, allowing no runs and just five hits. Meanwhile, Knoblauch, the former Rookie of the Year, was continuing to make life miserable for Texas starter Roger Pavlik.

Pavlik entered the game with a 7–1 win-loss record, but Knoblauch improved his batting average against him to .500 (12-for-24) with four singles and two runs scored.

The happy story, however, changed quickly in the eighth. Radke coughed up a leadoff homer to Rusty Greer. Considerable mayhem followed against Radke and three successors. By the time the Rangers were done, the Twins trailed 5–3 with Mike Henneman, a longtime nemesis who had 15 saves to his credit in just two months, entering the game to replace Pavlik.

Greg Myers struck out to open the ninth inning but the next six batters rapped singles. The fifth of those hits belonged to Knoblauch, giving him the first five-hit game of his career. Rich Becker followed suit with a looper to right that broke a 5-all tie and gave the Twins a one-run lead. Paul Molitor hit a three-run homer to make it 9–5 to cap the six-pack outburst. The Rangers put a couple of runners on base in the bottom of the inning, but Greg Hansell whiffed Pudge Rodriguez and induced Will Clark to hit a harmless fly ball to center field, putting a happy ending on a long, interesting day. —⁓—

At a Glance

WP: Milchin (2–1)

HR: Molitor (3)

Key stats: Knoblauch 5-for-5, 3 runs; Twins 6 runs, 7 hits in ninth

Shorthanded Twins Find a Way Despite Injuries

Under most circumstances, the story of this afternoon would probably have been how Minnesota starter Johan Santana extended his league-leading strikeout total to 105 with 14 Ks in a marvelous eight-inning effort. After giving up a pair of first-inning runs, Santana allowed only one more run (a Victor Martinez homer), retiring 13 of the last 14 batters he faced.

But baseball is often anything but fair, and Santana's effort ended up as just one of several intriguing stories in a 4–3, 13-inning victory over the Indians at the Metrodome. Santana left the game with the score tied at 3-all. It stayed that way until the Twins got to Rafael Betancourt for the winning run several innings later on an RBI-single by Jacque Jones.

Much of the postgame talk was centered over the fact that the Twins had managed to win despite losing three regulars during the game to injury. First baseman Justin Morneau left in the fifth inning with an injury. Two innings later, second baseman Nick Punto tore his hamstring while trying to steal a base. Later, catcher Joe Mauer left the game with a reoccurrence of the groin problems that had sidelined him for the previous five games.

Fortunately, there were a few healthy bodies left. With one out in the 13th, Lew Ford doubled and sprinted home on Jones' two-out single. It was the fourth time in ten days the Twins and Indians had played an extra-inning game. ⁓

At a Glance

WP: Romero (1–2)

HR: Mauer (5), Punto (1)

Key stats: Ford doubles, scores on Jones single in 13th

Did You Know?

Jacque Jones holds the club record for most leadoff home runs in team history (20). Chuck Knoblauch ranks second with 14. Dan Gladden is the only other player in double digits with 12 longballs at the top of the order.

The Killer Goes Upstairs

He had hit tape-measure homers before. There was the one that went off the batter's eye in Chicago's Comiskey Park in 1961, the jolt over the left-field roof at Detroit's Tiger Stadium in 1962, and the rocket in Baltimore two years later that measured at 471 feet—the longest one in Memorial Stadium history.

But the drive Harmon Killebrew hit on a Saturday afternoon remains the most talked-about home run in Met Stadium's 25-year history. What other hit would draw such attention that it is still memorialized by a plaque nearly three decades after the ballpark where it was struck was razed?

The irony is that, if this shot had occurred a couple years before, it probably would haven't been as big a deal. When the Twins first moved to Met Stadium

Harmon Killebrew hit a 520-foot home run on June 3, 1967, at Met Stadium that instantly made its way into Twins lore. Killebrew's shot is still honored at the Mall of America, where Met Stadium once sat.

in 1961, left field was simply a one-level bleacher. But the success of the NFL's Minnesota Vikings (who also played their home games there), led to the construction of a second deck in 1965.

Angels	AB	R	H	RBI
Cardenal cf	5	0	1	0
Schaal 3b	2	1	2	0
Fregosi ss	4	0	1	1
Mincher 1b	4	2	2	0
Hall rf	4	1	0	0
Reichardt lf	5	1	2	3
Satriano c	5	1	2	2
Knoop 2b	4	0	1	0
McFarlane ph	1	0	0	0
Brunet p	1	0	0	0
Burdette p	0	0	0	0
Johnstone ph	1	0	0	0
Coates p	0	0	0	0
Morton ph	1	0	1	0
Kelso p	0	0	0	0
Skowron ph	1	0	1	0
Wallace pr	0	0	0	0
Rojas p	0	0	0	0
Cimino p	0	0	0	0
Totals	38	6	13	6

Twins	AB	R	H	RBI
Tovar cf	3	0	2	0
Uhlaender pr-cf	0	1	0	0
Carew 2b	4	3	2	1
Rollins 3b	3	2	2	0
Killebrew 1b	3	1	1	3
Allison lf	4	0	1	3
Valdespino rf	3	0	1	0
Versalles ss	4	0	1	1
Zimmerman c	3	0	0	0
Boswell p	2	1	0	0
Ollom p	0	0	0	0
Perry p	1	0	1	0
Nixon ph	1	0	0	0
Kline p	0	0	0	0
Totals	31	8	11	8

```
CAL  0 0 1 0 0 4 0 0 1 - 6 13 0
MIN  0 0 2 4 0 0 0 2 x - 8 11 0
```

Angels	IP	H	R	ER	BB	SO
Brunet L(1–9)	3.2	7	4	4	3	2
Burdette	0.1	1	2	2	0	0
Coates	1	1	0	0	0	1
Kelso	2	1	0	0	3	3
Rojas	0.1	1	2	2	3	0
Cimino	0.2	0	0	0	0	1
Totals	8	11	8	8	9	7

Twins	IP	H	R	ER	BB	SO
Boswell W(2–3)	5	6	4	4	4	4
Ollom	0	2	1	1	0	0
Perry	2	2	0	0	1	0
Kline S(1)	2	3	1	1	1	2
Totals	9	13	6	6	6	6

DP—California 1. Minnesota 1. 2B—California Schaal, Mincher 2, Satriano. Minnesota 2B: Rollins, Allison. HR—California Reichardt (5), Satriano (2). Minnesota HR: Killebrew (11). SH—Minnesota Zimmerman, Rollins. HBP—Minnesota Rollins, Versalles. LOB—California 11. Minnesota 12. Attendance—12,337.

A year later, Boston's George Scott tempted fate when he crushed a ball in batting practice that went off the façade of the upper deck some 70 feet above ground level. But nobody had successfully found the upper tier until this day.

The Angels came to town in last place but they did have a decent pitching staff. Jim McGlothlin, an impressive young right-hander, had blanked Minnesota on five hits the night before. George Brunet, the scheduled Saturday starter, didn't have a good win-loss record, but he was considered a crafty buzzard and a potentially difficult opponent.

The Twins had been one of the big boppers of the American League for several years. But they had hit just 34 home runs all year, by far the lowest total at this stage of the season in their history. With 10 longballs, Killebrew was the only one holding up his end of the deal.

California grabbed an early lead but the Twins chased Brunet from the mound, grabbing a 3–1 lead in the fourth inning. Enter Lew Burdette, who was in the final stages of his 18-year major league career. (In fact, he pitched only six more times after this game and retired in mid-July.)

With Rod Carew on first base, Burdette got off to a bad start by hitting Rich Rollins with his first pitch. Killebrew had been hitless in five previous at-bats against Burdette. This time, however, he got a knuckleball that didn't flutter and sent it spiraling into the second row of the second deck. Angel leftfielder Rick Reichardt looked like a junior astronomer as he watched the ball disappear out of view.

"I got all of it," was all Killebrew could say later.

Years before, Twins public relations director Tom Mee had worked out a mathematical system for measuring home runs. Since this one landed in uncharted waters, it took Mee a few seconds, but he came up with 520 feet as the estimated distance.

Other people chimed in with different ideas, but all acknowledged they had never seen a ball hit like that before. Even Twins coach Billy Martin, who had been a teammate of Mickey Mantle when that gentleman hit a celebrated home run in Washington, agreed this was the longest one he had ever seen.

There was, however, one person, who didn't seem too impressed—Selva Lewis Burdette.

"I've thrown longer ones than that," Burdette told reporters after the game. Then he seemed to soften a bit. Asked what pitch he threw, Burdette sighed, "It was a knuckleball that started too high and it got higher."

THE AFTERMATH

The day after Killebrew's home run, the team painted the seat where the ball landed a different color. It stayed that way for the rest of the ballpark's life. When Met Stadium was razed, the seat was transported and now has a place of honor at the Mall of America on the approximate spot where those bleachers stood. —⁓—

Did You Know?

It was a good thing the Twins' bats were hot against the Yankees on May 2, 1967. Minnesota slapped out 13 hits in a 13–4 win that night. The game time temperature was the coldest record in team history: 32 degrees.

The Streak Ends in Style

This turned out to be one of the pivotal days in club history—for more reasons than one.

The Twins' first year in their new stadium, the Metrodome, wasn't going well. The club started off decently, going 5–4 in a nine-game homestand to open the season. But when they went 2–8 on the season's first road trip, the young team headed in a direction they had a hard time correcting for the rest of the season.

In an attempt to shake things up, the club made three major trades (two with the Yankees) in the first six weeks of the season. They bade farewell to several players who had been regular contributors for years (Roy Smalley, Doug Corbett, Rob Wilfong, Roger Erickson, and Butch Wynegar). Of the eight players acquired in those transactions, three of them—pitcher Ron Davis, shortstop Greg Gagne, and outfielder Tom Brunansky—would become significant players for the team in the future.

But little of this was noticeable when the Orioles came to town for a series in early June. Baltimore was scuffling with a 23–25 record, eight games out of first place in the AL East. But they looked like world-beaters compared to the young Twins, who entered the weekend at the Metrodome on a team-record 14-game losing streak and with MLB's worst win-loss mark at 12–41.

To make matters worse, Baltimore lefty Scott McGregor, a solid pitcher, was on the mound against one of the team's many youngsters still learning the game, lefty Brad Havens.

To juice attendance, Twins president Calvin Griffith promised fans who attended the game they could purchase tickets for a future game for just a dollar if the Twins won that night.

Some 8,517 folks took Calvin up on his offer, going home delighted when the unlikely combo of Havens and Terry Felton combined for a six-hit shutout in a 6–0 win.

McGregor entered the game with a career 8–1 win-loss mark against Minnesota. On this night, however, Havens bettered him from the start. The southpaw went 5 2/3 innings, giving up five singles. Felton, who had been winless in his 16 career decisions, took it from there for the first of three career saves. It was also Minnesota's first shutout of the season.

Blanking the solid Baltimore lineup was one thing. The team still needed to score some runs. The Twins finally broke through when Ron Washington lèd off the fourth inning with his second home run of the season. Before the inning was over, Gary Ward hit a two-run homer, and Minnesota suddenly had a 4–0 lead.

Sal Butera singled home a run in the seventh, and Jesus Vega's sacrifice fly in the eighth produced another run. Compared to the team's offensive problems during the long losing streak, this was a plethora of runs.

But there were still moments of tension. Havens had been struggling with holding onto leads. So, when it was still 4–0 in the sixth and the Orioles loaded the bases with two outs with Cal Ripken Jr. at the plate, manager Billy Gardner took no chances. He waved in Felton, who promptly whiffed Ripken to end the threat.

Washington didn't seem surprised. "Worry? There was no reason to worry," he said after the game. "Terry had things under control."

Although it was 6–0 by the ninth inning, the Twins felt plenty of anxiety when Baltimore again loaded the bases. But Felton got Rich Dauer to hit into a game-ending force play and there were huge sighs of relief everywhere—a crowd reaction that seemed louder than just 8,000 plus fans.

"I thought it was the seventh game of the World Series," Gardner said. Griffith, who rarely came to the manager's office, popped in after the game to offer congratulations and encouragement. "It was something to see," he beamed.

Kent Hrbek was thinking ahead. "Hey, what's the longest winning streak the Twins have ever had?" he asked.

At the time, the answer was 12 games. Nine years later, however, Hrbek would be on the team that would break that record and set the standard that exists to this day: 15 consecutive wins. It was a main impetus for the team that would go on to claim Minnesota's second World Series championship.

A FUTURE STAR ARRIVES

Although Hrbek had no way of knowing it, one other occurrence that day—the signing of an outfielder selected in the January free agent draft—would play a major role in the eventual team-record winning streak. The fellow had played that spring with a junior college team and was headed to Elizabethton, Tennessee, to start his pro career in a few days.

His name? Kirby Puckett. —⌇—

Orioles	AB	R	H	RBI
Bumbry cf	4	0	1	0
Dauer 2b	5	0	1	0
Ford rf	4	0	1	0
Murray 1b	4	0	1	0
Ayala lf	3	0	1	0
Lowenstein ph-lf	1	0	0	0
Singleton dh	2	0	1	0
Ripken 3b	3	0	0	0
Dwyer ph	1	0	0	0
Dempsey c	3	0	0	0
Crowley ph	0	0	0	0
Sakata ss	2	0	0	0
Nolan ph	1	0	0	0
McGregor p	0	0	0	0
Stoddard p	0	0	0	0
Totals	33	0	6	0

Twins	AB	R	H	RBI
Milbourne 2b	4	0	0	0
Washington ss	4	2	3	1
Brunansky cf	3	1	0	0
Hrbek 1b	4	0	1	0
Vega dh	3	1	1	2
Ward rf	4	1	1	2
Hatcher lf	3	1	1	0
Gaetti 3b	3	0	1	0
Butera c	2	0	1	1
Havens p	0	0	0	0
Felton p	0	0	0	0
Totals	30	6	9	6

```
BAL  0 0 0 0 0 0 0 0 - 0  6 0
MIN  0 0 0 4 0 0 1 1 x - 6  9 0
```

Orioles	IP	H	R	ER	BB	SO
McGregor L(6–4)	6.1	7	5	4	2	1
Stoddard	1.2	2	1	1	0	0
Totals	8	9	6	5	2	1

Twins	IP	H	R	ER	BB	SO
Havens W(2–4)	5.2	5	0	0	2	3
Felton S(1)	3.1	1	0	0	3	6
Totals	9	6	0	0	5	9

DP—Baltimore 1. 2B—Baltimore Singleton. Minnesota Vega, Gaetti. HR—Minnesota Washington (2), Ward (6). SF—Minnesota Vega. LOB—Baltimore 11. Minnesota 3. Attendance—8,517.

The Kid Makes a Good (Second) Impression

It wasn't the best of ways for Rik Aalbert Blyleven to start his major league career. His manager, Bill Rigney, misspelled his name on the lineup card. Then the first batter he faced in the bigs—Lee Maye—hit a home run to allow the hometown Washington Senators to tie the game.

But a funny thing happened after that.

Blyleven started pitching like a wily veteran instead of a 19-year old who had only appeared in 21 minor league games. Two hours later, the Twins had a 2–1 victory and a 22-year MLB pitching career was under way. "I was a little nervous and dazed when I went out to start pitching," Blyleven admitted later. "That home run startled me and made me concentrate more."

Here is an advertisement for the power of concentration:

After Maye's home run, Blyleven allowed only four more hits, walked one batter, and struck out seven in a seven-inning effort. He even had a role in the winning run in the fifth inning. With the game tied at 1-all, Frank Quilici led off with a single. Blyleven moved him to second with a perfect sacrifice bunt. Cesar Tovar promptly singled Quilici home with the night's final run.

At a Glance

WP: Blyleven (1–0)

S: Perranoski (13)

Key stats: Blyleven allows 5 hits, has 7 Ks in 7 IP

In the eighth inning, Maye was scheduled to lead off and Rigney decided his rookie had done enough, replacing him with veteran Ron Perranoski. It turned out to be a wise move. Perranoski retired all six batters he faced to preserve the win, the first of 287 Blyleven would achieve in his career. —

Zimmerman Finally Gets to Do a Home Run Trot

The 1965 season was going along well. Minnesota had a two-game lead on the White Sox and had already pounded the ninth-place Senators in the series opener when the largest crowd of the season at Met Stadium—30,665—made their way in on a sunny Sunday afternoon.

The team wasn't the only attraction that day—club owner Calvin Griffith was giving away Little League bats as well. Little did the crowd know they were going to witness a major league first.

An injury to regular catcher Earl Battey had forced Jerry Zimmerman into regular duty. He was a fine defensive player (manager Sam Mele once said he was the best "mechanical" catcher in the league), but he was nowhere near the hitter Battey that was. In his fifth big league season, Zimmerman had never hit a home run.

In the second inning, Zim singled home a run (just his fifth RBI of the season) to break a 1-all tie. Minnesota led 3–2 in the bottom of the fourth when Zimmerman caught a Phil Ortega pitch just right and hit it on a line to straight center field. It flew over the fence and landed against the batter's eye for Zimmerman's first four-bagger in 499 major league at-bats.

At a Glance

WP: Pleis (3–0)

HR: Oliva (10), Zimmerman (1)

Key stats: Zimmerman 3-for-4, 3 RBIs; Hall 3-for-4, 2 RBIs

His teammates picked up the attack from there, rapping out 14 hits in an 11–2 win. Zimmerman later added a single, finishing 3-for-4 with two runs and three RBIs. Afterward, he seemed unimpressed with the whole thing. "Any man with a bat in is hands has a chance to hit one out," he said.

Perhaps so. But it was an event that happened just twice more in an eight-year, 994 at-bat career. —⁓—

Hrbek's Five-Hit Night

If you polled the majority of Twins fans who followed the team during Kent Hrbek's 14-year career and asked what they remember the most about him, you would probably get replies about his home run prowess and the fact he was a much better fielder than many people suspected.

But he was also a .282 lifetime hitter. When he was swinging a hot bat, as was the case in this Twins' 4–1 victory over Kansas City, he was a handful to deal with at the plate. Because of pitching problems, Minnesota had fallen nine games off the lead two months into the season. On this night, however, Bert Blyleven was on top of his game, silencing the defending World Series champs with a complete-game seven-hitter.

Hrbek and his longtime running mate, Gary Gaetti, provided all the offensive punch that was needed. In the first inning, with one out and Mickey Hatcher on second, the big guy doubled to deep center for the game's initial run. Gaetti then followed with a home run for a quick 3–0 lead. Hrbek singled his next two times up off starter Danny Jackson but was stranded on base.

In the seventh inning, Hrbek took matters into his own hands with a home run off reliever Steve Farr. He capped his big night with a ninth-inning single. The five-hit game—the only one of Hrbek's career—raised his batting average 18 points to .306. After the game, though, gaudy numbers seemed the furthest thing from Hrbek's mind. There had been rumors the team might trade Gaetti or outfielder Tom Brunansky to shake things up. Hrbek, never shy, had a definite view on the subject. "Let's get something going right here and put an end to all this crap about a trade," he said. ⁓ᴡ⁓

> ## At a Glance
>
> **WP:** Blyleven (5–5)
>
> **HR:** Gaetti (14), Hrbek (11)
>
> **Key stats:** Blyleven 7-hitter, 5 Ks; Hrbek 5-for-5, 2 RBIs

How Do You Spell Relief? S-O-U-P

The pregame plan was simple: have starter Pete Redfern throw 60 pitches to test his sore elbow in a game situation at Cleveland. After that, it would be up to the bullpen to pull the game out. Dave Goltz had tossed a complete game the night before, so manager Gene Mauch felt everybody should be well rested.

Redfern lasted 68 pitches, leaving in the fourth inning with a 2–1 lead and two runners on base. It was a dicey situation, so Mauch went to the relief pitcher he trusted the most. Bill Campbell was often used as the closer. But he also had already pitched four or more innings four times that season.

Campbell proved his manager to be a smart guy: he induced Doug Howard to ground out to end the inning and start one of the most remarkable relief efforts in team history. Campbell ended up facing just 17 batters the rest of the game (one over the minimum), only allowing a single, a walk, and no runs. He was the winning pitcher in a 3–1 decision. Rod Carew had three hits, three stolen bases and two runs scored—plenty of offense for Campbell.

> ## At a Glance
>
> **WP:** Campbell (7–2)
>
> **Key stats:** Campbell allows 1 hit in 5 2/3 IP in relief; Carew 3-for-4

Afterward, Mauch could only shake his head in amazement at Campbell, who was making his sixth relief appearance in eight days. In that time, he had thrown 16 innings, almost the equivalent of two complete games. "I hope he knows how good he is," Mauch said.

A ROUGH TREND BEGINS

Campbell, who had signed with Minnesota as a free agent, was in his fourth season with the team. He went on to have a terrific 1976 season for the Twins, leading the team in appearances (78), wins (17), and ERA (3.00), the only time this unlikely hat trick of stats has occurred in team history. (The 17 wins is still an AL record for relievers and one short of the major league mark.) Unfortunately for the Twins, this was the beginning of the free agent era. Campbell left the team for Boston in the winter, signing for a reported $210,000. He had a great first year at Fenway, saving 31 games, and was named to the All-Star team. But he hurt his arm the next season and, although he stayed in the majors for another decade with half a dozen franchises, he never regained his status as a team's primary closer.

Campbell does hold one other unusual distinction with the Twins. He is the only player with actual military combat experience who has ever played for them. —⁓—

An Out-of-Order Win

Ask longtime Twins' fans for memories of Cleveland's cavernous Municipal Stadium and you may get some funny looks. Some might recall the final weekend of 1984 when Jamie Quirk and friends ruined a late run for the West Division flag. Others might recall the trouble the team had in the otherwise wonderful 1965 campaign. The Indians were the only team to win a season series against the Twins that year, winning nine of 12 games played in Cleveland.

But there were happy memories there, too. Minnesota's 11–10 victory on a June night in 1975 was no work of art—unless you like high comedy. Still, as Shakespeare once pointed out, the play's the thing. In this case, the team survived a series of mistakes and emerged with one of the strangest wins in club history.

The fun started before the first pitch. Twins manager Frank Quilici had made two lineup cards before the game. One had Rod Carew, (who was hitting .418 but was hurting) in the game. The other one didn't. When he determined Carew was healthy enough to play, Quilici handed in the official card to the umpires, listing center fielder Dan Ford hitting seventh and shortstop Danny Thompson batting eighth.

However, in the lineup card he put up in the dugout, Ford and Thompson's places in the order were reversed. When Thompson flied out as the No. 7 batter to end the first inning, nobody said anything in the Cleveland dugout. They remained silent in the second when Ford was disposed of with no problem.

The Twins continued to hit out of order for eight innings with middling success. Ford tripled and scored a run and Thompson had a single. But the Indians seemed to have a good reason for staying mum: their hitters were having their way with Minnesota starter Jim Hughes and reliever Bill Butler, racing to a 10–6 lead after seven innings.

It was still that way in the ninth when things really went askew. Tony Oliva had led off the inning and eventually scored when Tom Kelly (yes, the future manager) was safe on an error by Rico Carty. It was now 10–7 with Thompson seemingly due at the

Twins	AB	R	H	RBI
Braun lf	5	1	1	1
Carew 2b	6	1	3	0
Hisle 3b	5	1	2	0
Oliva dh	4	1	2	1
Gomez pr-dh	0	1	0	0
Darwin ph-dh	1	0	0	0
Soderholm 3b	4	3	3	2
Kelly 1b	5	1	1	2
Ford cf	6	1	1	1
Thompson ss	6	0	2	2
Borgmann c	2	0	0	0
Terrell ph	1	0	0	0
Roof c	0	0	0	0
Walton ph-c	2	1	1	1
Totals	47	11	16	10

Indians	AB	R	H	RBI
Bell 3b	5	0	2	0
Manning rf-lf	6	1	1	1
Hendrick cf	6	2	1	0
Powell dh	5	2	2	2
Lowenstein lf	2	0	0	1
Spikes ph-rf	4	2	2	1
McCraw ph-1b	2	0	0	0
Carty ph-1b	3	0	2	2
Ellis c	5	0	0	0
Duffy ss	4	1	0	1
Kuiper 2b	3	2	2	1
Totals	45	10	12	9

MIN 2 0 1 0 2 1 0 0 4 0 1 - 11 16 3
CLE 0 0 4 1 3 0 2 0 0 0 0 - 10 12 1

Twins	IP	H	R	ER	BB	SO
Hughes	4.1	6	6	3	1	3
Butler	1.2	6	4	3	1	2
Albury W(4–2)	5	0	0	0	2	5
Totals	11	12	10	6	4	10

Indians	IP	H	R	ER	BB	SO
Harrison	5.2	9	6	6	3	0
Beene	2.1	4	2	1	1	0
Buskey L(2–3)	3	3	3	1	0	1
Totals	11	16	11	8	4	1

E—Minnesota Braun 2, Soderholm. Cleveland Carty. 2B—Minnesota Kelly, Soderholm. Cleveland Spikes. 3B—Minnesota Ford. Cleveland Kuiper. HR—Minnesota Oliva (4), Walton (1). Cleveland Powell (8). SH—Minnesota Hisle, Borgmann, Kelly. HBP—Cleveland Kuiper. LOB—Minnesota 10. Cleveland 7. Attendance—6,912.

plate. For reasons no one ever explained, Ford suddenly decided to bat where he should have been all along. Cleveland manager Frank Robinson never questioned this as another run scored on Ford's grounder that was the first out of the inning. Thompson followed with another ground out that plated another run to make it 10–9.

The issue might have never been discussed except for what happened next: Danny Walton was sent to pinch-hit for Phil Roof. Walton had once hit 17 home runs for Milwaukee but had done little in two seasons in limited duty in Minnesota.

Until now.

Walton drilled a Tom Buskey fastball over the right-field fence to tie the game at 10–10.

In the next inning, there was more fun. Vic Albury, who had not allowed a hit since relieving Butler in the seventh inning, walked Duane Kuiper. He promptly caught Kuiper so far off first base that Thompson, the second baseman, had no choice but to bolt for second. In the ensuing rundown, Thompson eventually tagged out Kuiper. But Quilici came out to argue the out should have happened even *sooner* because Kuiper had left the baseline during the rundown. Umpire Dave Phillips thought otherwise and ended up ejecting the Minnesota manager for the night.

In the 11th inning, Eric Soderholm singled and Kelly sacrificed him to second base. Buskey wild-pitched Soderholm to third, but Ford, batting for the second time all night where he was supposed to, fanned. Thompson, getting used to hitting eighth, then singled to center to give Minnesota an 11–10 lead. Walton, his role in the drama finished, flew out to end the inning.

Albury, in one of the best outings of his career (5 IP, 0 H, 0 ER, 2 BB), then pitched a perfect bottom of the inning to wrap up the zany night.

In the end, it was a game that saw the Twins bat out of order eight times, a guy (Walton) hit the final home run of his career, a future manager play first base and the current manager get ejected for arguing over a play in which his team recorded an out.

All in all, a very interesting and—for a change in Cleveland—happy night at the ballpark. —⁓—

Long Day's Journey Ends on Happy Note

The Twins and Mets had already played two tight, low-scoring games, managing just 11 runs between them. So it made sense the finale of the series would be a four-hour plus, 15-inning affair with a grand total of five runs scored. Thanks to solid relief pitching, solid fielding by Torii Hunter, and a clutch hit by little-used Michael Ryan, Minnesota escaped with a 3–2 win that gave them a sweep in the only games the Mets ever played at the Metrodome.

Minnesota had used an unearned run to win one game and a terrific effort from Johan Santana to get a second win. A sweep didn't look very promising when the Mets jumped on Kyle Lohse for a 2–0 lead after 2½ innings in Game 3. But Lohse and five successors held the visitors to just five hits the rest of the day.

Still, it was 2–1 in the ninth inning with two out and nobody on when Matt LeCroy singled. Jose Offerman doubled to left-center and LeCroy, whose running style would fit in well in Pamplona,

> ## At a Glance
>
> **WP:** Balfour (1–0)
>
> **Key stat:** Rivas scores GW run on Ryan single in bottom of 15th inning

kept going toward home. When center fielder Mike Cameron airmailed a throw to the backstop, the game was suddenly tied. ("That was entertaining," manager Tom Kelly said later.)

Nothing much happened until the 15th inning, when, with a runner on first and one out, Jason Phillips drove a ball to deep center. Hunter managed to run it down. Later, Todd Zeile drove a ball to the gap only to see Hunter repeat himself. Duly inspired, the Twins loaded the bases in the bottom of the inning on three straight singles. Ryan, who had entered the game as a pinch-runner for Joe Mauer in the eighth, then slapped the ball through the right side, and the sweep was complete.

Later, Kelly marveled at Hunter's defensive prowess on the Phillips' ball. "If Willie Mays was watching, he'd had been proud of that one," he said. —⌁—

Finally, the Twins Get a Win at Dodger Stadium

All Justin Morneau cared about was coming out of a 1-for-22 funk. But Twins fans with a long memory had other reasons to celebrate the team's 5–3 win on a Saturday night at Dodger Stadium. Granted, that wasn't Sandy Koufax or Don Drysdale on the mound. But when you have waited 40 years to get a victory on enemy soil, you take it any way you can get it.

When the interleague opponents were announced for the 2005 season, Minnesota lobbied hard to have the Dodgers' games played at the Metrodome. It would be the 20th anniversary of the team's first World Series appearance— against the team that narrowly defeated them, four games to three.

Justin Morneau shows his power during a June 11, 2005, win in Los Angeles. Morneau drove in the first four runs in a 5–3 win, the Twins' first-ever win at Dodger Stadium.

But the MLB folks were unimpressed. Minnesota was assigned to go to L.A. after a series in Arizona. The Dodgers weren't spending a lot of time reminiscing about 1965. No, their focus was on the 1955 team, Brooklyn's only World Series crown achieved over the rival Yankees.

The Twins brought in Jim "Mudcat" Grant, who had been the team's pitching hero in the 1965 Series, for the local telecast. The Dodgers? They rounded up the locals from that club who were still living in town and had them wave to the crowd. In a very Hollywood-like ending (fan favorite Hee-Sop Choi homered in the bottom of the ninth), the Dodgers then won the series opener, 6–5.

At a Glance

WP: Silva (5–3)

S: Nathan (18)

HR: Morneau (9), Hunter (10)

Key stats: Morneau 2-for-4, 4 RBIs

The next night, though, Morneau helped achieve what Harmon Killebrew, Bob Allison, and Camilo Pascual could not do—win a game at Dodger Stadium. Morneau started early, with a two-run single in the first inning that gave the Twins a quick lead. He knocked in two more on his next at-bat, a booming two-run homer that made it 4–0.

Los Angeles crept back into it against starter Carlos Silva, but, after two shutout frames from J. C. Romero, Joe Nathan tossed a perfect ninth, and the Twins finally had a win at Dodger Stadium.

For Morneau, the win had extra importance. He had been dogged by newspaper reports that he had intentionally recovered slowly from a bone spur injury on his elbow. He said, however, the rumors didn't matter to him. He was just happy to snap a skid that had seen him get just one RBI in 14 games.

Joe Nathan

An unknown quantity when acquired from the Giants in an off-season trade, he quickly developed into one of the top closers in the game, setting a team record for saves in 2009 with 47. In 2006, he led the AL in appearances with 61. For the most part, however, he morphed into the role as Ron Gardenhire's trusted guy in the ninth inning of big games. His peers took proper note, too, picking him for the All-Star Game four times.

A Good Trend Starts

The Twins seemed to be in good humor when they arrived at the Astrodome for their first interleague game ever. "I want [Paul] Molitor to teach me how to hit," said pitcher Bob Tewksbury, scheduled to start the final game of the series. "I better take him to lunch. I need a few tips." And this was from a guy who had spent nine of his 10 previous MLB seasons in the National League.

Not to worry. The Twins had to make a few adjustments. Minnesota manager Tom Kelly had to go to his Houston counterpart, Larry Dierker, for a lineup card. The AL tradition is the home team supplies lineup cards for the visitors. In the NL, everybody is on their own in this regard. Games like this one—an 8–1 victory—had a lot to do with getting comfortable with the new format.

Once Kelly solved the lineup card issue, he had to decide on a bigger issue: whether to use Molitor, who had been serving primarily as the team's DH, at first base. There was also the matter of how much leeway at the plate to give his pitchers, most of whom had never batted in a major league game.

These thorny issues went on the backburner in a hurry. Second baseman Chuck Knoblauch, who spent the week at his parents' house, went 4-for-4 with three RBIs. Molitor played first base for the second time all season and hit a two-run homer. Brad Radke did what he was known for, pitching a solid eight innings to earn the victory. Although he went hitless at the plate, Radke surprised many folks by hitting three fly-ball outs.

Interleague play for the Twins was off to a smashing start at the Astrodome.

Knoblauch was a big reason why. The local lad (he was raised in nearby Bellaire) had a walk, two singles, a double, and a triple in his first game home as he raised his batting average 13 points to .280. Joked Molitor afterward: "People say that baseball players don't give back to their community. Chuck comes home, and first day back, puts on a clinic." (As it turned out, he kept it up all week, going 8-for-12 with three walks as the Twins won two of three games.)

Molitor did OK himself. He had only played one other game at first base all season prior to this night at the Astrodome. But he looked like Kent Hrbek as he handled 10 chances perfectly, capping his night with a two-run homer off Jose Lima in the seventh inning that stretched Minnesota's lead to 6–1.

Radke took it from there, allowing a solo run on six hits before giving way to Mike Trombley who pitched an uneventful ninth to end the game.

As they like say at another place in Houston, "Mission accomplished."

At a Glance

WP: Radke (6–5)

HR: Molitor (3)

Key stats: Knoblauch 4-for-4, 3 RBIs

INTERLEAGUE PHENOMS

With an overall win-loss mark of 132–96, the Twins have the second best all-time interleague mark among MLB teams. (Only the Yankees, at 133–95, have done better.) The club hit its peak in 2006, when they swept the Cubs, Dodgers, and Brewers at home and finished with a 16–2 standard. It was very appropriate they played their first interleague games ever at Houston. In all, they have made four visits there, coming away with a 7–4 mark. When Milwaukee changed leagues in 1998, they soon became the Twins' "regular" interleague opponent. Since 2002, the teams have played each other six times a season. Ironically, the only city Minnesota hasn't visited is their old stomping grounds of Washington, D.C. Minnesota did visit Montreal in 2004, sweeping a series there. Since the club became the Nationals, they have made a pair of visits to the Metrodome. But Minnesota has yet to visit Nationals Park. ―〜―

A Starter Takes His Turn at Closing

At first glance, the boxscore looks upside down. Did Jim Perry, who started 447 games in his career, actually get a save in relief of Lee Stange, who is best remembered for his relief work?

The answer was yes, indeed—and there was a method in what appeared to be madness.

At the time in 1964, Stange, later well known for his relief work with the Red Sox, was starting a lot for the Twins, who were in fourth place—4½ games behind the White Sox when the doubleheader in Washington began. In Game 1, Stange gave up a pair of home runs and struggled at times but worked his way through 5 2/3 innings to get the win. Perry picked up the pieces, going 3 1/3 innings and leaving the winning run on base as the Twins escaped with a 6–5 win. It was one of only 10 saves he recorded in his career.

The Twins scored their runs in an accustomed manner. Harmon Killebrew hit a pair of home runs with supporting solo shots from Bob Allison and Zoilo Versalles. Minnesota also benefited from a June 11 trade with the Angels. Second baseman Jerry Kindall, a St. Paul native, had been acquired as an insurance in-fielder. When Bernie Allen ripped his knee up two days later, Kindall moved into the starting lineup, went 1-for-4, and made two sparkling plays in the field.

Although he didn't know it at the time, Stange was actually auditioning for the Cleveland Indians, who were talking a trade with the Twins. The next day, the teams made their deal. Stange and utility player George Banks headed for Ohio in exchange for a fellow who was considered to be a talented but moody pitcher.

His name? Jim "Mudcat" Grant. —⁓—

At a Glance

WP: Stange (3–6)

S: Perry (1)

HR: Killebrew 2 (19), Allison (14), Versalles (5)

Key stats: Killebrew 2-for-3, 2 HRs, 2 RBIs

No Worries as Kaat Takes His Usual Turn

Your have to be very durable to last long enough to make 898 major league appearances and pitch more than 4,500 innings. A little stubbornness doesn't hurt, either.

Jim Kaat put both those traits on display in the second game of the double-header in the city where his 25-year career started. The day before, talk centered on whether Kaat, who had left a game in Detroit five days before with a sore shoulder, would make his scheduled start. Kaat put those issues to rest, saying, "I have a Novocain shoulder now [he had received a shot the day before]. I'll be ready."

To their chagrin, the Senators found out how ready he was. Kaat tossed a complete-game nine-hitter and hit a home run as Minnesota romped to a 9–2 win and a sweep of the twin bill.

Harmon Killebrew and Jimmie Hall had already gone deep to give the Twins a 5–1 lead in the sixth inning when Washington pitcher Jim Duckworth hit Minnesota second baseman Johnny Goryl with a curve ball. Goryl didn't like it, charged the mound, and was promptly ejected. A rally seemed looming when Jerry Zimmerman singled, but Jerry Kindall (running for Goryl) was thrown out at third base. That left it up to Kaat, who was often used as a pinch-hitter and already had one 1964 homer to his credit. He made it two with a two-run shot off Duckworth that blew the game open.

Later, Bob Allison hit the team's fourth home run of the game, and the rout was on. Kaat shrugged off his bad shoulder and went the rest of the way to improve his season mark to 6–3. "My shoulder feels fine," he said afterward. A complete game and a home run will do that to a fellow. —⁓—

> ## At a Glance
>
> **WP:** Kaat (6–3)
>
> **HR:** Killebrew (20), Hall (13), Kaat (2), Allison (15)
>
> **Key stats:** Kaat 9-hitter and hits a HR; Zimmerman 3-for-4, RBI

When You Win 15 in a Row, the Game Is Really a Lot of Fun

It had started innocently enough with an 8–4 win in Kansas City that had moved the team within one game of .500. But then the Twins won the next day and, even though it was June, things began to snowball. There was a 10-game homestand in which the team swept Baltimore, Cleveland, and the Yankees. Now the Twins were at Municipal Stadium in Cleveland, the scene of so many previous heartbreaks. But the Twins won the first two games of the series as well and boasted the longest winning streak in the American League in 15 years.

Still, something was missing. Despite the impressive win steak, Minnesota was still in second place in the West Division standings, a half-game behind Oakland. By day's end, that would change. Thanks to some clutch hitting by Kirby Puckett and others and a three-inning relief effort by Rick Aguilera, Minnesota won its team-record 15th game in a row 4–2 in 10 innings. The Twins went home in first place alone for the first time since the last day of the 1987 season. "That means more than the winning streak," Kent Hrbek would say later. "Who would have guessed we could do this the way we started out?"

At a Glance

WP: Aguilera (2–2)

HR: Puckett (8)

Key stat: Newman, Puckett score in 10th to win

Indeed, Minnesota had started the 1991 season losing nine of its first 11 games. The Twins recovered quickly, though, and were at .500 by May 15. But they went back and forth from there until hitting this hot streak at the start of June.

The win in Cleveland was atypical of the streak. Minnesota simply hunted and pecked until they managed to get a lead. Cleveland led 1–0 into the sixth inning when Puckett homered to tie the game. The next inning, Gene Larkin led off with a double and scored on Al Newman's two-out single.

Twins starter Kevin Tapani worked seven commendable innings and, as frequently happened, turned the game over to first-year closer Aguilera in the eighth. This time, however, things went wrong quickly. Carlos Baerga walked, moved to third on Alex Cole's single and scored on Felix Fermin's single. Things got even messier when right fielder Shane Mack muffed Fermin's hit and the runners moved up a base. Designated hitter Mike Aldrete was intentionally walked, a move that worked out when Chris James bounced into an inning-ending double play.

You keep long winning streaks alive by taking advantage of second chances. It took an extra inning, but the Twins did just that when Newman walked and moved to third on Puckett's single. Chili Davis' sacrifice fly broke the tie. Later, Puckett scored on a Brian Harper single. Aguilera, working a rare third inning of relief, closed out the deal, and the Twins were in first place to stay.

The streak ended the next night when the Orioles victimized Aguilera for three runs in the bottom of the ninth for a 6–5 win. But that didn't seem to matter much. "How can anybody hang their heads? We just have to go get 'em tomorrow," Puckett said.

The Twins did just that and, by the time they returned home a week later, they had a 3½-game lead in the West. They eventually won by eight games, defeated Toronto in the AL playoffs, and then edged Atlanta to win their second World Series in four years. But everybody remembers where the seed was planted. —⁓—

Gardy's Happy Return to Shea Stadium

This was no run-of-the-mill interleague game for Twins' manager Ron Gardenhire. No, this was his first trip back to Shea Stadium since October 6, 1985, when he went 1-for-4 in what would be his final game as an infielder for the New York Mets. "It means a lot to me to go back to where I started. There is always an electric atmosphere there. You can feel it. There is always something going on here," he told reporters before the game.

Afterward, the manager felt even better. A solid pitching effort by Johan Santana that sparked a 6–1 victory will do that for you.

At a Glance

WP: Santana (2–1)

HR: Mohr (5), Hunter (16), Pierzynski (4)

Key stats: Santana 7 Ks in 6 IP; Pierzynski 2-for-4, 2 RBIs

Santana, who had started 2002 at AAA Edmonton recovering from an elbow injury, was working in just his fourth game of the season for the Twins. His first three efforts had produced a lot of strikeouts but too many hits and walks. On this night, however, he started strong by fanning the side in the first inning. He went on to show the form that would later become his trademark, handcuffing the Mets on a walk, three singles, seven strikeouts, and a solo run in what was, to that point, the longest outing of his career—six innings. "He went after the hitters and that's a great lineup over there," Gardenhire gushed after the game.

The Twins had plenty of offense, too. A. J. Pierzynski, Torii Hunter and Dustan Mohr homered as part of a 12-hit attack that proved Thomas Wolfe's old adage that "you can't go home again" doesn't necessarily apply to baseball. —

Blyleven's Bet Inspires Santana Shutout

Perhaps he got the inspiration from Twins broadcaster Bert Blyleven. Perhaps he remembered what had happened in his first appearance at Shea Stadium. Maybe he was auditioning for the team that later became his employer. Or maybe he had watched his teammates get smoked 8–1 the night before and was determined not to let that happen two nights.

Whatever the reason, Santana pitched one of the top games in his career on this night at Shea Stadium—a four-hit complete-game shutout. As a bonus, he also hit a double and scored a run in a 9–0 romp.

The good night may have actually started as the team rode the bus to the stadium. Blyleven said to Santana, "Don't be afraid to throw a shutout. In fact, if you do, I'll shave my head." Santana took the challenge head on, replying. "Believe me, it's going to happen."

Two hours and 26 minutes later—after the Mets had failed to even get a runner to third base—Santana proved he was as good as his word.

The free-swinging Mets helped out a bit. Santana walked nobody and only one batter—Paul Lo Duca in the ninth inning—struck out. Minnesota third baseman Jeff Cirillo, one of the hitting heroes of the night (he was 3-for-5 with a run scored and an RBI), also observed, "He had some luck on his side because they were smoking some of those balls." Still, the fact remained that Santana was constantly ahead in the count.

Helped out by a five-run second inning, the southpaw cruised through the Mets' order, retiring 15 of the last 16 batters he faced. Manager Ron Gardenhire had decided ahead of time that he would limit his pitcher to no more than 110 pitches. As it turned out, this caution wasn't needed. Santana used only 92 in working his masterpiece.

His teammates helped out with a 13-hit attack, including Santana's first extra-base hit ever, a fifth-inning two-bagger off Aaron Sele. In addition to Cirillo, three J boys—Mauer, Morneau, and Jason Bartlett—had two hits each off five helpless Met hurlers.

As for Blyleven, he was as good as his word. The next night, prior to the game, Santana got out the clippers and collected his winnings. —⁓—

Johan Santana shined in his 2007 appearance at Shea Stadium, which later became his home park. But first, Santana won two Cy Young awards for the Twins.

A Day to Remember at Yankee Stadium

Calvin Griffith was never a fellow to mince words. After the Twins beat the Yankees the first three times the teams played in 1965, it was suggested to Griffith this occurred because some New York players were injured. Griffith wasn't so sure of that. "We'd beat the Yankees even if they were healthy," he replied.

Those words had come back to the haunt the Twins' owner a bit when New York took the first two games of a four-game set on a mid-June visit to the Big Apple. But, in what manager Sam Mele

later said was his "most pleasant day I ever spent managing," Minnesota then swept a Sunday afternoon twin bill before the largest crowd ever to see the team play—71,245.

It was the first doubleheader sweep at Yankee Stadium for the franchise since 1924.

Minnesota's lead over the second-place White Sox had dropped to a half-game going into the day. To right the ship, veteran Camilo Pascual took the ball against one of the few young Yankee prospects, Mel Stottlemyre. Minnesota recovered from an early deficit to take a 3–2 lead, but Roger Maris' two-run homer off reliever Jerry Fosnow in the seventh inning put New York ahead, 4–3. Harmon Killebrew quickly tied the game with a home run in the eighth, setting up an unusual winning rally.

It was 4–4 with one out in the ninth when Zoilo Versalles walked and Sandy Valdespino singled him to third base. A Bob Tiefenauer knuckleball then eluded veteran catcher Elson Howard, and Versalles ran home to make it 5–4. Tiefenauer then walked Tony Oliva intentionally and Harmon Killebrew un-intentionally to load the bases. Hal Reniff replaced Tiefenauer and unloaded a wild pitch. Valdespino scored easily with the insurance run. Oliva, who could really scoot when he was young, tried to score from second but was thrown out at home.

In the process of the messy inning, Joe Nossek had pinch-hit for Al Worthington, the team's regular closer, leaving Mele looking for a pitcher. Jim Kaat, who had pitched a nine-inning complete game in Chicago two days before, volunteered for duty. He survived a Versalles error to record what, at the time, was just the fourth save in his seven seasons in the bigs. —

Killebrew Refuses to Knuckle Under

Having used a wily veteran in game 1, Twins' manager Sam Mele went the youth route for the second game. Twenty-year-old Dave Boswell had joined the team the previous September and had become the fifth starter a month before. Paired against Al Downing, Boswell fared well and ended up as the winning pitcher in a 7–4 decision. Mele mixed up his lineup, placing Joe Nossek at third base for the first time in his major league career, while the regular incumbent there, Rich Rollins, handled second base. Harmon Killebrew set up shop at first base after playing third base in the opener.

At a Glance

WP: Boswell (4–3)

S: Stigman (2)

HR: Killebrew (13)

Key stats: Killebrew 2-for-5, 3 RBIs; Stigman no hits, 4 Ks in 3 1/3 IP

The unusual setup held up defensively and paid dividends on offense, shelling Downing for five runs in the first three innings. But the Yankees didn't go quietly in front of their big crowd. Minnesota's lead had shrunk to 5–4 in the ninth when Bob Tiefenauer, who had played such a critical role in the first game, returned to the mound to start the ninth inning. Tiefenauer fooled Zoilo Versalles badly on a knuckle ball for strike three. The pitch, however, also fooled catcher Doc Edwards and Versalles ended up on first base because of a passed ball.

Two outs later, Tiefenauer tried to best Killebrew with another knuckle ball. But the big fellow was ready for it and drilled it into the left-field seats for a two-run homer that put the game out of reach at 7–4.

Boswell lasted long enough (5 2/3 innings) to get the win. Dick Stigman, the Nimrod, Minnesota, native who was being moved to the bullpen to basically make way for Boswell, picked up the save with 3 1/3 innings of work. Never had the Twins performed better on the big stage of New York than they did on this long afternoon. —⁓—

A Record-Setting Extra-Inning Outburst

There are times where baseball makes little sense. Take the unusual events that ocurred on a summery Saturday at Oakland-Alameda Coliseum as Exhibit A in this regard. The night before, Minnesota banged out 15 hits, including a home run by pitcher Dave Boswell, but left 18 runners on base and lost 3–2 in 14 innings. The next day, they tied a 41-year old AL record for most runs in an extra inning by scoring 11 times in the 10th inning in a 14–4 victory.

Go figure.

For most of the afternoon, the Twins picked up where they had left off the night before, leaving runners on base in key situations. Jim Perry and Ron Perranoski kept the A's at bay until Danny Cater's eighth-inning home run tied the game at 3-all. It took two more relievers to do so, but the Twins squelched a ninth-inning threat and the game headed for extra innings.

It was there, however, that the game took a very unusual turn. The Twins sent as many batters to the plate in the 10th inning as they had in the previous four innings *combined*. Thanks to some fumbling by the A's in the field, eight hits, and four walks, Minnesota tied a record set by the 1928 Yankees.

Manager Billy Martin could only shake his head about the whole thing. "Here we were on Friday dying for a hit," he sighed after the game. "Then, today, once we got going, I didn't think we'd ever stop."

For the record, it started with a Ted Uhlaender single and ended when Leo Cardenas lined into a double play. In between, three Oakland pitchers were on hand to personally witness a Harmon Killebrew three-run homer, a pair of Rod Carew singles, three others players with a single and a walk, three infield errors and a Cesar Tovar stolen base.

> ## At a Glance
>
> **WP:** Grzenda (2–1)
>
> **HR:** Killebrew (17)
>
> **Key stats:** Killebrew 2-for-4, 4 RBIs; Carew 3-for-6, RBI; Twins 11 runs in 10th inning

The beneficiary of all this was Joe Grzenda, who had entered the game in the ninth with Bert Campaneris on second base and two outs. He promptly struck out Reggie Jackson, then an up-and-coming Oakland outfielder. "If Jackson gets a hit," Perranoski said later. "The game's over."

But he didn't, and the rest became baseball history.

IT'S A FUNNY GAME

Grzenda, who had been picked up from the Mets in 1967, was a true journeyman reliever, appearing in 219 games for six teams in an 11-year period. He appeared in 38 games that season, winning four games in his only season in a Minnesota uniform. The Twins traded Grzenda and Charley Walters, later a newspaper columnist in the Twin Cities, to Washington the following spring for outfielder Brant Alyea. Reggie Jackson may have hit 563 career home runs in a Hall of Fame career, but Grzenda wasn't impressed. Jackson had 10 official at-bats against Grzenda—and struck out six times. ⁓

Did You Know?

Cesar Tovar is one of just four Twins position players to ever pitch in a regular season game—and the only one not to allow a run. Julio Becquer allowed three runs in a 1 1/3-inning stint in a 1961 game at Kansas City. Dan Gladden appeared twice as a pitcher, giving up a run in two total innings of work. Outfielder John Moses appeared in three games in 1989–90, surrendering three runs in three innings. None of them gave up a home run.

Youth Shall Be Served

It had all the makings of a rough night for the Twins. A national TV audience was set to tune in to watch Minnesota, which had kicked away a two-run lead the night before in a 5–3 loss, take on the Astros at Minute Maid Park. The home team was sending the ageless wonder Roger Clemens to the mound for his first start of the major league season. The Twins were responding with Francisco Liriano, who was born the year Clemens began his pro career. To make matters worse, Clemens had always done well against Minnesota, posting a career win-loss record of 23–12.

Liriano, however, didn't seem too awed, telling reporters before the game, "I'm facing the hitters. I don't want to even think about him (Clemens)." His manager, Ron Gardenhire, seem unconcerned as well. "I think he is at the point in his career where he will handle himself just fine," he said.

It turned out that the 43-year-old veteran was the one who ended up in awe after Minnesota's 4–2 win. Although Clemens fared well in his first MLB start of the year (5 IP, 2 ER, 4 K), Liriano was terrific, holding the Astros to two runs on four hits with seven strikeouts in eight innings. Justin Morneau had three hits (including a home run off reliever Russ Springer) and Jason Kubel had a pair of hits. The Twins' defense was sharp, turning three double plays.

> ## At a Glance
>
> **WP:** Liriano (7–1)
>
> **S:** Nathan (11)
>
> **HR:** Morneau (18)
>
> **Key stats:** Liriano 7 Ks in 8 IP; Morneau 3-for-3, RBI

By the time the Astros got on the scoreboard in the eighth inning, Minnesota had a comfortable 4–0 lead. Joe Nathan gave up a ninth-inning single but also recorded two strikeouts to wrap up the game.

Afterward, Liriano—not Clemens—was the talk of both clubhouses. "That's the best young pitcher I've seen since (Houston ace) Roy Oswalt came up," Astros catcher Brad Ausmus said. "He's got three quality pitches. I'd love to have him on my team."

Liriano's manager was duly impressed as well. "We all got a chance to see something special tonight," Gardenhire said.

And he was talking about the guy who was born in 1983, not the guy who started his pro career that year. —⁓—

The Metrodome Giveth . . . and Taketh Away

For 8 1/3 innings, White Sox pitcher Richard Dotson had a 2–0 lead and was working on a nifty six-hit shutout at the Metrodome. Then he threw a pitch to Twins second baseman Tim Teufel, who hit a broken-bat fly ball to right-center field and started running hard.

At a Glance

WP: Schrom (1–2)

HR: Teufel (7)

Key stats: Teufel 2-out, 3-run, inside-the-park HR in bottom of ninth for win; Schrom 7-hitter

Teufel kept running. And running. And running—all the way around the bases for an inside-the-park three-run homer that produced an improbable 3–2 victory. It was the sort of thing that left many who saw it speechless—except the losing team.

"It was a joke to lose that way," grumped Dotson afterward. "Teufel didn't hit the ball well at all."

The perpetrator didn't disagree at all. Instead, he waxed philosophically about the quirky place where he played his home games. "This place can eat you up," he said. "But you got to be aggressive. You're busting your butt and the next thing you know the ball is bouncing over your head because you didn't get there in time. If you let it play you, it's going to bounce out over your head anyway."

For most of the afternoon, it was a tame affair. Minnesota's Ken Schrom, a 15-game winner the year before, didn't make his first start of the season until early June due to arm issues. Thus, he was still looking for his first win of the season when matched against Dotson, a 22-game winner in 1983 who was on his way to the All-Star Game that year.

Schrom pitched well, giving up a run in the second inning when the unlikely combination of Joel Skinner and Tom Paciorek worked a perfect double steal and another in the third inning on a pair of singles and a sacrifice fly by Harold Baines. After that, the right-hander retired 21 of the last 23 batters he faced.

That seemed to be it for offense for the day until the fateful happenings in the bottom of the ninth inning. Although Mickey Hatcher and Kirby Puckett each had two hits (and each had gotten as far as third base once), the rest of the Twins' lineup had gone out meekly against Dotson.

The small crowd of 12,696 started to stir, however, when Dave Engle singled to right to open the ninth. Randy Bush, who had hit an inside-the-park homer the night before in a 4–3 win, popped out, but Tom Brunansky redirected a Dotson fastball into left field for a single to set the stage for Teufel's theatrics.

Dotson jammed him with a fastball and Teufel barely connected, sending it softly toward the outfield. Baines, playing right field, broke late and watched in horror as the ball bounced straight over his head and headed for the right field corner. Engle knew he was going to score easily. At first, Brunansky was a bit more hesitant. "I'm the tying run and I don't want to get caught off (base) if Baines catches it," he recalled after the game. "Then, all of a sudden, I saw the ball bounce and I said, 'No one is stopping me. I've got to score.'"

What Brunansky didn't know was third base coach Tom Kelly was also waving Teufel frantically around third base. Brunansky crossed home and turned around in surprise to see Teufel right behind him.

Game over. As they used to say on Mitch Miller's old TV show, "Follow the bouncing ball."

Once he calmed down, Schrom reflected on the unusual occurrences of the day. "Losing like Rich did, he might be crying," Schrom told reporters. "But he's got nine wins already. This is my first one. You gotta spread 'em around a bit." —∿—

Did You Know?

It only makes sense a June 26 game is used in this book. Minnesota's 32 wins on that date is their highest single day total in team history through the end of the 2009 season. June 24 and July 21 rank as the next best dates with 31 wins apiece.

Battey Legs One Out

Until that kid from St. Paul came along, a nice case could be built that Earl Battey was the best catcher in Minnesota Twins history. Although never fleet afoot (he once hit a one-hop line drive to right field and was thrown out at first base by Detroit's Al Kaline), he was an excellent defensive catcher who was also a solid hitter with a .270 lifetime batting average.

By 1967, however, injuries had battered Battey down to a part-time role. He was now sharing the job behind the plate with Russ Nixon and Jerry Zimmerman. Still, as was shown at Met Stadium on this Sunday, the ol' fellow was able to come through with a clutch hit when needed.

With two outs in the bottom of the eighth inning, Chicago's Tommy John was shutting down the Twins on just two singles and had a 1–0 lead. Zoilo Versalles singled to keep hopes flickering. Pinch-hitter Frank Kostro did the same. Battey was sent up to bat for pitcher Jim Merritt. Why pinch-hit a guy who was hitting .174 and had just two RBI in the last month? Battey gave the media a good reason why after the game. "I won't hit the long fly ball often but I seldom strike out," he said. "I usually put the ball in play."

Chicago center fielder Tommie Agee found this out to his chagrin. Battey drilled a shot into right-center field that escaped Agee's diving attempt and rolled to the fence. By the time the smoke cleared, Battey had a triple and Minnesota was ahead 2–1. Cesar Tovar followed with another single to clinch a 3–1 victory, chopping a game off the first-place White Sox's lead. It was the 17th—and last—three-bagger of Battey's 13-year, 3,586-at-bat career. —⚂—

An original Twin, Battey batted .277 in his seven seasons behind the plate, appearing in five All-Star Games. Despite a lack of speed, Battey had six straight seasons in which he recorded at least 17 doubles. He was also a very good defensive player, leading his fellow AL backstops in assists three straight years and winning three Gold Gloves.

Earl Battey

Hitters' Delight

The sun was shining brightly. The combination of the good weather, two teams tied for first place playing, plus a jersey giveaway all helped draw 46,463 fans (at that time, the largest crowd ever at Met Stadium for a Twins' game) for the Sunday matinee with the White Sox.

What they saw was a hitting show for the ages—a game that saw Rod Carew bang out four hits, score five runs, and tally six RBIs, only to be upstaged by DH Glenn Adams, who also had four hits but had eight RBIs. It was a game that saw relief pitcher Tom Johnson pitch more innings and allow more runs than the starter Bill Butler, but still get the win.

There was a lot more to talk about as well in the Twins' 19–12 win.

Rod Carew

The sweet-swinging Carew hit from the moment he arrived in town, making the All-Star team every season he played here. He went on to win seven batting titles here, including the memorable 1977 season when he flirted with the .400 mark and finished at .388. That same season, he led the AL in runs, hits, and triples. Earlier in his career, he was known for his daring base running, including stealing home seven times in 1969. He was an easy pick for baseball's Hall of Fame in 1991.

"This was a game—and there are a few like that every season—that a manager can do nothing about," Twins manager Gene Mauch said. "This was a great day for hitting. There were some very good ones swinging the bat today . . . and one unreal hitter."

The latter would be Carew, who had two singles, a double, and a home run in five official at-bats. He ended the day with his batting average at .403 and was honored with several standing ovations. "Those gave me butterflies," he admitted later.

The wild day started early and, for the first four innings, didn't seem to let up for a second. The White Sox nicked Butler for a run in the top of the first inning. Adams, acquired from the Giants for his hitting prowess, responded with a two-run double in the bottom of the inning for a 2–1 lead.

That was a warmup act for the second inning. Adams ended one of the roughest outings of White Sox starter Steve Stone's career with a grand slam that made the game 8–1.

Rod Carew acknowledges a standing ovation from the Met Stadium crowd after his batting average topped the .400 mark on June 26, 1977.

This seemed like a safe lead but the White Sox turned on Butler for a pair of home runs in the top of the third. Before long, Johnson replaced Butler. But the hits kept on coming and it was now 8–7 when the Twins came to bat in the bottom of the inning. Adams chipped in with another RBI (on a single) and the Sox seemed pleased to hold the Twins to four runs on four hits.

Carew resumed his carnage the next inning with an RBI single. When the fourth inning ended, the teams had been playing for over two hours and Minnesota led 15–8.

Chicago wasn't quite done. Jim Essian, a longtime Twins' tormentor, and Chet Lemon homered off Johnson to make it 15–10, but the Twins got two more runs in the seventh (Adams had another RBI on a sacrifice fly) and duplicated that effort in the eighth when Carew ignited another ovation with a two-run homer.

In the ninth inning, the Sox roughed up Johnson a bit more, but he ended up the winning pitcher despite allowing seven runs on 10 hits in 6 2/3 innings of relief. Mauch usually had a lot to say after games. This one, however, stupefied him. "I've never had a game like this in my life," he said after the game. "Nothing else comes close."

At a Glance

WP: T. Johnson (9–2)

HR: Adams (2), Carew (6)

Key stats: Adams 4 hits, 8 RBIs; Carew 4 hits, 5 Rs, 6 RBIs

"HE PLAYS BAT"

When Minnesota acquired the left-handed hitting Glenn Adams from the Giants the previous winter, he was a real unknown commodity to many folks. Mauch, however, had a definite idea on how to use Adams, telling reporters, "He plays bat."

"I always could hit," Adams said later. "It was just a matter of finding a place to play." Although the Astros selected him in the first round of the 1968 draft, he never knew why. "Houston only wanted an outfielder who could run the 100 in 9 flat. That isn't me." Eventually, he went to the Giants, where he appeared in 130 games (and batted just 164 times) over two seasons. "The Giants thought they had better players," he said.

For five years, though, he had a home in Minnesota. In 1977, he was platooned against right-handed pitchers and hit a solid .338. Although he did see some action in the field, the majority of his time was spent as a DH. He played more and averaged 80 points less the next year, but he recovered quickly to become a solid DH for the next two seasons, batting .301 and .286 respectively. By 1981, the team was going young and Adams knew his days were numbered. He spent one season in Toronto before retiring. But he goes down in team history as one of their best DHs ever. —〰—

A Proper Farewell

One can understand why the Twins were in a bit of a nostalgic mood when they entered Detroit's Tiger Stadium for the final time—and not just because of the great players who had worked there in days gone by.

This was the ballpark where the Twins set their team record for most runs in a game. It was the place where they celebrated the 1987 American League pennant. Tiger Stadium is one of just two AL home fields (Chicago's Comiskey Park is the other) in which they hold an all-time winning record.

But this series was different from many that had been played there. Detroit had won the first game 2–0. The next night, Joe Mays threw six shutout innings before giving way to Bob Wells and Mike Trombley, who preserved a 1–0 victory.

At a Glance
WP: Hawkins (4–8)
HR: Gates (2)
Key stats: Hocking 5-for-6; Mientkiewicz 3-for-4, RBI

But the final game between the two teams at Michigan and Trumbull was a hitter's battle all day. It lasted 3 ½ hours. The two teams used 11 pitchers, who allowed nine doubles and two home runs among a total of 28 hits. The Twins made better use of their hits and left the old park with a 12–7 victory.

Detroit starter Jeff Weaver had gained his first major league victory by going five scoreless, one-hit innings against the Twins in April. This time, he was shelled quickly, exiting after giving up seven runs in 1 2/3 innings. His six successors fared a little better but still gave up five runs in the final three innings.

Denny Hocking whacked three doubles among a career-high five hits. Doug Mientkiewicz contributed three singles. Brent Gates, a Michigan native, homered off the facing of the upper deck in right field. Jacque Jones and Todd Walker also had a pair of hits.

However, as often happened during Tiger Stadium's 87-year tenure, the home team made things interesting before the game ended. Minnesota had a 7–2 lead after an inning and a half. By the end of the seventh inning, the margin was down to 9–6. But an error by Detroit outfielder Bobby Higginson opened the door for three more runs to put the game put of reach. LaTroy Hawkins started and went the minimum five innings to gain the victory.

Twins manager Tom Kelly always had a soft spot for The Corner. In addition to being the park where he watched his team win the 1987 AL pennant, it was also the site of his only career major league homer, off Vern Ruhle in 1975. But he had a good idea why the time had come to move on. "I like Tiger Stadium obviously but you have to understand that you need new ball parks if you want to be successful," he said before the final meeting there. "I think we all understand that." —⌒⌒—

Sweet Music's Last Blanking for Twins

Less than a year after winning the Cy Young award, Frank Viola was struggling. Although the Twins were still in the West Division race, Viola only had a 5–8 win-loss mark when the team hit the field for a game against Oakland. There had been considerable grumbling that the Twins were not getting their money's worth out of the league's highest paid pitcher ($3.4 million a year). Even when he pitched well, there was controversy. In his previous start, Viola was publicly unhappy to be pulled with a 10–0 lead in favor of Jeff Reardon after throwing eight scoreless, six-hit innings at Boston.

That was all in the background, however. The main attraction on this night was Viola matched up against Oakland ace Dave Stewart, who had a laudable 12–3 record.

Viola, however, was on top of his game from the start, scattering seven hits as he outdueled Stewart for a 2–0 victory.

Minnesota didn't get much going against Stewart, either. In the third inning, Greg Gagne singled and Wally Backman doubled him home. Four innings later, Randy Bush hit a one-out triple and came in on Jim Dwyer's double.

> ### At a Glance
>
> **WP:** Viola (6–8)
>
> **Key stats:** Viola 7-hitter, 4 Ks; Dwyer 2-for-3, RBI

That was basically it for the Twins for the day. But it didn't matter. The A's couldn't touch Viola down the stretch—he retired the last nine batters in a row.

"Hell of a ballgame," Twins manager Tom Kelly said. "It was all it was cranked up to be."

Even Stewart was impressed. "There's only a few pitchers in the league I admire and Viola is one of them," he said.

AND THEN THE MUSIC STOPPED

Four days after blanking the A's, Viola produced another dandy effort—a complete-game 2–1 victory over the Angels with only four hits as his ERA shrunk to a season-low 3.54. Ironically, as Viola was finding his touch, his teammates were losing theirs. His shutout of the A's had moved the Twins to a 40–37 record, only 5 ½ games out of first place. Unfortunately, Minnesota lost 11 of its next 12 games. By July 14, they were 13 games behind and it became apparent that the team would consider shopping Viola around before the trade deadline at the end of the month. On July 31, the rumors became reality. Viola went to the New York Mets in exchange for five pitchers. —⁓—

A Six-Pitch Victory

As Yogi Berra once observed, "In baseball, you don't know nuthin." One day, you can throw 150 pitches and end up with a no-decision or, worse, a defeat. On another night, you can throw six pitches to two batters, walk one of them and end up the winning pitcher.

With some nifty relief help from Rick Aguilera, that is exactly what happened to provide pitcher Kevin Wade Campbell with his only victory in a Twins uniform as part of a 6–4 win over Texas. Campbell had signed with the Twins in the winter after three years in Oakland. He started the season in AAA ball and had only been with the big league team for five days when he was called upon to replace starter Pat Mahomes and face Rusty Greer in the seventh inning with the bases loaded and Texas leading 4–2. On the second pitch, Greer popped out to left to end the threat.

The Twins then combined three singles, a double, a wild pitch, and a hit batter for three runs and a 5–4 lead. Campbell walked Doug Strange to start the Texas eighth. Larry Casian replaced him and got one out. Aguilera had been tinged for two runs in the ninth inning the night before in a 11–10 loss. Baseball, however, is a game of second chances. Aguilera put the memories of the night before out of his head quickly by fanning four of the five batters he faced for the save.

Campbell, who had thrown just six pitches, emerged the winning pitcher, his only decision in 20 games with the Twins over two seasons. Sometimes, less is more. —

At a Glance

WP: Campbell (1–0)

S: Aguilera (17)

HR: Winfield (8)

Key stat: Campbell pitches 1/3 of an inning for win

Kaat's 'Imperfect' Game Is Still Good Enough

The California Angels had a grand plan. They would play a rare 6 p.m. home game on a Sunday night and shoot off fireworks after the game. As it developed, there were few fireworks during the game, and the team had to wait for over an hour to do their postgame air show. That's because Minnesota pitcher Jim Kaat also had a plan, and his was not in sync with the Angels'.

Kaat allowed just one hit—a Frank Robinson home run—and just one other base runner in what might have been the best pitching outing of his long career. Bill Singer, who would later join the Twins' staff, was nearly as good, allowing just four Twins to reach base in the game. Unfortunately for Singer, one of those was Rod Carew, whose two-run single made the difference in a 2–1 victory.

Neither pitcher walked a batter. As a result, the game was played in a snappy hour and 40 minutes, causing the lengthy delay before the fireworks went off.

"I've never had a one-hitter before, not even in Little League," Kaat said afterward. "Why, I can't even hold my son to one hit when we play Whiffle ball in the backyard."

But Kaat's games with his son weren't played at twilight with Disneyland in the background. When he arrived at the Big A that day, Kaat took note of the time of day and the sky and suggested to catcher George Mitterwald (and his eventual replacement, Phil Roof) that it would be a good idea to work as fast as possible.

The only blot on Kaat's day was Robinson's home run that led off the second inning that snapped a 0-for-15 slump and gave the Angels a 1–0 lead.

But the Twins responded quickly in the next inning. With one out, Mitterwald was hit by a pitch. Although not known for his speed, Mitterwald still beat Ken Berry's throw to third on Jim Holt's subsequent single. Holt took advantage by moving to second base.

> ## At a Glance
>
> **WP:** Kaat (9–6)
>
> **Key stat:** Kaat 1-hitter, 7 Ks; Holt 3-for-3; Carew 2-run single

Carew then dropped a single in front of left fielder Vada Pinson that easily scored Mitterwald. Holt's trip was a bit more adventurous. He stopped short of the plate and nimbly went around catcher Jeff Torborg for what proved to be the final run of the night.

Kaat took over from there. The only Angel who got on base the rest of the night was Winston Llenas, who was safe when third baseman Steve Braun booted his grounder for an error. Kaat, however, wasn't fazed. He struck out Robinson and Bob Oliver to end the inning. He retired the next six Angels as well, finishing with a flourish by whiffing Lee Stanton to end the game.

Roof, who had replaced Mitterwald during the game, was duly impressed. Noting it was almost a year to the day that Kaat's season ended early with a broken wrist, Roof did some quick math. "He was 10–2 when he got hurt last year," Roof said. "Now he is 9–6 this year. That's 19–8 in a span of roughly one season. Not too shabby."

NEAR MISSES

No-hitters are a tricky business at any time. Kaat's near-miss in Anaheim put him in some nice company. Greg Maddux (355 career wins), Tom Glavine (305) and Lefty Grove (300) are among the big winners who never tossed a no-no. The Twins have had 15 one-hitters in their first 49 years of existence. The list has some names you might expect. Bert Blyleven threw three. Scott Erickson, who did throw a no-hitter in 1994, also had a complete game one-hitter and a shared effort with Mark Guthrie. Other well-known names on the list include Jim Grant (1965), Dave Goltz (1977) and Geoff Zahn (1980).

The unlikeliest name on that list is probably lefty Gerry Arrigo. Plucked out of the White Sox system a month after the Twins came into existence, Arrigo spent scant time with the big club in 1961–63, appearing in just 13 games.

But he made the team in spring training in 1964 as a short reliever and a fill-in starter. He was in the latter role for the first game of a doubleheader against the White Sox on June 26, 1964 at Met Stadium. In the first eight innings, Arrigo fanned eight batters, allowing four baserunners (two hit by pitches, one walk, and one on a Zoilo Versalles error).

Thanks to Harmon Killebrew's two run homer, Arrigo took to the mound in the ninth inning three outs from duplicating Jack Kralick's effort two years prior with a 2–0 lead. But Mike Hershberger ended the drama with a clean single to center field to lead off the inning. There was nothing for Arrigo to do but sigh and retire the next three batters he faced (Don Buford, Jim Landis, and Pete Ward) to gain the win. It was the highlight of the southpaw's tenure with the team. He finished 1964 with a 7–4 win-loss mark and was traded to Cincinnati in December. He went on to pitch six more years in the majors. In addition to the Reds, he spent time with the Mets and White Sox and even threw another one-hitter. On the way out the door, though, Arrigo helped the Twins obtain a player who would play a key role for the team for years to come, including a brief stint as a pitcher. His name? Cesar Tovar. —⋙—

Liriano Lights Up Brewers

Even though he had not joined the regular starting rotation until mid-May, Francisco Liriano had been putting up some nifty statistics. Although he was not named to the All-Star team that was announced later that day, Liriano was still on the top of most Twins' fans minds after he shut down the Brewers for eight innings as part of an 8–0 romp at the Metrodome. For good measure, Liriano, who now had a 9–1 win-loss record, racked up a dozen strikeouts, putting him within one of the league lead.

Those were pretty good numbers for a guy who didn't make his first start until May 19. Since that time (ironically, a win at Milwaukee), Liriano had won seven of eight, lowering his ERA by nearly a run to 1.99. "I don't know how many different ways you can describe how he is throwing the baseball," Twins manager Ron Gardenhire said. "But it's nasty." The Brewers, whose collective team batting average against Liriano was .114, ruefully agreed.

The only mishap came in the first inning, when Liriano stumbled and fell awkwardly off the mound for a balk. A quick check showed he was OK. After that, he made the Brewers sick, allowing just three singles and a walk. Former Twin Jack Morris took note of the third inning, when Liriano fanned the side on just 11 total pitches. "More than anything else, Liriano throws strikes," Morris said.

On the flip side, the Twins ate up Milwaukee starter Zach Jackson for five third-inning runs. Later, Justin Morneau hit his 21st homer of the season. Liriano had more than enough runs to make the rest of the day relaxing.

At a Glance

WP: Liriano (9–1)

HR: Morneau (21)

Key stat: Liriano 3 hits, 1 BB, 12 Ks in 8 IP; Morneau 2-for-4, 2 RBIs

NO ALL-STAR APPEARANCE, THOUGH

White Sox manager Ozzie Guillen didn't select Liriano for his All-Star squad. But the rookie was one of the five finalists for the last spot on the team. The player would be determined by online balloting. Liriano had a good showing of votes but lost out to White Sox catcher A. J. Pierzynski—one of the players Minnesota had originally sent to the Giants in the trade that had brought the lefty to town. —⚊—

Landreaux Enters the MLB Record Book

Mike Augustin of the St. Paul *Pioneer Press* once wrote, "If you are looking for humility, Ken Landreaux is not your man." But if you can back it up, it ain't bragging. For most of the 1980 season, Landreaux let his bat do the majority of the talking. It started in the second home game of the season, when he doubled with one out in the ninth inning to break up Bruce Kison's attempt at a no-hitter. That hit jumpstarted what is still the team record for most games in a row with a hit: 31.

Although his average had fallen to just under .300 by early July, Landreaux was still named to the AL squad for the All-Star Game. In this 10–3 win over the Texas Rangers, he added another notch to his offensive belt by tying an MLB record with three triples in one game. This time, he was reserved in his comments. "I'm not really a triples hitter," he said. "Just luck, I guess. Those balls were right in the gaps."

In addition, he scored two runs and knocked in one as part of a 13-hit attack that included seven for extra bases. Rick Sofield, Glenn Adams, and John Castino also had two hits each and drove in four between them. But Landreaux, who tripled in the third, sixth, and eighth innings off three different pitchers, was the story of the night.

> ## At a Glance
>
> **WP:** Erickson (3–5)
>
> **S:** Corbett (8)
>
> **HR:** Sofield (6)
>
> **Key stat:** Landreaux 3-for-5, RBI

Earlier, he had told reporters he was thinking of turning down the All-Star bid because he felt he needed a rest. After torching the Rangers, he was having second thoughts. "I'm normally a second-half hitter," he said after the game. "I guess I started the second half a little early this time."

ON THE MOVE

Landreaux, who had hit .305 in 1979 after being acquired from the Angels, finished the 1980 season with a .281 batting average. He did go to the All-Star Game and lined out to left in his only at-bat. The Twins traded him to the Dodgers for three players near the end of spring training in 1981. Of the three acquired from L.A., only Mickey Hatcher ever played regularly for the team. Although he never quite reached the same levels he had in Minnesota, Landreaux hit .263 in a seven-year stint there. —◦◦◦—

Becquer to the Rescue

Before the Twins came to town, one of the area's great traditions was the annual holiday doubleheaders between the St. Paul Saints and Minneapolis Millers of the American Association. Each Memorial, Independence, and Labor Day, the two teams would play in one city at 10 a.m. and then head over to the other town for a 3 p.m. nightcap. Fans (and occasionally players) took the trolley back and forth and all who attended seemed to have a good time.

The Twins played a doubleheader at Cleveland on Memorial Day and paid homage to the old tradition with a July 4 pair against the White Sox. What occurred is sometimes forgotten in the team's lore. Next to winning the first game as a franchise in New York, however, this might have been the high-water mark of the inaugural season.

> ## At a Glance
>
> **WP:** Stobbs (2–3)
>
> **HR:** Tuttle (1), Lemon (8), Becquer (4)
>
> **Key stat:** Becquer grand slam in ninth for win

In Game 1, Twins' starting pitcher Bert Cueto struggled into the fourth inning before leaving the game due to a blister on his pitching hand. Bill Pleis and Chuck Stobbs then stepped in and did a solid job of keeping the game close. Despite home runs by Bill Tuttle and Jim Lemon, though, Minnesota trailed 4–2 entering the last of the ninth inning. Sox lefty Billy Pierce appeared headed for success when he disposed of Harmon Killebrew on a fly to center to open the inning. Bob Allison, however, followed with a single that chased Pierce in favor of Russ Kemmerer, who quickly eliminated Lemon on a fly ball.

When Earl Battey, who had started his career with the White Sox, singled to center to keep hope alive, Sox manager Al Lopez turned to Frank Baumann to finish matters. Lenny Green, however, had other ideas and worked a walk to load the bases.

This left Lopez with a dilemma. Would he stick with the lefty Baumann against the right-handed batting Tuttle? Or would he turn to 36-year-old right-hander Warren Hacker, who was the closest thing the team had to a closer? Lopez knew that if he did that, Twins skipper Sam Mele had a warm body waiting to swing.

Harmon Killebrew

The first Twin to enter the baseball Hall of Fame (in 1984), Killebrew hit 475 home runs during his 14 seasons here. In 1969, he was named the American League's MVP when he hit 49 home runs, drove in 140 runs, and drew 145 walks, all Twins' single-season records that still stand. One of the most feared slugger of his era, Killebrew was selected to 10 consecutive All-Star teams.

Lopez went with Hacker, and Mele made his move, sending Julio Becquer to the plate. Acquired from the Phillies a month before, Becquer had been hot, forging a .286 batting average with a pair of pinch-hit home runs, including a ninth-inning game-winner against Baltimore on June 20. Since he had not walked once in 36 plate appearances since joining the Twins, it will surprise few to learn what he had in mind as he went to the plate to face Hacker. "I went up to hit the first pitch," he said later.

He did just that, lining a drive over the 365 mark in right field for a game-winning grand slam home run, the only time in team history it has happened in the bottom of the ninth inning to win a game.

Later, Mele was asked why Becquer was used so often as a pinch-hitter and rarely as a starter. "He tends to swing at bad balls," Mele explained. "Over time, that will catch up to him. But in a situation like this, where the pitcher has to throw a strike or get the ball near the plate, Becquer is tough." —⋙—

Did You Know?

Ah, the glorious life of a baseball player. On August 15, 1965, Minnesota split a doubleheader at Cleveland. They played on August 17 at Detroit but got rained out the next day. So, on August 19, they played two games at Tiger Stadium, winning both. The team then flew west and played another doubleheader the next night at Dodger Stadium, splitting a pair of games with the Angels. Thus, the club played three doubleheaders in five days.

Not Your Standard Killebrew Home Run

Doubtless, there were a few folks among the 23,592 who paid their way into Met Stadium who didn't stick around for the second game of the holiday twin bill with the White Sox. Those who didn't stay missed a rare event. Oh, it wasn't the first time that Harmon Killebrew had hit a three-run homer to break a tight game open. But it was the first time (at least in the major leagues), he did it by running it out all the way.

For 7½ innings, Minnesota's Jack Kralick and Chicago's Calvin Coolidge Julius Caesar Tuskahoma McLish tossed zeroes at each other. The Twins were the first to break through. Lenny Green led off the eighth with a single and was sacrificed to second. Kralick was a decent hitter for a pitcher, and he promptly broke the scoreless tie with a single to center. Zoilo Versalles, the next batter, also singled. With two outs, as per usual, the Sox outfield shifted slightly toward left for Killebrew. This time, however, Harmon went the other way. Sox center fielder Jim Landis gave pursuit but he only got a piece of the ball in right center. The ball rolled behind Landis, and Killebrew kept going around the bases for the first inside-the-park homer in Twins' history.

At a Glance
WP: Kralick (8–5)
HR: Killebrew (25)
Key stats: Kralick 10-hitter, 6 Ks; Green 2-for-3

Given a 4–0 lead, Kralick tired a bit in the ninth inning but held on for the complete-game win. Afterward, Killebrew seemed amused that people kept asking about his home run. "I hit one like that in Charleston (in the minor leagues)," he said. "I actually thought I hit it well enough to go out. When the ball rolled free, I saw a chance to go all the way."

It was the capper to one of the most memorable twofers in Met Stadium history. —∿—

Reggie Gets Headlines but Twins Get the Win

The headlines the next day trumpeted Reggie Jackson's mammoth home run that nearly took out the top of the Met Stadium scoreboard. As a result—to all but the 21,673 in attendance and the folks who resided in the first base dugout—the final score was almost an afterthought.

Minnesota's 13–1 win, however, broke a tie for first place in the Western Division with the A's. The Twins never left the top again the rest of the year, going on to claim the mini-pennant under first-year manager Billy Martin.

The tight division race—plus the attraction of seeing Oakland's Jackson, whose 33 home runs put him ahead of the pace Roger Maris had in his 61-home run season eight years earlier—was enough to get NBC in town to air the game to a national audience.

Jackson did his part early, connecting off Jim Perry in the first inning with a high shot that nearly went over the big scoreboard in right-center field. Later, Jackson said he had hit "four or five" balls harder than this one, which was estimated at 450-feet plus. The debate over how far the ball actually did travel continued until Twins pitching coach Art Fowler said, "You want to see how far it went? Check out the dent in the scoreboard."

After Jackson's blow, however, Perry stuffed the A's on just four hits the rest of the way.

At a Glance

WP: Perry (7–4)

HR: Killebrew 2 (22)

Key stats: Perry 5-hitter, 5 Ks; Killebrew 3-for-4, 2 HRs, 6 RBIs; Oliva 4-for-4, RBI

In the bottom of the inning, the first four Twins to face Oakland starter Chuck Dobson reached base. The fourth of these was Harmon Killebrew, whose two-run home run didn't go as far as Jackson's (it was measured at a mere 418 feet), but it did give Minnesota a 4–1 lead.

Things went downhill from there for Oakland. In the second inning, Killebrew faced Dobson again, this time with two runners on base. It ended with the same result—a home run—and Minnesota had a 7–1 lead. By the time the big fellow was done for the day, he had three hits and six RBIs. Tony Oliva and Leo Cardenas had four hits each as the Twins totaled 16 hits off five Oakland pitchers.

Jackson may have drawn the headlines, but the real story of the game was the first four hitters in Minnesota's batting order. Ted Uhlaender, Rod Carew, Oliva and Killebrew went a combined 10-for-17 with nine runs scored and nine RBIs. It may not have been as dramatic or as memorable as Jackson's homer. But the Twins will gladly make that trade anytime. —

Winning by a Touchdown

As a rule, ballplayers hate day-night doubleheaders. No matter how you slice it, a 10–12 hour day at the ballpark is tiring for everybody. The Twins, however, found a way to make this sunshine-nighttime twin bill at U.S. Cellular Field enjoyable. They banged out 32 runs and swept their divisional foes right out to the Dan Ryan Expressway.

Almost everyone had a good time in Game 1. Catcher Joe Mauer went 4-for-6 with four runs scored and five RBIs. But he had to take second billing to left fielder Jason Kubel, who knocked in *seven* runs. These figures made Justin Morneau and Torii Hunter's three-RBI efforts look miniscule in comparison.

Minnesota had four runs on the board before the Sox came to the plate in the first inning and never let up. It was sort of necessary to do so because starting pitcher Scott Baker, whose previous effort was a complete-game 1–0 loss at Detroit with only three hits, was off his form. Accordingly, Minnesota led just 6–4 after three innings.

Kubel's grand slam highlighted a six-run fourth inning that appeared to blow the game open at 12–4. But the Sox kept pecking at Baker and his first replacement, Ramon Ortiz. As a result, the lead was down to 14–8 as the game entered the seventh inning. That's when Morneau singled home a run and Hunter followed with an RBI double. RBIs by Jason Kubel and Nick Punto pushed the lead back to 10 runs at 18–8.

But the Sox still had some sting left in their bats. They kept gnawing away at the lead, causing closer Joe Nathan to actually get up in the bullpen and start to loosen up until Juan Rincon whiffed ex-Twin A. J. Pierzynski with the bases loaded to finally put an end to the offensive onslaught. The final combined totals showed 34 runs, 39 hits, and six errors. Under the circumstances, a game time of three hours and 42 minutes seemed almost quick.

Earlier in the season, Chicago manager Ozzie Guillen had compared Minnesota's attack to a bunch of piranhas nibbling away at all times. By the end of the game, he was seeing a different type of mammal. "They're not piranhas anymore," Guillen sighed. "That's a shark attack." —⁓—

At a Glance

WP: Baker (3–3)

HR: Hunter (18), Kubel (7)

Key stats: Mauer 4-for-6, 5 RBIs; Kubel 2-for-3, 7 RBIs

Morneau's Memorable Night in Chicago

Justin Morneau described it best. "There are days you put in a memory bank and never expect to happen again," he said after swatting three home runs in a 12–0 romp over the White Sox in the night half of the doubleheader.

It was a rude welcome to the American League for Chicago pitcher Gavin Floyd, who had been acquired from the Phillies over the winter but was working his first game on the South Side. Four home runs and 5 2/3 innings later, Floyd left with an ERA of 9.53 in his new league.

Morneau was a big reason why. He hit a three-run homer in the top of the first inning. In the third, he lined a solo shot. (Torii Hunter followed suit four pitches later.) In the fifth, Michael Cuddyer took his turn going deep to make it 6–0.

Morneau's third longball came off reliever Boone Logan in the seventh inning. Before the inning was over, pinch-hitter Jeff Cirillo joined in the fun with a three-run homer of his own. This was more than enough for starter Matt Garza, who scattered five hits through six innings to gain the win. Garza might have been more tired from having to swing the bat. In the first inning, catcher Mike Redmond got hit in the head with a bat and had to leave the game. Joe Mauer was already in the lineup as the DH and had to move behind the plate. This sent Garza into the batting order, the first Twins' pitcher to hit in an AL game in seven years. (He grounded out once, struck out once, and sacrificed.)

There was only one piece of drama remaining. By going deep thrice, Morneau joined some elite company. Harmon Killebrew, Bob Allison, and Tony Oliva are the only other Twins to hit three home runs in a game. In the eighth inning, Morneau had his chance to break the tie but flied out to left.

Justin Morneau

Picked in the third round of the 1999 amateur draft, Morneau moved quickly up the chain, making it to the big club four years later. In 2006, he was named the American League MVP when he hit .321 with 34 home runs and 130 RBIs. Two years later, he set the team record for doubles in a season (47) and won the Home Run Derby the day before the 2008 All-Star Game. The next night, he scored the winning run in the 15th inning in the AL's 4–3 triumph.

Quilici Takes Over in Style

Frank Quilici's last season as a player with the Twins was 1970. He wanted to manage, but there were no openings in the team's minor league system. Calvin Griffith liked Quilici, however, and hired him as an extra coach on manager Bill Rigney's staff. The problem was that Rigney didn't assign specific duties to Quilici. For a year and a half, Quilici wandered to and fro as a coach without a portfolio.

But when the team returned from getting swept in Boston, Griffith decided he could give Quilici some very specific duties. Thus it was that Rigney was fired and Quilici, who had never run a team a day in his life, was named manager. Asked why he chose Quilici over more experienced members of the team's coaching staff, Griffith offered this non-baseball explanation: "Frank is as well-known around the state as Hubert Humphrey."

Translation: the club is sinking quickly and nobody is coming out to games at Met Stadium. Maybe Quilici can spark the team a bit and this, in turn, will bring some people to the ballpark.

Frank Quilici (right) with Mudcat Grant, members of the 1965 American League champion Twins, celebrated the team's 40-year anniversary in 2005. Quilici is still the only person to have played, coached, managed, and broadcasted for the Twins.

Most first dates don't work out this well. On Quilici's first full day on the job, the Twins, who had been shut out two games in a row at Fenway Park, erupted for a season-high 16 hits in a 5–2 win over the Yankees. Even better news for Griffith: 19,514 fans— the largest crowd of the season to date at the Met—came out to watch the game.

In the pregame meeting, Quilici was so nervous he called New York manager Ralph Houk "Sir." The Twins did little to ease his nerves, falling behind 2–0 after three innings. In the last six innings, however, starter Dick Woodson and successors Jim Strickland and Wayne Granger only allowed two more hits.

Meanwhile, Minnesota snipped away at New York starter Fritz Peterson but could only manage one run on eight hits in the first six innings of play. It took two old reliables—Rod Carew and Harmon Killebrew—to bring the crowd to life. With two outs in the seventh, Carew singled. Killebrew followed by hitting a 2–1 pitch far over the left-field fence for a 3–2 lead. Quilici was a little excited, telling reporters later, "I wanted to jump through the top of the dugout."

There was excitement of a different sort the next inning. George Mitterwald was on third and Cesar Tovar was at second with two outs with Danny Thompson batting. Quilici decided it was time for a suicide squeeze. A second later, he changed his mind and took the play off. Thompson got the sign and swung away, hitting a fly ball to left. Mitterwald, however, thought the squeeze was still on and nearly had heart failure when he saw Thompson swinging freely. He scrambled back to third base to keep the inning going as Thompson flied out.

Good thing. Carew tapped a ball to the right side and then raced Yankee first baseman Felipe Alou for the bag. Alou thought he had won the race and tagged the base with his foot. Umpire Bill Kunkel disagreed, ruling Carew safe as Mitterwald scored easily. Alou turned around to argue the point. Because Alou didn't remember to call time, he was

Yankees	AB	R	H	RBI
Clarke 2b	4	1	1	0
Munson c	3	0	0	0
Murcer cf	3	0	1	1
White lf	2	0	0	0
Blomberg 1b	2	1	1	0
Torres ph-rf	2	0	0	0
Alou rf-1b	4	0	2	1
Sanchez 3b	4	0	1	1
Michael ss	4	0	1	0
Peterson p	3	0	0	0
McDaniel p	0	0	0	0
Totals	31	2	7	2

Twins	AB	R	H	RBI
Tovar rf	5	1	2	0
Thompson ss	4	0	2	0
Carew 2b	5	1	3	2
Killebrew 1b	4	1	2	2
Reese pr-1b	0	0	0	0
Darwin cf	5	1	3	0
Brye lf	4	0	2	0
Soderholm 3b	4	0	0	0
Mitterwald c	4	1	2	1
Woodson p	2	0	0	0
Strickland p	0	0	0	0
Renick ph	1	0	0	0
Granger p	1	0	0	0
Totals	39	5	16	5

NY	0	1	1	0	0	0	0	0	0	-	2	7	0
MIN	0	0	0	1	0	0	2	2	x	-	5	16	1

Yankees	IP	H	R	ER	BB	SO
Peterson L(7–10)	6.2	12	3	3	1	5
McDaniel	1.1	4	2	2	0	1
Totals	8	16	5	5	1	6

Twins	IP	H	R	ER	BB	SO
Woodson	5.1	5	2	1	3	1
Strickland	0.2	0	0	0	0	1
Granger W(3–0)	3	2	0	0	1	2
Totals	9	7	2	1	4	4

E—Minnesota Woodson. DP—Minnesota 1. 2B—Minnesota Tovar. HR—Minnesota Killebrew (12). SH—Minnesota Thompson. LOB—New York 6. Minnesota 12. Attendance—19,514.

unaware that Tovar kept on running and scored as well. Shakespeare had it right: all's well that ends well . . . at least for one night.

After the game, Quilici was still excited and somewhat relieved. "I didn't sleep too well last night," he said. "I want to savor this one for a while."

A MULTI-FACETED GUY

Quilici holds a unique place in Twins' history as the only man to play, coach, manage, and work for the team as a broadcaster. He played 405 games over five seasons, finishing with a lifetime batting average of .214. He basically lost his job in 1967 when Carew joined the team. When he took over the reins of the team as manager, the Twins were 36–34. A month later, they were eight games over .500 and just 5½ games out of first place in the West Division. An eight-game losing streak (including three extra-inning losses in a row at Detroit) ruined the season, however, and the Twins finished third at 77–77. The Twins finished in third place the next two seasons as well. When Quilici's 1975 team staggered badly down the stretch, ending up in fourth place, 20½ games out of first, Griffith decided it was time to make a move again and brought in veteran skipper Gene Mauch.

Quilici moved upstairs to the radio booth, where he teamed with play-by-play man Herb Carneal for the next two seasons. He left for two years and returned to work three more seasons with Carneal. He stayed in town afterward and has remained one of the most popular ex-Twins of all time. —⁓—

Frank Quilici

The most versatile member ever to work for the Twins, he played 405 games in five seasons as a good-glove, occasional-hitting infielder. (He played most of his games at second base but also filled in at third base and shortstop.) Then, he served two seasons as a coach before replacing Bill Rigney as manager in 1972. He stayed nearly four seasons in that role before moving to the radio broadcast booth for two separate terms.

Winfield Shows He Still Has What It Takes

For 20 seasons, Twins fans had always wondered what it might have been like to have Dave Winfield in the lineup. San Diego had taken the St. Paul native with the fourth pick in the draft on June 5, 1973. Two weeks later, he made his major league debut with a single in four at-bats against Houston and rarely looked back.

He spent eight years on the West Coast, followed by nine interesting seasons with the Yankees. After that, there were side trips to California and Toronto. Finally, in his 20th season as a major leaguer, he came home, signing with the Twins as a free agent to serve as a designated hitter and occasional outfielder. He got off to a good start in 1993 with a pair of home runs and nine RBIs in his first four games. But things went downhill quickly, and Winfield managed just one home run and eight RBIs in the next month of games.

Things improved slightly from there but, as the calendar turned to July, Winfield was only hitting .234. Then, he made an unspecified adjustment to his swing. Suddenly, he resembled the Winfield the locals remembered. The eighth of those games saw Winfield nearly hit for the cycle, helping the Twins run away from the Brewers 10–6 at County Stadium.

At a Glance

WP: Willis (2–0)

HR: Winfield (12)

Key stats: Winfield 4-for-4, 3 RBIs

Winfield's timing couldn't have been better. The team had started the second half of the season the night before with a dispiriting 15–3 loss. Kent Hrbek was in a terrible funk as well, struggling with a 5-for-37 slump. For one night, however, prospects looked a lot brighter.

Winfield singled in the first inning and then doubled a run home in the second to help Minnesota to an early 6–0 lead. By the fourth inning, Brewers starter Jaime Navarro had left in favor of Matt Maysey, who had pitched a perfect inning in relief the night before. This time, the Twins turned on Maysey quickly as Winfield drilled a two-run homer that bounced off the team bus behind the left field fence to push the margin to 10–2.

There were five innings remaining for Winfield to bid for his second career cycle (he had one with California in 1991). He had two more at-bats but settled for a walk and an infield single. His 4-for-4 night had jumped his batting average 11 points in that game and 35 points overall in a little over a week. "That was unfamiliar territory for me," Winfield said of his old stats. "I believe I've got it going now."

IN A WAY, HE WAS RIGHT

It turned out Winfield was partially correct. His 1993 average continued to rise the rest of the season. By August, he seemed to be headed for the .300 mark until he fell back slightly and finished at .271. His totals of 21 home runs and 76 RBIs ranked third on the team, behind Kirby Puckett and Hrbek. Only Puckett and Chuck Knoblauch had more plate appearances by the end of the season. The highlight came on September 16, when Winfield lined a ninth-inning single off Oakland's Dennis Eckersley for his 3,000th career hit, the first time this had happened for a player wearing a Twins uniform. (Later, Paul Molitor did it as well. Rod Carew, who recorded his 3,000th hit while playing for the Angels, is the only other ex-Twin in this exclusive club.)

However, Winfield's stay in town didn't last very long. He struggled in 1994 with a .252 average and was traded to Cleveland for a player to be named later while the baseball strike was going on. Winfield hit just .191 in 46 games for the Indians and retired at the end of the season. In 2001, he was a no-brainer electee to baseball's Hall of Fame. —w—

Killebrew Snuffs Out the Yankees with Late Blast

In each major league team's history, there are two or three games that stand out as milestones among the rest. The last game before the 1965 All-Star break is one such event for the Minnesota Twins. It's not just how it ended, because there had been a similar ending the year before. It is what the final result seemed to signify at the time, a theory that proved to be prescient afterward.

There was considerable excitement and anxiety at Met Stadium that afternoon. The area was getting ready to host the All-Star Game two days later. The Twins had exceeded all expectations and had a four-game lead over the Indians. But the Yankees, the defending AL champs, had ended the team's nine-game winning streak the night before. And if New York won again, well, they would only be 12½ games behind Minnesota. These were, after all, THE YANKEES.

So it was that 35,623 fans on hand seemed a bit anxious when the very reliable Jim Kaat was knocked out of the game in the fifth inning. When reliever Bill Pleis uncorked a wild pitch in the seventh inning that tied the game at 4-all, the anxiety level jumped considerably.

Jerry Fosnow was pitching for the Twins with runners on the corners and two outs in the ninth inning when a 4–4 game took a detour toward a legendary affair.

It started innocently enough. Roger Repoz hit a slow roller up the first base line. Fosnow picked up the ball and went to tag Repoz. The ball suddenly flew up in the air and Elston Howard, who had been on third, crossed the plate.

But home plate umpire Ed Hurley ruled that Repoz had interfered with Fosnow and was out to end the inning. Before the crowd could breathe a sigh of relief, first base umpire John Flaherty stepped

Yankees	AB	R	H	RBI
Richardson 2b	4	0	1	0
Linz ss	5	1	1	0
Mantle lf	4	2	2	0
Ramos p	0	0	0	0
Mikkelsen p	0	0	0	0
Howard c	4	2	3	2
H. Lopez rf	4	0	2	0
Pepitone 1b	5	0	0	0
Boyer 3b	3	0	0	0
Repoz cf	4	0	0	0
Downing p	2	0	0	0
Barker ph	1	0	1	0
Reniff p	0	0	0	0
Hamilton p	0	0	0	0
Tresh ph	1	0	0	0
Moschitto lf	1	0	0	0
Totals	**38**	**5**	**10**	**2**

Twins	AB	R	H	RBI
Versalles ss	3	2	1	1
Rollins 3b	4	1	1	1
Oliva rf	5	1	2	0
Killebrew 1b-lf	4	2	3	2
Nossek cf	3	0	0	0
Mincher ph-1b	1	0	0	0
Hall lf-cf	3	0	1	1
Battey c	4	0	2	1
Grant pr	0	0	0	0
Zimmerman c	0	0	0	0
Kindall 2b	3	0	1	0
Allen ph-2b	1	0	0	0
Kaat p	1	0	0	0
Worthington p	2	0	0	0
Pleis p	0	0	0	0
Klippstein p	0	0	0	0
Valdespino ph	1	0	0	0
Fosnow p	0	0	0	0
Totals	**35**	**6**	**11**	**6**

											R	H	E
NY	1	0	0	0	2	0	1	0	1	-	5	10	0
MIN	0	0	1	2	1	0	0	0	2	-	6	11	4

Yankees	IP	H	R	ER	BB	SO
Downing	5	6	4	4	2	6
Reniff	1.1	3	0	0	1	2
Hamilton	0.2	0	0	0	0	1
Ramos	1	1	0	0	0	1
Mikkelsen L(2–5)	0.2	1	2	2	1	0
Totals	**8.2**	**11**	**6**	**6**	**4**	**10**

Twins	IP	H	R	ER	BB	SO
Kaat	4.1	7	3	2	3	1
Worthington	2	2	1	1	2	2
Pleis	1	0	0	0	2	1
Klippstein	0.2	0	0	0	0	2
Fosnow W(3–3)	1	1	1	0	0	0
Totals	**9**	**10**	**5**	**3**	**7**	**6**

E—Minnesota Rollins, Battey, Kaat, Fosnow. DP—Minnesota 1. 2B—New York Howard. Minnesota Rollins, Kindall, Battey. HR—Minnesota Versalles (10), Killebrew (16). SF—Minnesota Hall. LOB—New York 13. Minnesota 8. Attendance—35,263.

in to say that wasn't so. He said Fosnow was at fault and Repoz was innocent of all charges. After a consultation, Flaherty's call stood and the Twins were suddenly behind 5–4.

Things looked grim when Zoilo Versalles grounded out to relief pitcher Pete Mikkelsen to open the last of the ninth. Rich Rollins offered some hope when he worked a walk, but the crowd looked anxious after Oliva hit a soft fly ball out to, of all people, Repoz.

That left only Harmon Killebrew standing at the plate.

"You just try to relax in those situations," Killebrew would say later. "You run into things like this in baseball—the chance to win the game. Either you do or you don't. But you do try a little harder."

Killebrew said later he didn't know that Mikkelsen, who had saved a dozen games the year before, had been having gopher ball trouble lately. But he did think he was going to get a fastball sooner or later. On a 3–2 pitch, Mikkelsen tried to fool him with a changeup that was fouled away. "That was a pretty good pitch," Howard said after the game. "There was nothing wrong with the next pitch selection, either . . . if it is down."

Mikkelsen, however, didn't get it down. His fastball was up and Killebrew turned on it, hitting a line drive that cleared the left-field fence by three or four rows as Met Stadium exploded in a mixture of joy and relief.

Killebrew had hit a bottom-of-the-ninth inning homer the year before off Al Downing (ironically, the New York starter that day) to win a game and tried to equate this one at the same level. After a while, however, even Killebrew gave up the ghost. "It's one of the sweetest of the sweet," he told reporters. That's as close as one ever got to hearing Killebrew brag about a home run.

Later that day, the Indians lost at California and the Twins went into the All-Star break five games ahead of the pack. They were never slowed down the rest of the way and went on to win the AL pennant by seven games.

More importantly, the Yankees, who had won five straight and nine of the previous 10 AL pennants, were dealt a blow from which they never recovered in 1965. They finished 25 games out of first place. ⁓

Viola Tames the Tigers

For most of their history, the Twins have been able to corral the Detroit Tigers. Their winning percentage against the Bengals is easily the best of all their regular AL foes.

The year 1984 was an exception to that rule. The Twins dropped the first two games of the season at home to Detroit. By the time the Tigers returned to town after the All-Star break, they had a seven-game lead in the East Division while Minnesota was tied with California for second in the West, a game behind Chicago.

It was an oddity—an afternoon game on the first day back after the All-Star Game. Minnesota manager Billy Gardner and pitching coach Johnny Podres missed the first pitch because their early morning flight out of Newark left late due to fog. By the time they arrived in the second inning, pitcher Frank Viola was already mowing the Tigers down. He retired 12 batters in a row at one point.

He kept the pace up most of the afternoon, stifling the powerful Detroit offense on a run, five hits, and a walk to improve his record to 10–7 before leaving with a sore shoulder. Ron Davis made things interesting in the ninth, but Minnesota held on for a sweet 4–2 victory.

The Twins took a while to get to Detroit starter Dan Petry. Eventually, the number eight and nine hitters in the order—third baseman Gary Gaetti and shortstop Houston Jimenez—finished with two hits and an RBI apiece.

Jimenez, who batted in just 28 runs in 384 at-bats over two seasons, ended up with a key hit. After Gaetti broke a 1–1 tie in the seventh with an RBI double, with two out, Gardner considered pinch-hitting Andre David for Jimenez, but decided he would just get walked anyway. So, he let Jimenez swing away and the shortstop, a .201 hitter that season, nailed a single that scored Gaetti with an insurance run.

At a Glance

WP: Viola (10–7)

S: Davis (17)

Key stats: Viola 5 hits, 1 BB, 1 ER in 8 IP

Minnesota's lead improved to 4–1 in the ninth when a walk and a pair of singles off Davis produced a run. With two outs, Lou Whitaker, a .300 hitter, came to the plate. But Davis always seemed to handle Whitaker well and fanned him to end the game.

Viola's sterling effort was saved in what proved to be Minnesota's only win at home all season against the Tigers, who went on to win 104 games and roll to a World Series title. —⁓—

Turning on an Old Tormentor—Guidry

If you had heard that Ron Guidry was the starting pitcher in a Yankees-Twins game that ended 6–1, you might have logically concluded the man known as "Louisiana Lightning" was the winning pitcher. After all, he finished with a 17–5 career mark against Minnesota. (The only team he beat more was Oakland.)

On this night at the Metrodome, however, it was Ken Schrom, who had joined the Twins after being released by Toronto, who was the commanding force on the mound. Tom Brunansky recorded the first four-hit game of his career as the Twins cuffed their nemesis for 13 hits in seven innings.

Good thing it was Camera Night. If there hadn't been so many pictures taken (fans were allowed on the field beforehand to shoot snapshots of their favorite players), many folks wouldn't have believed this occurred.

Although Minnesota was 9½ games out of first place, it was clear the dismal memory of the 1982 season had faded and the young team was making baby steps toward maturing. Schrom, for example, now had eight victories after going a solid 8 2/3 innings. "I feel like I've arrived as a big leaguer when I beat the Yankees," he said afterward.

Minnesota manager Billy Gardner was thinking of an even bigger picture. "It was just a matter of getting good pitching into the sixth and seventh innings," he said. "If we get some more of that, we can keep it up and be a very good team."

At a Glance

WP: Schrom (8–3)

S: Davis (15)

Key stats: Schrom 1 ER in 8 2/3 IP; Castino 3-for-4, 2 RBIs

The 1983 Twins weren't quite ready for prime time. But they did win 10 more games than the year before. And, as they showed on this night against a guy who ended up third in the majors with 21 victories that season, they could be a handful at times. —⁓—

Not Your Everyday Shutout for Grant

Jim "Mudcat" Grant once gave up 14 hits in a complete-game victory. But he had a good excuse. The game went 14 innings. His second-highest total of hits allowed in a game—13—resulted in one of the strangest shutouts in baseball history.

Grant may have allowed a baker's dozen worth of hits to the Washington Senators at Met Stadium, but he emerged with the result that truly mattered—a 6–0 victory. "You might say I utilized the presence of my fielders handsomely," Grant said later in dissecting the odd result.

There were defensive gems everywhere. It started with center fielder Jimmie Hall's leaping catch off Dick Phillips in the second inning. It ended with Grant himself, jumping off the mound to snare Jim King's grounder and turn it into a game-ending double play. Toss in a few Zoilo Versalles gems at shortstop and a solid throw from left fielder Harmon Killebrew that kept a runner at third base, and you have the makings of an untidy shutout.

The Senators left a dozen runners on base. Amazingly, though, they only managed to get two as far as third base. That's because all 13 hits were singles. Outside of the hits, Grant had good control. He only walked one batter.

At a Glance

WP: Grant (7–5)

HR: Snyder (1), Hall (16), Rollins (9)

Key stats: Grant 13-hit shutout; Allison 2-for-4, 2 RBIs

As for offense, the Twins hit three homers, including the only home run of second baseman Jim Snyder's 86 at-bat major league career. Hall and Rich Rollins also went deep in an 11-hit attack that was slightly more efficient than the Senators'.

Grant, who had been acquired a month before from Cleveland, seemed to appreciate the oddness of a night that included a lot of at-em balls. "The way they were hitting me, it's a wonder somebody didn't get killed out there," he said. ~

Carew Cops Home (Again)

Rod Carew stood on third base in disbelief. With the bases loaded, White Sox lefty Jerry Nyman had decided to pitch from the windup. What Nyman didn't know was that Carew had larceny in his heart—and his feet. "It's been a while since somebody did that with me on third," he said later.

Carew swiped home successfully for what turned out to be an important run in a 9–8 win. It was the seventh time Carew had stolen home that season, tying the major league mark set by Pete Reiser 25 years before. In this case, it was part of an unusual triple steal that featured two guys not normally seen in such supporting roles—third baseman Harmon Killebrew (19 stolen bases in 2,435 career games) and left fielder Charlie Manuel, who recorded the only pilfer of his six-year career. It was part of a five-stolen-base night against four pitchers and beleaguered catcher Don Pavletich. "Usually, the White Sox are the ones doing the running," Carew said after the game. "We simply turned it around on them."

Fleet-footed Rod Carew stole home in a 9–8 win over the Chicago White Sox on July 16, 1969. It was Carew's record-breaking seventh steal of home that season, part of a unique triple steal.

Minnesota had plenty of other offense, too. Rich Reese hit a pair of home runs and finished with five RBIs. But it was Carew, who had three hits and scored three times, who was the main subject of the postgame chatter. Minnesota was leading 8–7 in the eighth inning when, with two out, Carew singled and promptly swiped second base. Reese followed with an RBI single, a run that proved vital when the Sox got a run in the ninth inning off reliever Al Worthington.

At a Glance

WP: Worthington (4–0)

HR: Reese 2 (10)

Key stats: Reese 3-for-4, 5 RBIs; Carew 3-for-5, 3 runs, 3 SBs

SO MUCH, THEN LITTLE MORE

This was the final time Carew stole home for the rest of the season. There were several reasons for this. For one thing, the Twins were in a tight battle for their first Western Division title and manager Billy Martin tightened the reins a bit as the season wore on. For another, Carew missed three weeks of the season when he had to report for military duty in August.

But old habits die hard, and Carew tried twice before the season's end. The first was against the White Sox again on September 10 at Comiskey Park. This time, Tommy John and Pavletich guessed right, pitched out, and nailed him at the plate. On September 26, Carew tried again in Seattle. This time, he pulled a leg muscle and was easily retired. He was forced to leave the game in the next inning.

Although he later recorded a few more steals of home, Carew never threatened Reiser's single-season mark. So, he had to settle for the AL record. There may be some comfort, however, in the knowledge of the man he displaced as the league's all-time single-season leader in home plate thefts. He was a fellow named Ty Cobb. —⁓—

Settling the Issue Early

There are days at the plate where you wish you could simply bottle what you do and recycle it for the next occasion. The first inning of this afternoon game at Met Stadium was one of those occasions.

The Twins sent 14 batters to the plate to get a look-see at Cleveland starter Barry Latman and his eventual replacement, Jim Perry. Eleven of those hitters liked the view so much they ended up crossing home and returning to the first base dugout. That was plenty of ammo for what ended up being a 14–3 romp.

The day started badly for Latman and got worse quickly. Bill Tuttle walked to open the first. Vic Power singled. Latman looked over, saw Power leaning and threw to first. But he tossed it over first baseman Tito Francona's head and the runners moved up a base. Rich Rollins singled to score a run, and Harmon Killebrew walked to load the bases. Bob Allison then waited for a 2–0 pitch he liked and dumped it in the left-field seats for a grand slam homer. The rout was on.

Earl Battey homered to end Latman's day early. Perry entered and mixed in a pair each of walks, hits, and outs. So it was now 7–0, the bases were loaded, and Killebrew was at the plate. "I didn't want to be the one to make the last out of the inning," he said after the game.

> ## At a Glance
>
> **WP:** Stigman (4–2)
>
> **HR:** Allison (11), Battey (6), Killebrew 2 (24)
>
> **Key stats:** Stigman 11 Ks; Killebrew 2-for-4, 2 HRs, 5 RBIs; Allison grand slam in 11-run first

He didn't, sending Perry's 2–0 offering almost over the left-field bleachers. It marked the first time in major league history the same team had hit two grand slam home runs in one inning.

Killebrew's shot upped the score to 11–0, a lead Minnesota starter Dick Stigman had no problem holding as he tossed a six-hit complete game. Stigman later contributed to the hit parade with a single, half his total for the season in 45 tries. He also added an RBI on a sacrifice fly. It was that kind of day for the Twins. —⁓—

Did You Know?

The Twins actually had a better batting average on the road than they did at home in both 1962 and 1963. This only occurred two times in the next 46 years (1978 and 2007).

The Master Struts His Stuff

Ted Williams, a fellow who knew a thing or two about hitting, once said Camilo Pascual had "the most feared curve ball in the American League for 18 years." When the Twins joined the American League in 1961, Pascual was easily their most established pitcher. He had won 57 games in his seven years in Washington—a nifty feat for a team that was 218 games under .500 in that time frame.

In Minnesota, he picked up where he had left off in Washington, tossing a complete-game victory in his first start. He remained an old reliable. By mid-July, he had recorded seven victories, three shutouts and a 3.66 ERA. He then outdid himself with one of the season's best efforts when he struck out 15 batters and scattered five singles in a 6–0 win over the Los Angeles Angels at old Wrigley Field. Center fielder Albie Pearson, who worked the Halos' only walk of the night, was also the only member of the starting batting order who did not strike out against crafty Camilo. To make up for this oversight, Pascual claimed shortstop Joe Koppe and catcher Earl Averill three times each. The Angels only got one runner to second all night, and that was due in part to an error by second baseman Ted Lepcio.

As for offense, Harmon Killebrew hit a two-run homer in the first inning and Bob Allison added a pair of four-baggers. The rest of the night belonged to Pascual, who later said it was the best night of curve balls (he threw a fast and a slow one) he had all season.

At a Glance

WP: Pascual (8–12)

HR: Killebrew (28), Allison 2 (19)

Key stats: Pascual 5-hitter, 15 Ks

After struggling through a six-game losing streak in June, Pascual had won three of his previous five starts. After watching Pascual carve up the Angels, his manager, Sam Mele, decreed, "I think he's found himself again."

The manager proved to be prescient. Pascual finished the season with a 15–16 win-loss record and a credible 3.46 ERA. He also led the league with eight shutouts and 221 strikeouts. His strikeout figure that night stood as a team single-game record (Joe Decker tied it once) until Johan Santana whiffed 17 in a 2007 game.

JUST THE BEGINNING

Having never played on a winning team in Washington, Pascual adapted quickly to the Twins' gains in the win column in later seasons. Pascual was a big reason the team jumped to 91 wins the next year. In addition to repeating as the shutout and strikeout champ, the Havana native led the league in complete games with 18. He matched that figure the next season and even claimed one more victory. But his supporting cast wasn't as strong, and the team fell back to 79–83.

After a decade in the majors as a workhorse, Pascual's arm began to falter a bit. He had enough left to win 15 games in 1964 and nine more for the 1965 team that went to the World Series. He started Game 3 of the Series, losing 4–0 at Dodger Stadium. When it came time for his turn again, Mele didn't think his pitcher had anything left, opting instead for Jim Grant on two days' rest. (It proved to be a smart move. Grant pitched a complete game and homered in a 5–1 win in Game 6.)

The old warrior went one more season in Minnesota before being traded back to the city where he had started, Washington, in December 1966. There, he conjured up the old magic, working his way to 27 wins in three years. There were pit stops in Los Angeles and Cleveland before Pascual finally retired in 1971 with career totals of 2,162 strikeouts, a 174–170 record and the respect of nearly every player who had ever faced him. He later returned to the Twin Cities for three seasons as a coach from 1979–81. He still ranks in the Twins' All-Time Top Ten in four single-season and eight career categories.

Remember Williams' bromide about how hard it was to face Pascual? That was from a guy who had a career .395 batting mark against him. Some other well-known hitters didn't fare as well against Pascual. Mickey Mantle could only produce a .258 batting average and struck out 39 times in 128 official at-bats. Yogi Berra hit just .237 (23-for-97) against him. That was better than a young Rod Carew, who checked in at .235 with 4-for-17 hitting numbers. Ex-teammate Jimmie Hall had even less luck at .182 (4-for-22). But few people suffered more than Detroit's Willie Horton, who was happy to see Pascual retire after managing just three hits in 27 at-bats, a .111 mark. —ᴡ—

Camilo Pascual

The man with the big, sweeping curve, Pascual was a three-time All-Star who was one of the AL's top pitchers in his first four seasons here. In the Twins' inaugural season, he led the AL with a remarkable eight shutouts and won 15 games. The next season, he won 20 games (and led the league in shutouts again with five). The next season, he won 21 games. Although dogged by arm problems, he won nine for the 1965 AL champs and started a World Series game. Later, he spent three seasons with the team as pitching coach.

Welcome Back, Scotty

There was a time where Scott Erickson could have owned the Twin Cities media market. In 1991, he led the league with 20 victories, helping the Twins to their second World Series title in five seasons. He later pitched the team's first no-hitter in 27 years. By 1995, however, it was clear Erickson and the Twin Cities were going to part ways.

The team was rebuilding. Erickson had made comments critical of team owner Carl Pohlad. His walk total, always a potential issue, was up, and his strikeout numbers were down. When he was traded to Baltimore for pitcher Scott Klingenbeck on July 7, a collective sigh of "Good riddance" could be heard at the Metrodome and elsewhere.

Erickson found a sympathetic ally in former pitcher Phil Regan, now the Orioles manager. He won two starts in a row there and tried to downplay his return to the Metrodome for a Thursday matinee against his old team. In the end, Minnesota got the last laugh, grinding out a 5–2 win that can be credited to perseverance and knowledge of the opponent.

The knock on Erickson had always been that he refused to listen to his coaches and add pitches to his repertoire. The fastball was humming early as Erickson zipped through the first nine batters with little issue. "It was odd looking at him the first time," admitted Kirby Puckett later. "But I thought we might get him the second time around."

Puckett knew something. Erickson later said it was his overdependence on his fastball that led to what happened in a fateful fourth. Whatever the reason, Baltimore had a 1–0 lead until the Twins rapped four singles that led to three runs in the inning. It stayed at 3–1 until the seventh, when Marty Cordova found a fastball he liked for his 13th homer of the season.

That was enough for the fellow who replaced Erickson in the Twins' starting rotation—Frankie Rodriguez—and a handful of relievers. Acquired from the Red Sox in the deal that sent Rick Aguilera away, Rodriguez gave up only one run on three hits in six innings to earn his first major league victory. It was the end of a fascinating 24 hours that introduced Rodriguez to the unusual world of Major League Baseball.

The night before, Twins pitcher Pat Mahomes was giving Rodriguez a ride home when Mahomes said he was also giving a ride to a former road roommate of his—a fellow named Scott Erickson. "Strange game sometimes, isn't it?" asked Rodriguez. —⁓—

At a Glance

WP: Rodriguez (1–3)

S: Stevens (3)

HR: Cordova (13)

Key stats: Rodriguez 3 hits in 6 IP; Twins turn 4 double plays

Fenway Sweep

You know you are doing well when, in mid-July, you feel confident enough to send a guy to play left field for the first time all season at Boston's Fenway Park. Granted, it was just for two innings and the Twins already had a 14–1 lead. But this is Fenway Park, home of the 37-foot wall and odd corner dimensions. But things were going very well for the Twins on this Sunday afternoon.

Going into the weekend, Minnesota had won only one season series at Boston since 1981. That was a season they paid only one visit and swept a four-game series. But the Twins had won three straight from the faltering Red Sox and were anxious for a chance to repeat history. Armed with a 4½-game lead over their nearest competitor (Chicago), the Twins seemed to be gaining confidence. As second baseman Chuck Knoblauch put it, "We've been in first place long enough for it no longer to be considered a fluke."

After this Sunday beating, the Bosox ruefully agreed. Scott Leius and Knoblauch, the No. 1 and 2 hitters in the order, scored three runs each. Kirby Puckett, in the third spot, had two hits and three RBIs. Cleanup hitter Chili Davis had three hits. No. 5 hitter Brian Harper? Two hits and two runs. Shane Mack, the six-hole guy, matched Davis' three hits. Gene Larkin, the No. 8 man in the lineup, had a two-run triple. Even Greg Gagne, the No. 9 guy, doubled, scored a run, and drove in a run.

It was the sort of whomping the Red Sox often doled out on unsuspecting visitors. Backed with this kind of attack, Kevin Tapani allowed only an unearned run on three hits in six innings to gain the victory. Tapani was out of the game when manager Tom Kelly did an unusual defensive change. In the eighth inning, he allowed Mack some respite from the 99-degree temps and sent Davis, who had been in his usual role of designated hitter, out to left for his first defensive appearance of the season. Davis had to run to the clubhouse to get his glove, which (he said later) had been cooling off.

But Davis still knew where to go, flagging down Jody Reed's fly ball near the Green Monster to end the eighth inning. In part, this absolved a creative base running move earlier in the game that resulted in Knoblauch and Davis both being picked off base for a double play without a pitch being thrown.

Kelly managed to forgive it all and marveled at the enjoyable weekend in Beantown. "You have to be fortunate to come to Boston and win four straight games," he smiled. —⁓—

At a Glance

WP: Tapani (6–7)

Key stats: Puckett 2-for-4, 3 RBIs; 11 Twins have hits

Passing the Mettle Test

Although the season still had 67 games to go, the Twins were faced with a crossroad game of sorts. After being hammered 7–1, they had bounced back to edge the Yankees, 2–1, on a Kent Hrbek RBI single in the bottom of the ninth inning. This was the last game at the Metrodome before leaving on a two-week, 13-game road sojourn. Heading out of town on a happy note seemed to be a vital task.

Fortunately, Frank Viola had the baseball in his hands. The New York native was top of his game from the start, skimming four hits and just one run in eight innings. Jeff Reardon mopped up the ninth. Hrbek hit a two-run home run and the Twins left town with a 3–1 victory that wasn't quite as simple as it looked.

Hrbek got it off to a good start with his shot off Yankee starter Rick Rhoden in the first inning. In the fifth, Kirby Puckett, who had been scrapping at the plate, homered to make it 3–0, but Claudell Washington got that one back with a similar shot for the Yankees in the top of the sixth.

At a Glance

WP: Viola (10–6)

S: Reardon (20)

HR: Hrbek (24), Puckett (15)

Key stats: Viola 4 hits, 1 ER, 6 Ks in 8 IP

It was still 3–1 in the eighth inning when Puckett gave the crowd of 40,054 a thrill—and a prelude to something that would happen on a bigger stage four years later. Henry Cotto led off the inning with a rope to straight-center field. Puckett took off in hot pursuit but it didn't appear he would be able to catch up in time. Suddenly, he jumped and extended his arms as far as his 5-foot-8 body would let them. What had looked like a possible leadoff home run to make it a 3–2 game was now just a fly out to center. "That was awesome—maybe his best one yet," Viola praised afterward.

The next two batters went out meekly. Reardon did his thing in the ninth, and the game was quickly over. This may have been a coincidence, but the Yankees, who had a three-game lead in the AL East at the time, lost their next two games at Chicago and began a gradual free-fall that ended in fourth place, nine games behind. Four years later, Henry Cotto could sit in front of his TV, watch Puckett perform another acrobatic piece of thievery off Ron Gant in Game 6 of the 1991 World Series, and say, "Welcome to the club." —⚉—

Thanks for the Nice Win; See Ya Later

It was one of those odd moments in a season when a team desperately needed a starting pitcher. The Twins were playing a makeup day-night doubleheader in Detroit. There were no bullpen candidates available to start the night game. So, the call went out to AAA Rochester and said, in essence, "You can have him back next week but we need him tonight."

The fellow in question was right-handed pitcher Scott Baker. Called up for one game, Baker made a case to stay longer when he silenced the Tigers on two runs and five hits in seven innings in a 5–2 victory. It was his first triumph in the bigs and, as manager Ron Gardenhire observed, "His time here is coming shortly."

Detroit wished it hadn't come at all. Matched against the Tigers' rising star, Justin Verlander, Baker held his own quite well. It was 1–1 in the fourth inning when first baseman Justin Morneau, who had been threatened with a trip to Rochester (outfielder Mike Ryan drew the short straw instead), doubled home a run to break the tie. Later, catcher Mike Redmond singled to score two more runs.

At a Glance
WP: Baker (1–1)
S: Nathan (27)
HR: Morneau (12)
Key stats: Morneau 2-for-3, 2 RBIs

Baker took it from there, walking only one and fanning five. Gardenhire followed established form with Jesse Crain working the eighth and Joe Nathan getting the save with a 1–2–3 ninth. After the game, Gardenhire stuck to his guns and sent Baker back east. But he added a codicil. "I think you're seeing what we hope to get out of this young man. It's very exciting." —⁓—

Did You Know?

Scott Baker's masterpiece was a considerably cleaner game than the Twins' win on August 31, 1993. That night, they tied the club record for most innings in a game when they went 22 frames before edging the Indians, 5–4, at the Metrodome. In the bottom of the ninth inning with two out and no runners on base, David McCarthy and Terry Jorgenson hit back-to-back doubles to tie the game. It remained deadlocked until Pedro Munoz led off the bottom of the 22nd with a home run off Cleveland's Jason Grimsley. Brett Merriman, who pitched the final three innings, earned the only win of his major league career in the game. The game lasted 6:17.

Bostock Cleans Up from the Cleanup Spot

Nearly 100 years before Lyman Bostock arrived at Met Stadium, the poet John Greenleaf Whittier had already written a proper epitaph for him: "Of all the sad words of tongue and pen, the saddest of these are what might have been."

Perhaps no other player ever came through town in such a whirlwind fashion. An obscure 26th round pick in 1972, Bostock quickly showed he could hit at every level of the minor leagues. By 1975 he was in the major leagues, scoring three runs in his first game at Texas. He made a brief side trips to AAA Tacoma but settled in with the big team and batted .282.

The next year, he finished fourth in the AL batting race and was doing even better the next season. This didn't bode well for Minnesota owner Calvin Griffith, who seemed resigned that he would lose Bostock to free agency in the offseason. Games like the one he had on a Saturday afternoon at Comiskey Park, as part of a 17–2 thumping of the White Sox, only accelerated the pace.

Here is Bostock's gaudy line for the day:

AB	R	H	BI
4	4	4	4

There was one of each type of hit, just the fourth cycle performance in team history.

Ironically enough, it came when Bostock was batting fourth in the lineup for the first time ever in the majors. "I hadn't looked at the lineup until just before game time," Bostock would say later. "When I saw it, I couldn't believe my eyes."

By the time the game was over, the White Sox were believers in Bostock. He started slow, getting a walk in a three-run first inning. In the three-run second inning, he plated two of the runs with a triple. It was still 6–0 in the fourth when Bostock hit his third home run of the season to push the lead to 7–0. He added a sacrifice fly in the sixth and then doubled in the eighth inning.

A bright comet whose time with the Twins was all too brief, Bostock improved his statistics notably each season, finishing with a stellar 1977 campaign (.336 BA, 36 2B, 12 3B, 14 HR). That's pretty impressive for a guy who was a 26th round pick in 1972. Sadly, Bostock was killed by gunfire late in the 1978 season.

Lyman Bostock

At a Glance

WP: Bane (3–2)

HR: Bostock (3), Braun (3), Ford (11)

Key stats: Bane 10-hitter with 6 Ks; Bostock 4-for-4, 4 runs, 4 RBIs; Ford 2-for-2, 3 RBIs

By the time he led off the ninth, Minnesota led 15–2. Bostock completed his day with a single.

The beneficiary of all this was pitcher Eddie Bane, who scattered 10 hits for the only complete game of his major league career. Bane had been the team's number-one pick in June 1973 and made his big league debut a month later. But he never quite lived to up to his promise and won only seven games in three seasons.

THE SAD AFTERMATH

Bostock, the 596th player taken in the 1972 winter draft, played just as many seasons for Minnesota as did Bane but fared slightly better. He finished 1977 second to teammate Rod Carew with a .336 batting average.

As expected, he entered the free agent waters and came up a winner, signing for big numbers with the California Angels for the 1978 season. After a slow start, he worked his average up to .296 near the end of the season. It is there where Whittier's words become particularly poignant. The Angels had played a game on a Saturday afternoon in, of all places, Chicago. As was his tradition, he drove to Gary, Indiana, after the game to visit an uncle. Later that day, he was a passenger in a car when a man fired a gun at his estranged wife, who was sitting next to Bostock in the back seat. Bostock died two hours later at a Gary hospital. —⚋—

Lyman Bostock, a 26th-round draft pick in 1972, became just the fourth member of the Twins to hit for the cycle. His final line after hitting a single, double, triple, and home run read 4–4–4–4.

GOLTZ
★ 30 ★

Goltz Guts It Out

The Twins had swept a long doubleheader the day before with the second game going a dozen innings. The bullpen was tired, and manager Gene Mauch was hoping his starting pitcher was up to the task of going several innings that night at Met Stadium.

Fortunately, Dave Goltz's right arm was up to the occasion. It took a while—180 pitches and 11 innings, to be precise—but Goltz hung around long enough to get the decision in a 2–1 win over Oakland. Mixing in his famed knuckle curve with a few well-placed fastballs, the Rothsay, Minnesota, native whiffed a career-high 14 batters and gave up only eight hits in the longest outing of his major league career.

"The man is pitching better than at any time in his life," Mauch praised afterward. "He certainly knows how to pitch."

Goltz had to go full bore because his mound opponent that night, Rick Langford, was being equally stingy. Mike Cubbage led off the third inning with a home run to give Minnesota an early lead. The A's tied it up in the fifth when Jeff Newman singled and Sheldon Mallory doubled him home.

After that, Goltz and Langford dueled magnificently until the 11th. By that point, Mauch had decided 180 pitches was enough for any man and had Gary Serum loosening in the bullpen for a possible 12th inning.

But the Twins, who had only managed four hits in the first 10 innings, suddenly got their offense going. Rod Carew started the 11th with a single and moved to third when Lyman Bostock singled to right. This necessitated an intentional walk to Glenn Adams. Larry Hisle, the next hitter, was certainly a threat to hit into a double play. As his team-leading 119 RBIs for the season also proved, Hisle was a threat to do other things, too. He singled to left to score Carew and allow Goltz to improve his season record to 12–6.

Mauch, whose team was now just five games out of first place in the West Division, was properly jubilant later, saying, "If Dave

Dave Goltz

It took him two seasons in the bigs to get going. Once he did, Goltz turned into one of the better starting pitchers in baseball for half a dozen seasons, winning 87 games. A reliable starter, he frequently finished as well, ranking third on the team's all-time list for complete games. In 1977, he had his only 20-win season as the Twins remained in the race until the final weeks.

After throwing 180 pitches, Dave Goltz shows he can still lift his left (non-pitching) arm, at least.

Goltz was only twins, we'd be in good shape."

The only visible sign of damage to Goltz was a blister on the index finger of his pitching hand. "I'll be ready for my next start," he said. "When this club is going good as they are right now, every pitcher is going to win games."

At a Glance

WP: Goltz (12–6)

HR: Cubbage (3)

Key stats: Goltz 8 hits, 14 Ks in 11-inning CG

ONE THAT DIDN'T GET AWAY . . . AT FIRST

Goltz, who went on to win 20 games that season for the only time in his career, was one of three players on the 1977 Twins who was eligible to test free agency after the season. Bostock left to go to California, and Hisle signed with Milwaukee. The day after his long outing against the A's, Goltz agreed to a two-year deal with the Twins. He fared fine, winning 29 games in 64 starts. When free agency came up again, team owner Calvin Griffith decided Goltz's price was too high, and the right-hander went west to the Dodgers. He spent two uncomfortable years there, getting tagged with the loss in a playoff game to Houston in 1980 for the West Division title. He was released in April 1982. He stuck around the area, though, signing with the nearby Angels as a part-time starter and reliever. He seemed more comfortable back in the AL, winning eight games over two seasons. He picked up a win in relief against the Twins in 1982, but lost twice to his old team before retiring for good in June 1983.

His 1977 season still ranks as one of the hardiest—and best in team history. Goltz's 19 complete games and 303 innings worked ranks third all-time on the team's single-season charts, while his 39 starts ranks tied for fifth best all-time. His 2.49 season ERA in 1978 ranks third as well. —⁓—

Did You Know?

Minnesota has never had a major leaguer who was born in Alaska, Hawaii, or New Mexico. Of the 15,000-plus American born players in major league history, only 11 have come from Alaska. The second lowest production belongs to North Dakota with 15. The Twins have had just one player from their neighbor, pitcher Gary Serum, who went 13–10 with one save in 62 games from 1977–79.

Mr. Walker Caps a Big Weekend vs. Texas

Todd Walker played a dozen seasons in the major leagues, retiring with a very solid lifetime batting average of .289. That's certainly a better mark than many other first-round draft choices ever accomplish. Had he been a little more proficient in the field—he played most of his career at second base—and a little less candid in his public appraisals, he might have had a longer career.

But there was never any question about his abilities as a hitter. As the Texas Rangers found out one weekend at the Metrodome, Walker was quite capable of going on the sort of tear that can practically lift a team by himself. He capped a 9-for-10 weekend in which he grabbed the American League batting lead by going 4-for-4 in an 11–3 romp over a Texas Rangers team that was leading the AL West at the time.

At a Glance

WP: Hawkins (7–9)

HR: Walker (8), Cordova (8)

Key stats: Cordova 2-for-4, 4 RBIs; Walker 4-for-4, 3 RBIs

The outburst, which saw his batting average jump 18 points to .352, left Walker one shy of the team record for most consecutive hits. As was often the case during his time in Minnesota, Walker mixed in the good on the field with some comments off it that didn't always sit well with folks. "The hard part about it is everybody wants to do well for themselves. Anybody who says he doesn't is lying," he told reporters after the series. "The really hard part is putting that out of your mind because you've got to put the team first."

Back to the field, though. The weekend started a little slow with a double and single in three official at-bats and a nifty base running ploy that allowed Paul Molitor to score the winning run in a 5–3 decision. The next night, he walked, doubled, and singled twice in four at-bats as Minnesota rallied from an early 5–0 deficit for a 7–6 victory.

Despite this sterling back-to-back effort, Walker was batting seventh for the series finale. In addition to three singles, Walker snapped the team's 59-inning longball drought with a three-run homer off Rick Helling in the fourth inning. Walker's hot streak now began to rub off on his teammates. Left fielder Marty Cordova, who had been 0-for-25 starting the afternoon, had a couple of hits, including a home run. LaTroy Hawkins and Eddie Guardado, Minnesota's moundsmen, scattered eight hits, and the rest of the day went smoothly. Walker entered the weekend eight points behind Texas' Pudge Rodriguez in the batting race and left 12 points ahead of him.

"It's been difficult at times but I put the personal things [said about his fielding] aside and concentrate on finding ways to help the team win," Walker said. "For me, that means getting on base."

Nobody ever doubted his ability there.

POSTSCRIPT

Two days after Walker's wild weekend, he singled in his first at-bat at Kansas City, tying the team mark of nine straight hits set by Tony Oliva and Chuck Knoblauch. It also meant he had been on base 11 straight times, tying a mark set by Carew and Knoblauch. The streak finally ended when he was called out on strikes in the fourth inning. This turned out to be the apex of the season—and perhaps his Twins career—for Walker. He finished 1998 with a .316 mark, easily the best of his Twins tenure. Two years later, Walker's average had slipped to .234 and he was traded to Colorado at mid-season. He would play for another half-dozen teams before calling it quits in 2007. —

An Unlikely Candidate for a Cycle Delivers In an Unlikely Way

A sturdy, competent third baseman, Mike Cubbage rarely faced southpaw pitchers during his four years in a Minnesota uniform. He had decent power but wasn't considered particularly quick.

On this gray Thursday afternoon, the second-year Toronto Blue Jays offered up righty Jim Clancy, their top winner, on the mound. Thus, Cubbage was given the starting nod and made the most of it, tagging Clancy for a second-inning double and a fourth-inning home run as Minnesota built an early 3–1 lead.

Clancy gave way to lefty Jerry Garvin, a former Minnesota farmhand. Normally, this meant that Cubbage would give way to Larry Wolfe, who handled third base most of the time when lefties were on the opposing mound. But with the Twins ahead, manager Gene Mauch decided to let Cubbage stay in. In the fifth inning, he was three-quarters of the way to the cycle after beating out an infield roller.

It was still a tight game—Minnesota led 4–2 in the seventh—when Cubbage's turn came up again. Mauch decided to let him go one more time and Cubbage responded with a shot to right-center that scored two runs. When he stopped at third base, he now had something in common with another left-handed hitter who called Met Stadium his home field when he was a minor leaguer, a fellow named Carl Yastrzemski.

Cubbage also ended his day with more RBIs (4) than he had recorded in his previous 17 games (2). Meanwhile, Minnesota starting pitcher Stan Perzanowski threw enough sinkers to give up only six hits and allow first baseman Rod Carew to record 21 putouts in the 6–3 victory.

After his big day, Cubbage was asked if he expected to see more at-bats against lefties on the team's upcoming trip. "Let's see, we're scheduled to face (California's) Frank Tanana and (New York's) Ron Guidry soon," he laughed. "Thanks a lot." —m—

At a Glance

WP: Perzanowski (1–0)

HR: Cubbage (5)

Key stats: Perzanowski 6-hitter with 4 Ks; Cubbage 4-for-4, 4 RBIs; Powell 3-for-3, 3 RBIs

Chance Delivers on the Mound and at the Plate

For much of the 1960s, teams looked forward to playing at Fenway Park. It wasn't just the short dimensions and wonderful atmosphere that made players look forward to the trip. For many years, the Bosox had struggled with their pitching and teams would come in, hit the tar out of the ball, and leave in a good mood.

But this trip was different for the Twins. It was the tail end of a road trip that had seen them win one game out of 10 played (and that was an exhausting 18-inning affair in which Jim Merritt came away with no decision after allowing just seven hits in 13 innings of pitching.)

The club had just spent three days in New York, starting with several players being fined for missing curfew. Then, in a span of 45 hours, they played 45 innings of baseball at Yankee Stadium. One game ended in a tie called by rain and had to be replayed in its entirety.

And these weren't the Red Sox of recent memory. No, this bunch, a 100–1 shot to win the AL pennant at the start of the season, was only a game out of first place. Jim Lonborg, who was 14–3, was starting that night for the Red Sox in what would be his final game before leaving for two weeks of National Guard duty. Just to add to the team's anxiety, the game was delayed nearly two hours by rain. As a result, second baseman Rod Carew had to be scratched from the starting lineup so he could catch a plane to go to his military reserve obligation.

Harmon Killebrew found a way to alleviate the tension with a first-inning home run. The Red Sox got that one back in the bottom of the inning off starter Dean Chance. The 1–1 tie stayed until the fourth inning when Cesar Tovar lined a two-run triple to give the Twins a lead they wouldn't lose. Before the inning was over, Lonborg was on his way to the National Guard and the Twins had moved back into the five-team pennant race with an unexpected 9–2 romp.

> ## At a Glance
>
> **WP:** Chance (12–8)
>
> **HR:** Killebrew (10)
>
> **Key stats:** Chance 8-hitter with 8 Ks

Normally, Chance's pitching effort, an eight-hitter with eight strikeouts, would be the entire story of the night. Chance later said, "I've pitched better games but none more important."

But an event that happened in the Twins' seven-run fourth inning was what many people came away talking about. Minnesota had inched to a 4–1 lead with runners on first and second as Chance headed to the plate. In his previous 78 at-bats, Chance had come away hitless, setting an American League record for consecutive hitless at-bats. But he knew his job and pushed a bunt to the right side. The ball went past Lonborg and Chance happily legged it out for an infield hit, his first in nearly a year. "I really wouldn't care if I ever got a hit. Winning is all I really care about."

ANOTHER MEMORABLE MEETING
Although Jim Lonborg was on National Guard duty, he was allowed to leave to pitch for his team. Nine days after that game at Fenway, Lonborg faced Chance on another rainy day, this time at Met Stadium. This time, Lonborg was able to keep Chance off the bases in both of his plate appearances and, in fact, fanned him as the last batter of the game.

But Chance was on the top of his game, retiring all 15 batters he faced. Minnesota worked out a pair of fourth-inning runs and then happily ran off the field with a 2–0 victory when the game was called in the bottom of the fifth inning. Since the game didn't go the full nine innings, it is not officially listed among major league no-hitters.

The shortened perfect game marked the 12th time Lonborg faced the Twins without gaining a victory. He faced Minnesota just once more that season. That was on October 1, the final game of the season. This time, he pitched a seven-hit complete game for a 5–3 victory that completed the Red Sox's "Impossible Dream" AL title.

The losing pitcher that day? Dean Chance. —⁓—

Oliva Sprints to Victory

One of the longest standing discussions during the Hot Stove League is the issue of whether Tony Oliva belongs in baseball's Hall of Fame. A check of the stats reveals he won three batting titles.

Good stuff.

He led the league in hits five times, and doubles four times.

Did we mention he had a nice arm, too?

But longevity means something to Hall voters, and Oliva finished his career with less than 2,000 career hits. Besides, he only played eight seasons as an out-fielder. Once the DH came into play, he never used his glove again.

For now, Oliva remains only a visitor to Cooperstown.

However, if there were a Hall of Fame for instinctive players, Oliva would have been a no-brainer pick. He often did the little things that made the difference between winning and losing a game. Exhibit A in this regard was his sudden sprint home from second base on a ground ball for the deciding run in a 2–1, 11-inning victory over Baltimore at Met Stadium.

Baltimore's John Miller was nursing a 1–0 lead and a three-hit shutout in the bottom of the ninth inning when Jimmie Hall doubled. Jim Kaat ran for him and scored when Harmon Killebrew singled.

Oliva led off the 11th inning with an infield hit. Pitcher Al Worthington sacrificed him to second. Killebrew was then walked to set up a double play. At this point, Minnesota third base coach Hal Naragon called time to remind Oliva this was not the time to try to steal third base, but he should be alert for all other running opportunities.

Such as the one that developed when Joe Nossek rolled a grounder to third baseman Brooks Robinson, who easily retired Killebrew at second. Nossek, however, beat Jerry Adair's relay at first to keep the inning going. Meanwhile, Oliva rounded third and motored toward home plate, a possibility that had not occurred to Oriole first baseman Boog Powell. By the time he noticed Oliva, Powell's late throw was way offline and the game was suddenly over. "I did that once before against Boston here this year," Oliva said later. "I thought I could make it, but if I'm out at home it's a bad play. Today it was a good play because I made it."

Instinctive players end up making good plays. —ᴧᴧ—

Tony Oliva

The only player ever to win batting titles in his first two seasons in the majors, his career was cut short by knee issues that limited him to designated hitter duty for his final four seasons. He retired with a .304 career batting average. In his heyday, however, he could run, hit with power, and throw with the best of them, as evidenced by his six All-Star appearances in a seven-year period. He hit .440 in his two American League Championship Series appearances. Later, he served nine seasons as a coach.

3,000 Ks . . . and Then Some

Bert Blyleven knew this day was coming. From the time he whiffed Washington's Ed Stroud—the second major league batter he ever faced—it seemed inevitable that he would someday become a member of one of baseball's most elite clans—the 3,000-strikeout club. But even after 16 years as a major league pitcher, he still had moments of anxiety. "I knew I needed just eight to get to 3,000," he said after firing a two-hitter against Oakland at the Metrodome. "I didn't want it to take three or four starts to get it done."

No worries. Blyleven nearly doubled the total he needed as he fanned a career-high 15 batters in a 10–1 victory before 14,855 delirious fans. It was such a memorable performance that Blyleven managed to turn Kirby Puckett's only career cycle performance into a side story. "I didn't have a prayer," said Oakland second baseman Tony Phillips, who went down three times. "He had me off balance all night. I knew he was going to get me."

Phillips had company. Donnie Hill joined him in the hat trick department. José Canseco, Mike Davis, Dwayne Murphy, and Mickey Tettleton were close behind with two whiffs each. Blyleven was so dominating that catcher Tim Laudner noted later he merely had to put his glove up and watch things happen. "It was a chair game," Laudner said. "I really had nothing to do with it all night."

Things started fast and got faster. After four innings, the Twins led 4–0, and the A's still hadn't had a base runner. Bruce Bochte singled to open the fifth and went to second

Bert Blyleven

In his first start, he recorded a victory at Washington—at age 19. Sixteen years later, in his second tour of duty with the team, he recorded his 3,000th career strikeout. A two-time All-Star, Blyleven led the league in shutouts three times and in innings pitched in back-to-back seasons. In 1987, he won 15 regular-season games, two ALCS starts, and one game as part of the team's World Series effort. He has been part of the team's TV broadcast unit since 1995.

Bert Blyleven frequently dominated hitters in his two stints with the Twins, but never more than in the game he topped 3,000 strikeouts for his career.

when Carney Lansford was safe on an error. Both runners, therefore, had good views as Blyleven mowed down Murphy and Davis on strikes, the latter being the magical 3,000th. Tettleton then worked a walk—Blyleven's only free pass of the night—to load the bases, but Alfredo Griffin grounded out to end the threat.

After dodging that bullet, Griffin's eighth-inning homer was the only runner Blyleven allowed the rest of the night. By that time, Puckett was three-quarters of the way to a cycle and the Twins had an 8–0 lead. Gary Gaetti and Tom Brunansky had hit home runs and Laudner had driven in three runs on a bases-loaded double. Puckett capped his night with a two-run homer in the bottom of the eighth and the attention went back to Blyleven.

"I knew I had 14 [a figure he had reached twice before] when I started the ninth inning," Blyleven said. "I wanted to do better than that. I don't get many chances to do something like this." After taking care of Hill on a comebacker, Blyleven got Canseco to chase one more sweeping curveball. Bochte then flied out, just the third outfield putout of the night, and the great game was over.

Puckett had been the hitting hero of the night, but he knew where the attention belonged. "That's the best pitching exhibition I've seen in my life," he said of Blyleven's effort. —⁓—

An Unexpected Comeback

For six innings, things seemed to be going according to form. The AL West Division-leading Angels were taking it to the team with the worst record in baseball. Minnesota starter Bobby Castillo only allowed five hits but two of them were home runs by Fred Lynn and Doug DeCinces. Throw in a two-run single by ex-Twin Rob Wilfong and the Angels had a seemingly secure 6–0 lead.

But nothing is ever totally safe in baseball. After managing just two hits in the first six innings against Angel righty Mike Witt, the Twins started the seventh with a Tom Brunansky double and back-to-back singles by Kent Hrbek and Gary Ward. A wild pitch and a sacrifice fly led to another run, and Witt's night was finished. Former Minnesota closer Doug Corbett entered and gave up another run before the inning ended. The Angels scored in the bottom of the inning to make it 7–3 but, in the eighth, Ward rocked Corbett (who would be sent to the minors the next day) with a three-run homer.

It was still 7–6 in the ninth when Luis Sanchez replaced Corbett. Unfazed, the Twins promptly loaded the bases and then took the lead with a Ron Washington two-run single. Brunansky, playing his first game at the Big A since being traded from the Angels (ironically, for Corbett and Wilfong) in May, doubled home an insurance run to make it 9–7.

At a Glance

WP: Little (2–0)

S: Davis (13)

HR: Ward (18)

Key stats: Ward 2-for-4, 3 RBIs

This time, there was no drama in a Ron Davis save. He dismissed a fairly impressive trio of Angels (Don Baylor, Lynn and DeCinces) in order, and the comeback win was complete. Manager Billy Gardner sounded more relieved than anything else. "At the beginning of the season, people were laughing at us and calling us a AAA team," Gardner said. "Well, they have something positive to write about now." —꿈—

No Decision, but a Lot of Attention for Niekro

It was one of the great nights of Gary Gaetti's career. He went 3-for-5 at the plate, scored twice, hit a home run, and had five RBIs in Minnesota's 11–3 victory at the Big A. Yet all that was barely a footnote to the odd events of the fourth inning when regarding Minnesota starting pitcher Joe Niekro.

Yes, indeed, this was the night when Gaetti surrendered the headlines to an emery board and a piece of sandpaper.

Ironically, the person in the middle of it all wasn't even supposed to be in the game. Niekro's turn had actually come up the day before when the Twins were in Oakland. But, since he had pitched well in some previous games at the Big A (including a near no-hitter), manager Tom Kelly held him out an extra day to face the Angels.

Gaetti's two-run single in the top of the third had tied the game at 2-all. In the bottom of the fourth, the score became insignificant. Home plate umpire Tim Tschida was already on the lookout, having seen some pitches earlier that moved strangely. Suddenly, after a strike to Brian Downing made the count 2–1, Tschida paid Niekro a visit at the mound. He asked to inspect his glove. While this was going on, an emery board suddenly flew out of Niekro's back pocket. Further inspection revealed there was a piece of sandpaper there, too. What had started as a small inspection turned into a quick ejection for violation of Rule 3.02. "The balls were defaced with something you can't do with your hands," Tschida said. "When you pull your hand out of your pocket and the smoking gun falls to the ground, there's nothing much you can do."

Not that Niekro didn't try. The 42-year-old knuckleballer pleaded innocence. "I've been carrying the emery board and sandpaper for 15 years, as long as I've been throwing the knuckleball," he said. "I was never questioned before, I don't feel like I did anything wrong. If I did, I'm sorry." Niekro added he used the implements to keep his nails sharp.

Crew chief Dave Phillips and his partners were disbelievers, however, and Niekro was excused for the night.

Once Niekro was no longer on the mound, the game became the focus again. Dan Schatzeder replaced Niekro and ended up going the rest of the way, giving up just a run and four hits in 5 2/3 innings.

> ## At a Glance
> **WP:** Schatzeder (6–1)
>
> **HR:** Gaetti (22)
>
> **Key stats:** Gaetti 3-for-5, 5 RBIs

The game remained 2–2 until the sixth, when Gene Larkin's bases-loaded walk off Mike Witt broke the tie. Minnesota got another run, but that was offset by Brian Downing's solo homer in the bottom of the inning. The game fell apart the next inning when the Twins combined three hits, two walks, and a balk for four runs. Gaetti's three-run homer in the eighth was the capper for the night. Minnesota now had a two-game lead over second-place Oakland and a 2½ game edge on the Angels.

A TRIAL, A CONVICTION, AND LIFE GOES ON

Niekro was given a 10-day suspension for his violation. As per agreement with the Players' Association, he was allowed to appeal. Four days after the Anaheim affair, he started and went a solid eight innings (2 ER, 5 H) to gain the victory in a 9–4 win over Oakland at the Metrodome. The next day, AL president Bobby Brown listened to Niekro's appeal but upheld the suspension. Things didn't go as well for Niekro when he returned to action. He lost five of six decisions and saw his ERA jump almost a run.

In the end, however, 1987 turned out to be a good year for the veteran. After two decades in the major leagues, he made it to his first World Series, pitching two scoreless innings in Game 4 in St. Louis. It was his only appearance for the World Series champs. In 1988, he survived a tight competition to be on the Opening Day roster and earned a victory in his first relief appearance of the season, April 12 at Cleveland. A week later, the Yankees tore into him for seven runs in 1 2/3 innings, and a downward spiral quickly began. After three more appearances, Niekro was released, ending his 22-year career with an overall record of 221–204 and a 3.59 ERA. The game at Anaheim was his only ejection in a 702-game career. —⁓—

Moving Into a Select Club

There was never anything fancy about Brad Radke's approach to pitching. He wasn't the type of guy who would blaze a ball past a hitter for a spectacular out. His career ERA of 4.22 isn't particularly impressive. At first (or even second) glance, Radke wasn't a guy who looked very impressive.

Except to his opponents. You see, all Radke ever did was come to beat you.

At a Glance

WP: Radke (16–5)

HR: Colbrunn (5)

Key stats: Radke no earned runs in 7 IP; Colbrunn grand slam

Never was this more apparent than in 1997 when the Floridian went seven innings to gain a 9–3 win over Toronto at the Metrodome. In doing so, he managed to do something that Sandy Koufax, Tom Seaver, Nolan Ryan, and many others never did—win 12 straight starts. Radke became only the third pitcher in the past 50 seasons (Bob Gibson and Pat Dobson were the others) to pull off such a remarkable feat. His victory that day was like so many others in the streak. It was so efficient that his manager, Tom Kelly, merely said, "I don't say anything to him (these days). I ain't going to be responsible for messing him up."

Radke had started his streak two months earlier with a six-hitter against the Angels. By the time the Blue Jays came to town, he had thrown two more complete games and had lowered his ERA nearly two runs. Normally the most quiet of souls, Radke had suddenly become a man in demand and had even made a guest appearance on the Howard Stern show when the Twins were in New York. The off-the-field attention was relentless. "It's more tiring than pitching," Radke admitted to reporters. "I'm getting worn out."

You will excuse the Blue Jays if they were disbelievers on this night. It didn't seem to matter much. Greg Colbrunn's grand slam homer and Matt Lawton's two RBIs had been the key blows in opening an 8–0 edge before Toronto got on the board in the seventh inning with a pair of unearned runs set up by a Pat Meares error.

But there was no need for Radke to go any further. Eddie Guardado and Mike Trombley finished the game off as Radke watched from the dugout. "I felt a little more nervous in the first inning that I had in past starts," he said. "Maybe I am starting to think about it [the streak] a little more."—

When Brad Radke won his 12th consecutive start on August 4, 1997, he became just the third pitcher in 50 years to accomplish such a feat. Radke went seven innings in a 9–3 win over Toronto.

A Little Confidence Goes a Long Way

It has only happened 18 times in the 49-year history of the Minnesota Twins. Camilo Pascual did it four times in his first two seasons with the team. Bert Blyleven did it on three occasions, once in 1971 and twice in 1973. Jim Grant and Dean Chance, mainstays of the staff in the late 1960s, managed this feat twice each. The list of hurlers who did it once include some of the great names from the team's past—Frank Viola, Scott Erickson, Jim Perry, and Dave Goltz.

One name you might not expect to see in that group was Dick Woodson, who recorded just 33 wins in 129 games for the Twins from 1969–74. But a little confidence can go a long way. So it was that when Woodson disabled the Oakland A's 4–0 on a Saturday afternoon at Met Stadium, he joined an august group of pitchers who tossed back-to-back shutouts.

"I'm more relaxed now," Woodson said after shutting out the future World Series champs on five singles.

For the first half of 1972, Woodson had been anything but comfortable. Despite winning his first three decisions,

> ### At a Glance
>
> **WP:** Woodson (9–9)
>
> **Key stats:** Woodson 5-hit shutout; Braun 2-run 2B

Woodson stood at 5–8 with a 3.56 ERA when manager Bill Rigney was fired in early July. His replacement, Frank Quilici, had played second base behind Woodson two years before and took a different method than the hands-on approach Rigney used. Instead of taking him out at the first sign of trouble, Quilici let Woodson try to get out of messes himself. The approach seemed to work, and Woodson, who had never thrown a shutout in the major leagues, blanked Texas on three hits on August 1.

Four days later, Woodson's teammates had jumped on Vida Blue early (Steve Braun's two-run double in the first inning was the big blow) for a 4–0 lead. It was still that way in the eighth inning when Oakland loaded the bases with one out. Sal Bando flew out for the second out. But that left Mike Epstein, a 230-pound left-handed hitter with 18 home runs to his name, at the plate. While everybody looked to the dugout, Quilici stayed put. "What's the worst thing that could happen?" he said later. "It would be a tie game, right?"

Relieved he wasn't seeing a replacement, Woodson retired Epstein on a meek fly to right and then dumped the side in order in the ninth. "Quilici has shown more confidence in me by letting me pitch out of certain situations," Woodson said after the game. "I think I've given the manager more reason for confidence by showing I can do the job." —⁓—

Luebber Comes Close to Making History

In the end, the wait was worth it for Steve Luebber. A decade after first being drafted by the Twins in the 13th round (1967), he had finally worked his way into a regular spot in the starting rotation. When he took the mound on a steamy Saturday night at Arlington Stadium, he had won his last two starts. By night's end, that streak was up to three in a row—with a near no-hitter to boot.

Luebber, whose previous effort was a complete-game shutout against Oakland, nearly topped that mark in a 3–1 victory. Only three of the first 29 batters Luebber faced reached base, two on walks and one on an error. Third baseman Roy Howell prevented the first Twins no-no in a decade with a clean single to center with two outs in the ninth. Luebber had missed history by a single out but was still happy with the night. "My overall reaction is one of happiness," he said at the time. "I have to establish myself as a big league pitcher. To do that, you need victories."

Thirty-three years later, he could remember the night—and the Howell at-bat—well. "Even though I had trouble with my breaking stuff, I had pitched pretty well in a start against the Rangers at Met Stadium [0 R, 3 H, 6 1/3 IP on July 28] and felt confident against them," he said. "That night in Texas, I had a good breaking ball from the start."

The game was still tight (3–0) when Howell stepped in against Luebber. "I got to 2–2 on him and threw a pitch exactly where we [catcher Butch Wynegar] wanted it—on the inside part of the plate," Luebber remembered. "I thought it was strike three. A few of the guys started to raise their hands. But the umpire (Art Frantz) called it a ball. Then, he fouled a good pitch off. It was either face him or Mike Hargrove, a very good hitter. So I tried the fastball again and he just hit it cleanly."

In a bizarre turn of events, Howell's single skipped through normally reliable center fielder Lyman Bostock's legs and he advanced to third base. Hargrove followed with a single and Luebber's shutout disappeared as well. At that point, Bill Campbell entered and fanned Jeff Burroughs to end the game.

Luebber remains philosophical about the night. "I've seen guys pitch 10-walk no-hitters and guys with great stuff not even come close to one," he said. "There is always a certain element of luck to getting one." —〰—

At a Glance

WP: Luebber (3–2)

S: Campbell (12)

HR: Hisle (9)

Key stats: Luebber 2 hits, 0 ER in 8 2/3 IP; Braun 3-for-4; Hisle 2-for-3, 2 RBIs

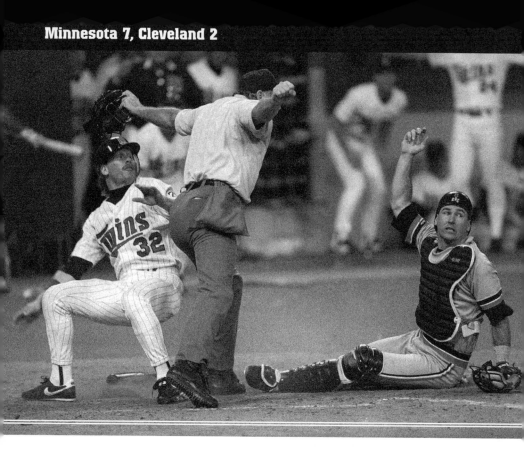

Triple the Pleasure

As a player, Dan Gladden's five-year tenure is best remembered by Twins' fans for his ability to get key hits, his hell-bent style of running the bases, and for his happy dash home with the winning run in Game 7 of the 1991 World Series.

But he could flash the leather, too. In Minnesota's 7–2 win over Cleveland, he showed off all the facets of his game. At the plate, he banged out three singles, scored a run, and knocked one in. He also swiped a base that opened the gates for a two-run inning that put the game out of reach.

But it was a catch he made that led to a rare 7–4–3 triple play that left the Metrodome crowd of 36,316 agog. Ex-Twin Ron Washington opened the fourth inning of a scoreless game with a single to center off Minnesota starter Allan Anderson. Willie Upshaw followed suit and Washington stopped at second.

Joe Carter, a very dangerous hitter, was now batting. Carter hit Anderson well (five home runs in 18 career at-bats) and this appearance was no exception. As soon as Carter made contact, Gladden took off for the left field fence.

"I was just hoping I could catch the ball," he said after the game. "I was a little surprised when it landed in my glove."

Washington and Upshaw joined Gladden in that department. After making the catch, Gladden turned and whistled a strike to second baseman Steve Lombardozzi, who tagged his bag and relayed the ball to Gene Larkin, playing first base. Upshaw was still five feet away. What looked like a ball that would give Cleveland a one- or two-run lead was suddenly an inning-ending triple play.

Even Tom Kelly, a man not known for giving gushing reviews, couldn't contain himself. "You're not going to see anything much better than that," he said.

Gladden had a sense of what would happen next. "Emotions are a big part of this game and that play was an example of that," he said. "I think it took the starch out of them."

Perhaps. Or it might just be the Twins figured out Cleveland starter Chris Codiroli as he made his second tour of the batting order. Whatever the reason, the facts are undisputable. Kirby Puckett led off the bottom of the fourth inning with a double. After Kent Hrbek popped out, Gary Gaetti tripled over Carter's head in center field to drive home the game's first run. Two more tallies quickly followed when Larkin hit a Codiroli pitch into the left-field seats.

One inning later, Gladden singled to start the inning. He then stole second and scored on Puckett's single to make it 4–1, and the Twins rolled home from there.

At a Glance

WP: Anderson (10–7)

S: Reardon (29)

HR: Larkin (5)

Key stats: Harper 4-for-4; Gladden 3-for-5, RBI

There were many happy stats to note. Catcher Brian Harper, whose first four-hit game of his career became a background item, doubled to start another two-run inning later in the game. Anderson pitched a sturdy 6 1/3 innings to gain the win. Jeff Reardon extricated the team out of possible messy eighth inning and recorded his 29th save.

But everybody left knowing that Dan Gladden had changed the direction of the game with a dramatic play. Again. ⎯⎯

Allen Finds a Way to Win Folks Over

Bernie Allen came to the Twins with two strikes against him. There was much local grumbling when Allen was named the team's main second baseman at the start of the 1962 season. For starters, he was replacing Billy Martin, who had endeared himself to fans at the end of the 1961 season. Secondly, many folks remembered Allen as the Purdue quarterback who bedeviled the University of Minnesota's defense for three seasons from 1958–60.

Allen found a way to quiet the multitudes. In his rookie season in the bigs, he hit a solid .269 and fielded his position well. And when he contributed as he did with a career-best four RBIs in a 12–10 win at Kansas City, even the hardcore Gopher football fans forgave him.

The game was tied at 2-all in the fourth inning when Allen led off the inning with a double and rode home on Zoilo Versalles' single. Minnesota added another run before the inning ended, but the A's rocked Minnesota starter Lee Stange for six runs in the bottom of the inning. Later, Allen and third baseman Rich Rollins each had RBI singles and the game eventually was tied at 9-all.

The same duo broke the game open in the top of the ninth with the game still knotted at 9-all. Rollins, who had come up to the Twins briefly in 1961, broke the tie with a two-run single to cap his four-RBI night. Four batters later, Allen rapped out his fourth hit of the night to send home one last run and make it 12–9. Kansas City actually brought the winning run to the plate before reliever Frank Sullivan finally induced pinch-hitter Deron Johnson to foul out and end the game.

"The kids [Rollins and Allen] were great again today," Minnesota manager Sam Mele said simply. "We'd be lost without them." —⁓—

> ## At a Glance
>
> **WP:** Sullivan (2–2)
>
> **Key stats:** Rollins 2-for-6, 4 RBIs; Allen 4-for-6, 4 RBIs

The Big Fellow Says Goodbye

As farewells go, this wasn't exactly like Ted Williams homering in his last at-bat. Or Brad Radke trudging sadly away in a playoff game with an aching shoulder and a breaking heart.

No, Kent Hrbek played his final major league game using the same low-key but effective technique he used in his other 1,746 efforts. There were no grandiose speeches because, frankly, nobody was sure at the time this really was his last game.

As it turned out, Minnesota's 17–7 win over the Red Sox was the last game of the 1994 season. The players' walkout that would cause the World Series to be cancelled for the only time in its history began the next day. And Kent Hrbek was now free to pursue his hunting and fishing interests full-time—something that still occupies his time and has turned into a second career with a syndicated television series.

But we digress.

A few days earlier, Hrbek had confirmed what many people figured would be the case. This would be the last go-around of a lively 14-year career that had seen the guy who grew up near old Met Stadium play a key role in a pair of World Series championships. The Big Fellow could still hit (his .270 batting average that year was the best he had recorded since 1991). But his body was aching more and more after each game. As is now the case in modern baseball, his old gang of teammates and pals had been broken up with a series of trades. Gary Gaetti and Tom Brunansky were playing elsewhere.

Four days before this final game with the Red Sox, Hrbek bombed a long home run against the Yankees. Did this cause him to have second thoughts? "Not any," he quickly replied. "I've had hits like that before. I'm gone."

Once unburdened of the questions regarding retirement, Hrbek finished strong. Despite an ankle injury suffered in the final week of his career, he whacked out hits in 15 of his last 18 games. As the Twins anxiously approached the date for the strike,

Twins	AB	R	H	RBI
Knoblauch 2b	5	2	3	2
Leius 3b	4	2	0	0
Puckett rf	3	4	2	7
Mack cf-lf	4	1	3	3
Winfield dh	1	0	0	0
Reboulet ph-dh	3	0	2	0
Hale pr-dh	1	1	1	0
Hrbek 1b	5	1	1	3
Munoz lf	4	1	2	0
Cole pr-cf	1	0	0	0
Walbeck c	5	2	2	0
Meares ss	5	2	2	2
Totals	41	17	18	17

BOS 1 1 1 0 0 3 1 0 0 - 7 11 0
MIN 1 4 0 1 3 0 8 0 x - 17 18 0

Red Sox	IP	H	R	ER	BB	SO
Nabholz	1	0	2	2	4	1
Bankhead L(3–2)	2.2	4	4	4	2	1
Howard	0.2	4	3	3	0	0
Frohwirth	1.2	4	3	3	4	1
Fossas	2	6	5	5	1	1
Totals	8	18	17	17	11	4

Twins	IP	H	R	ER	BB	SO
Deshaies W(6–12)	5.1	7	5	5	2	0
Trombley	1.2	3	2	2	0	1
Willis	1	1	0	0	0	1
Schullstrom	1	0	0	0	0	0
Totals	9	11	7	7	2	2

DP—Boston 1. 2B—Boston Fletcher, Vaughn, Brunansky. Minnesota Hale. HR—Boston Rowland 2 (9), Vaughn (26). Minnesota Puckett 2 (20). SH—Minnesota Meares. HBP—Minnesota Hrbek. LOB—Boston 5. Minnesota 13. SB—Boston Fletcher. Minnesota Knoblauch 2. Attendance—23,492.

the area's concern seemed to be more on Hrbek playing in the game than the ramifications of a walkout. As usual, Hrbek cut through the hullabaloo and got straight to the point. "If I don't think I can do the job, I won't go out there," he said, regarding involvement in the final game, adding, "Of course, it wouldn't hinder my running a bit."

As for the game, it was a wild one from the start. Puckett's second-inning grand slam homer helped the Twins take an early lead. In the fifth inning, Shane Mack's two-RBI single helped push the margin to 9–3. Minnesota starter Jim Deshaies and reliever Mike Trombley then got into trouble, and the lead was down to 9–7 when the Twins came to bat in the last of the seventh inning. Two walks and a single loaded the bases with no one out as Hrbek came to the plate, the fourth time in the game he had been up in that type of situation. He gave the crowd one last thrill with a single off second baseman Scott Fletcher's glove. Two runs scored and it was 11–7. Later (after a Puckett three-run homer), Hrbek came up in the seventh inning again—the 13th Minnesota batsman in the frame. This time, however, he flied out to center field to end the inning.

Kent Hrbek

The hometown boy made an immediate impact in his first game, hitting a home run at Yankee Stadium. The big fellow remained an impressive force for his entire career, hitting 293 home runs with 1,086 RBIs. He still ranks near the top in nearly every all-time team hitting category. He hit memorable home runs in each of his World Series appearances. Despite his size, he was a surprisingly agile first baseman, finishing with a career fielding mark of .994.

The crowd reaction, however, was the same for both at-bats: a standing ovation. As it turned out, Hrbek had the last word on the season. Shortstop Carlos Rodriguez popped out to Hrbek to end the game, the season, and his career. The normally unsentimental Hrbek decided to keep this ball as a souvenir and ran off the field quickly. "I'm not looking at it as my last game," he said to reporters later. "But if it is, it is."

Time to go hunting and fishing. —∿∿—

Kent Hrbek's 14-year career came to a premature end when the baseball players' strike ended the season on August 10, 1994. Hrbek finished with 293 home runs and 1,086 RBIs.

Kooz Shuts Them Down

It was exactly the type of game the Minnesota Twins hoped they would see from Jerry Koosman. Everybody knew he didn't have the high, hard one that he threw when he helped the 1969 New York Mets win the World Series. A decade later, he relied more on guile than speed. But the man still could pitch. On this day at Met Stadium, Koosman gave up 10 hits (twice as many as Oakland's Rick Langford) but ended up a 1–0 winner.

"He may not be fast as he once was," observed A's manager Jim Marshall. "But he is able to get his good curve across the plate anytime he needs it."

Throwing a 10-hit shutout isn't an easy thing to do. In the first seven innings, the A's placed at least one runner on base. But Koosman kept working his way out of trouble. In the first inning, a double play stopped a threat. In the fourth inning, catcher Butch Wynegar ended a potential rally when he picked Jim Essian off first base.

The game stayed scoreless until the seventh inning when a failed bunt attempt led to a run. In the second inning, Mike Cubbage led off with a single. DH Danny Goodwin bunted him to second, the Twins' club-record 110th such occurrence of the season. But Langford retired the next two batters.

Cubbage started off the seventh with another single. As was his wont, Minnesota manager Gene Mauch flashed the bunt sign. Goodwin fouled the pitch off. Mauch now changed his mind and told Goodwin to swing away. This he did, lining a double to right that scored Cubbage easily with the game's only run.

Armed with a lead, Koosman retired the A's in order in the eighth inning.

> ## At a Glance
>
> **WP:** Koosman (14–10)
>
> **Key stats:** Koosman 10-hit shutout; Cubbage 3-for-3

Essian, who always seemed to hit the Twins well, led off the ninth inning with a single. Remembering what had happened the last time Essian was on base, Dwayne Murphy went in to run for him. Wynegar did not attempt to pick Murphy off first. Koosman, however, did, and nailed him on his first try. The southpaw promptly fanned the next two batters to put the finishing touch on his first shutout in his home state. It raised his record to 14–10, a number that Mauch thought could have been much better. "He won his first seven decisions of the year but I think he pitched better when he lost his next six starts," Mauch said. "We just didn't get him any runs. He should have 20 wins by now."

Koosman preferred to dwell on the present. "I didn't know what to expect today because I hadn't pitched against Oakland since 1973 (in the World Series)," he said. "Fortunately, this was my best location of the year."

Timing is everything. —〰—

Radke Stops 'Em One Last Time

In his heyday, Brad Radke's fastball never scared anybody. However, as they say in the real estate business, it was always about location, location, location.

This was never more true than in 2006, when Radke's aching shoulder had reduced the speed on his heater down to the mid-80s range. By the time the Twins took the field against the Blue Jays on this Sunday afternoon at the Metrodome, the righty was close to running on fumes.

His manager, Tom Kelly, a longtime admirer, took note of this when he told reporters, "Brad pitches the baseball. He doesn't just throw it."

He needed to do some serious pitching against a team that led the league in hitting and had already won the first two games of the series. But pitch he did. Radke worked the corners like a surgeon performing at Walter Reed Hospital. He threw 96 pitches over seven innings, leaving the Blue Jays just enough room for five singles. Only one Toronto player visited second base, and he didn't stay long. Five pitches after arriving there, he had to head for the field after Reed Johnson bounced into a double play to end the inning. The catcher that day, Mike Redmond, later marveled, "He hit the corner every time we asked for it."

Held to one run in two games, the Twins broke out a bit on offense. Jason Tyner had three hits. Michael Cuddyer clubbed a home run. Justin Morneau drove in two runs. It added up to five runs and that was plenty for Radke.

After seven innings, Radke turned the game over to Matt Guerrier and Joe Nathan, who each recorded 1–2–3 innings. It was the 148th—and last—regular season victory for Radke. It was a performance reminiscent of Vin Scully's description of another master craftsman who got 'em out with guile more than speed—Tom Glavine. Said Scully, "He's like a tailor; a little off here, a little off there, and you're done, take a seat." —⌇—

At a Glance

WP: Radke (12–8)

HR: Cuddyer (17)

Key stats: Radke 7 shutout innings; Tyner 3-for-4, 2 RBIs

The Mouse That Roared

Jackie Hernandez batted just .143 and knocked in only three runs in 1967. But it takes a little bit of everything to stay in a pennant race. So it was that Hernandez ended up as an unlikely hero in a 2–1 victory over the Angels that moved the Twins a game ahead of the tight AL pack.

It has generally been forgotten that the AL race was actually a five-team tango for much of the 1967 season. This was the first day of a 14-day, 16-game road odyssey that some folks figured could be the Twins' demise. The trek was opening at Anaheim Stadium, where the Angels were in fourth place but only 1½ games out of the top spot.

For six innings, Minnesota's Dave Boswell and California's George Brunet matched goose eggs. In the seventh, catcher Jerry Zimmerman led off with a single and Hernandez, who had played the entire previous season with the Angels (but only came to the plate 23 times), ran for him. Two more singles followed to load the bases, but Brunet wriggled his way out of trouble with no runs crossing the plate.

In the bottom of the inning, Roger Repoz homered for the Angels to break the scoreless tie.

Minnesota, however, recovered in the eighth. With two outs and nobody on, catcher Hank Izquierdo ended up on second base after a rare throwing error by Angels shortstop Jim Fregosi. Hernandez had stayed in the game to play shortstop. Facing his old teammate, he guessed a curve ball was coming and drilled it into left field. Izquierdo scored and, when Jose Cardenal's throw went awry, Hernandez jogged to second. Ted Uhlaender then hit Brunet's first pitch for a double, and the Twins suddenly had a 2–1 lead.

> ## At a Glance
>
> **WP:** Boswell (10–8)
>
> **S:** Worthington (14)
>
> **Key stats:** Boswell 7 hits, 1 ER in 8 1/3 IP: Uhlaender 2-for-4, RBI

Boswell needed some late help (Jim Kaat retired one batter in the ninth and Al Worthington got the last one for the save), and the long road swing got off to a good start.

The decision was the beginning of the end for the Angels, who lost the next two games of the series against the Twins and then dropped four in a row on the weekend at Boston.

As for Hernandez, it was his last RBI of the season. —~~

The B Team Gets an A in Win over O's

Baltimore in mid-August can be a very uncomfortable place due to heat and humidity. When the Twins arrived at Memorial Stadium, they were already in a foul frame of mind. They had fallen out of first place after dropping the final two games of a series in Detroit. Manager Gene Mauch sensed some of his stalwarts were tired and went to the bench for help.

Rod Carew and Lyman Bostock, who merely stood first and second in the AL batting race, got the night off. Backup catcher Bud Bulling, sporting a .154 batting average, was inserted as the designated hitter. It looked like it would be a challenge to succeed against Orioles starting pitcher Rudy May, who had 13 wins to his credit.

Looks were deceiving. Bostock's replacement in left field was Bob Gorinski, a lumbering sort with a better nickname (Shoedog) than batting average (.189). But Shoedog made his presence felt early when he unloaded a two-run homer in the second inning to give Minnesota a 3–2 lead.

But Twins starter Dave Goltz was having a rough night. Baltimore led 5–3 in the fifth inning when Craig Kusick, standing in for Carew, drilled a three-run shot to left to put the Twins back ahead 6–5. Three more runs in the sixth chased May in favor of lefty Mike Flanagan. Kusick hit his second homer of the night, a bomb that made his first longball seem like a bunt, to make it 11–5.

The Orioles worked reliever Gary Serum over to creep within 11–8 after seven innings. It was the time for starters to return. Dick Drago, a right-hander, entered the game in relief, prompting Carew to leave the bench to hit for Kusick. Carew singled home a run. In the ninth, Bostock batted for Gorinski and justified the decision with a double. Bulling, who had batted only 13 times in the six weeks he had been with the team, then singled him home with Minnesota's final run of the night.

At a Glance

WP: Schueler (5–4)

HR: Gorinski (2), Kusick 2 (10)

Key stats: Kusick 2-for-4, 2 HRs, 5 RBIs; Gorinski 2-for-4, HR, 2 RBIs; Schueler 2 hits in 3 IP

Mauch's magic had worked. All in all, the reserves (including Jerry Terrell, who was in for Mike Cubbage at third base) scored three runs with six hits and eight RBIs. The mini-slump was over. The Twins went to bed in first place by a half game over the White Sox, who lost that night in New York. Later, Kusick was asked about being pulled from the game after hitting two home runs and knocking in five runs. "When a guy who is going to the Hall of Fame hits for you, what the hell," he smiled. —⌇—

Perry Multitasks to Earn a Win over the Angels

Jim Perry had one of the best seasons of his career in 1966. What's that, you say? After all, he only won 11 games. A few years later, he won 20 games in 1969 and took the AL Cy Young Award home when he garnered 24 the next year.

But Perry did have a good year in 1966—at the plate. He ended up with a higher slugging average than teammates Earl Battey and Cesar Tovar. Despite fewer at-bats, he ended up with more extra base hits than non-pitchers such as Sandy Valdespino or Russ Nixon.

And when things came together—as they did in an 8–1 win over California at Met Stadium on a Tuesday night—it was a nice package indeed. On the mound, Perry overwhelmed the Halos easily, scattering three hits and striking out 10 in a complete-game effort. The latter stat was no surprise—Minnesota led the AL with 37 complete games at that stage of the year.

At the plate, Perry was more proficient than the man he was facing that night, Dean Chance. He had a single off his future teammate in a four-run fourth inning that severed a scoreless tie. Two innings later, he doubled off reliever Lew Burdette. In the eighth, he capped his good night with an RBI double off relief pitcher Bob Lee. Manager Sam Mele was unsurprised. "This is the best hitting staff of pitchers in the league," he said.

> ### At a Glance
>
> **WP:** Perry (7–5)
>
> **HR:** Killebrew (27), Kosco (2), Oliva (20), Mincher (12)
>
> **Key stats:** Perry 3-hitter with 10 Ks

Afterward, Perry seemed more interested in talking about his mound work. "I wasn't pitching for strikeouts tonight," he said. "I just tried to throw the ball over the plate with something on it." He would go on to win a total of 215 games in 17 big league seasons—99 fewer than his Hall of Fame brother, Gaylord.

It was no contest at the plate, though. Gaylord finished his career with a lifetime .131 batting average. Older bro Jim, who hit .220 in 1966, ended up at a much gaudier .199. ⸺

Oliva Shares the Spotlight on Big Night

It was a night to remember for Tony Oliva. His knee problems were such that he was already limited to serving as a designated hitter and coming off the bench to pinch-hit. After a slow start, he adapted to his new role and had inched his average near the .300 mark when the Twins trooped into Municipal Stadium to open a three-game series with the Indians.

He helped his cause considerably on this night with a pair of home runs and a career-tying six-RBI night. In itself, this was newsworthy material. But what really made this game unique was his companions in the home run brigade.

For example, there was Jerry Terrell, who led off the game with a line drive that ended up in the left-field seats. Since this was his first home run in 319 major league at-bats, he was understandably a bit rusty as to procedure. "I didn't see it because I was running for a double," he said later. "I got to second base and the umpire [Merle Anthony] had a shocked look on his face. So I looked at third and the guy there [Ron Luciano] was signaling home run. Then I was shocked."

It was the start of a memorable night for Terrell, who ended up with four hits and two RBIs on the night. It was also the beginning of a very bad night for Cleveland starter Dick Bosman. Minnesota scored a pair in the first inning. In the second frame, Oliva ended Bosman's night with a grand slam home run. Milt Wilcox replaced him and fared just as poorly, facing six batters and retiring only one of them. The last man he faced was catcher Phil Roof, who slammed a three-run homer to break the game wide open. Although Roof hit 13 home runs in 110 games one season in Milwaukee, his power seemed to have evaporated in Minnesota. This was just his fourth longball since he had joined the Twins in 1971 and his only one of the 1973 season. "I don't like the idea of the little guys getting ahead of the Babe," he joked afterward.

At a Glance

WP: Blyleven (15–12)

HR: Terrell (1), Oliva 2 (14), Roof (1)

Key stat: Blyleven 7-hitter

As far as the Indians were concerned, there was nothing funny about Oliva's work that night. He hit a two-run shot in the fifth to cap his night, giving Minnesota starter Bert Blyleven plenty of room to cruise to a seven-hit complete-game win. "Al Worthington [pitching coach] had to keep reminding me to pitch like 0–0," Blyleven said. It's a problem many pitchers wouldn't mind in the least. —⁓—

Santana Paints a Masterpiece

Ron Gardenhire foresaw the problem. When Texas catcher Jarrod Saltalamacchia went down swinging to end the eighth inning, Twins starting pitcher Johan Santana had already set a team record with 17 strikeouts and was within reach of the major league mark of 20 in a game. Gardenhire might be the Twins field manager but, on this afternoon at the Metrodome, he was in the dual role of fan as well. "You want to sit in my seat and try to make that decision with all the people hooting and hollering for to him to go back out there?" he said after Minnesota's 1–0 win was complete.

Fortunately for Gardenhire, Santana figured 112 pitches was enough for one day and doffed his cap to the crowd in the matter of a matador who had slain the bull. "I still felt good but we knew that situation that [Joe] Nathan would be the right guy to go back out there," Santana said. "He's one of the best closers in the game and I trust him." (Good call. Nathan fanned two more batters to make it a team-record 19 for the day.)

Thus, Santana put an exclamation point on one of the best pitching performances in team history. As Texas manager Ron Washington put it, "The way Santana threw today, he could have gotten 17 strikeouts against the 1927 Yankees."

Nobody in the Rangers' lineup was spared. Michael Young struck out four times. Brad Wilkerson, Marlon Byrd, and Gerald Laird went down thrice. Saltalamacchia walked back to the dugout twice. In all, 15 of the 17 Ks went via swings—a sure sign that Santana had his magic going in several directions.

> ## At a Glance
>
> **WP:** Santana (13–9)
>
> **S:** Nathan (27)
>
> **HR:** Cuddyer (12)
>
> **Key stats:** Santana 2 hits, 17 Ks, 0 BBs in 8 scoreless IP

The Rangers had gotten a preview of coming attractions in May when Santana struck out a baker's dozen in a win at Texas. But he was even better this time. Sighed Young afterward, "In the past, I've had some good at-bats against him. But once he gets a full head of steam, it's tough to break his rhythm." The only Ranger to reach base against Santana was DH Sammy Sosa, who singled in the fifth inning and doubled in the seventh inning.

It was a good thing Santana was on top of his game. The Twins' offense was not. Michael Cuddyer's second-inning home run was one of just four hits Kevin Millwood allowed in the course of his duties. Third baseman Tommy Watkins got as far as third a couple times but that was about it for the offense. ⏤✖⏤

Landreaux Lives Up to His Own Hype

Ken Landreaux picked an interesting way to make his acquaintance with Minnesota fans. When he was acquired from the Angels the previous winter in a trade for longtime star Rod Carew, Landreaux's opening salvo to local fans was, "I don't think the Angels got enough for me." Although he didn't quite match up with Carew's past exploits, games like this one—when he banged out three extra-base hits and knocked in a career-high six runs in a 10–5 win over Boston at Met Stadium—eased the locals' pain a bit.

Landreaux's big night pushed his batting average up to .313, a good standard for most hitters. Landreaux, however, sounded almost disappointed. "It's about 17 points short of what I can do," he said. "I'm a big dreamer. I used to dream of being in the major leagues and I made it. And now that I'm in the big leagues, I'm dreaming of being a superstar."

He was one this night. It started early when he tagged Boston starter Mike Torrez for a run-scoring double in the bottom of the first inning for the game's first run. In the sixth, he ended Torrez's night with a three-run homer that gave Minnesota a 7–2 lead. He capped his big night with a two-run triple in the eighth inning. By season's end, however, Landreaux may have found himself still a bit wanting. His final batting average was .305.

> ## At a Glance
>
> **WP:** Erickson (1–7)
>
> **HR:** Landreaux (8)
>
> **Key stats:** Landreaux 3-for-5, 3 runs, 6 RBIs

A WIN, AND A NICKNAME LOST

Landreaux's big night helped Minnesota starting pitcher Roger Erickson get his first major league victory in over 11 months. Erickson had been solid as a rookie, posting a 14–13 win-loss mark, but he had struggled so badly in 1979 that he went back to AAA ball for six weeks. Pressed into a starting role because Geoff Zahn had a blister, he went 8 1/3 innings to accomplish two things. The victory was his first in the bigs since September 15 of the previous season. It also meant an end to being called "James Bond" by his teammates. Erickson didn't earn the name because he looked like Sean Connery or Roger Moore. He also didn't drive an Aston Martin, or, as was the case in the Ian Fleming novels, a 1933 Bentley. No, Erickson's nickname was strictly baseball humor. Before getting the win against the Red Sox that night, Erickson's win-loss record was . . . 0–7. ⟿

'Tish The Great' Comes to the Rescue

Twins' manager Bill Rigney had a problem. George Mitterwald, the team's regular catcher, was absent due to a military commitment. Paul Ratliff was a little sore. So, Rigney turned to Thomas Arthur Tischinski, who had started exactly 14 games all season behind the plate, to handle the duties. "I knew that Rig didn't like me a lot and would be looking for a chance to hit for me late in the game if he could," Tischinski said. "But I didn't care. I just wanted to play."

Turned out the man once dubbed "Tish The Great" by teammate Frank Quilici did more than that. His solo home run in the seventh inning provided the difference in a 4–3 win over Washington at Met Stadium that extended the Twins' divisional lead to six games. "Funny thing about that homer," Tischinski recalled 39 years later. "I hit it off Casey Cox, who was a guy I had batted against a lot in the minors. It seemed I was always facing him as I came up the Twins' chain."

Minnesota was trailing 3–1 in the sixth inning when Cesar Tovar tripled home a run and scored himself on Danny Thompson's single. That set the stage for the seventh when Tischinki turned on a pitch and sent it 373 feet to left field. "I was so surprised that I didn't know whether to run fast or slow or if I should run backwards or not," he told reporters after the game. "I usually hit my homers at 5 p.m. [during batting practice]."

Tischinski didn't impress his manager much with the only homer in 82 career games with the Twins. He batted just three more times during the rest of the season.

At a Glance

WP: Williams (8–0)

HR: Tishinski (1)

Key stat: Williams allows 1 hit in final 3 innings in relief

FRIENDS IN THE RIGHT PLACES

Although Tischinski never saw a lot of action for the Twins, he seemed to have a lot of fun. "My road roommate was Jim Kaat. We played a lot of golf together, even on days we weren't supposed to," he recalled. When the Twins came to Oakland, Tischinski frequently got together with A's pitcher Chuck Dobson, who was the best man in his wedding. Dobson had some connections, too. On one trip, he arranged for Tischinski and Kaat to join him and Catfish Hunter for a round at the prestigious Pebble Beach links. It was a day off, so it was permissible to play. As luck would have it, the foursome ran into Rigney, who was playing a round with team exec Howard Fox. Both had paid the going rate to play the course. Later, Rigney told Tischinski it was a beautiful place but very expensive to play. "I just smiled," Tischinski said. "Dobson knew some people and had gotten us on the course for free." —⁓—

The Comeback Kids Strike Again

The week had already included come-from-behind wins over such stalwart pitchers as Bob Welch and Dave Stewart. But there was no denying that things looked a little bleak when Seattle roughed up Twins starter Jack Morris and reliever Steve Bedrosian for a 4–1 lead. Thanks to some late dramatics supplied by Randy Bush and Scott Leius, Minnesota finished off a 6–1 week with a come-from-behind 5–4, 10-inning victory that extended their AL West Division lead to a season-high six games.

It was still 4–1 in the bottom of the ninth when the theatrics began in earnest. With one out, Al Newman walked and Chuck Knoblauch, who earlier had snuffed out a Twins' rally by being thrown out at third to end the seventh inning, beat out an infield roller for a single. That brought up Bush, who had been hitting over .400 since the All-Star break. He had always been considered a solid singles-doubles type of hitter. Now, he redirected a Mike Schooler fastball over the baggie in right for his fifth home run of the season to tie the game at 4-all.

In the tenth, Junior Ortiz opened with a single but was quickly erased off the bases when Shane Mack hit into a double play.

No matter. Scott Leius ended the game when he sent an 0–1 pitch into the seats for his fourth longball of the season.

"That's the great thing about baseball. You screw up one time but all it takes is a little rally to make people forget all about it," Knoblauch said.

> ## At a Glance
>
> **WP:** Aguilera (4–4)
>
> **HR:** Bush (5), Leius (4)
>
> **Key stats:** Bush 2-for-4, 3 RBIs, game-winning HR in 9th

Schooler saw it—and the Twins—differently. "We ran into a buzzsaw this series," he sighed after the game. "If they keep playing like this the rest of the way, I don't think anyone will catch them."

Schooler turned out to be right. Minnesota won the division by eight games. ~~~

> ## Did You Know?
>
> Randy Bush played 12 seasons in Minnesota from 1982–93. A .251 lifetime hitter in 3,045 career at-bats, his biggest contribution to the team was as a pinch-hitter. His 74 hits is easily the most in team history. Chip Hale (1989–96) is a distant second at 51.

The New Math: 1 Is Sometimes More Than 3

There were six weeks to go in the season and the Twins were getting desperate. The first-place White Sox were coming to town with a 10½-game lead over them in the AL West. That was a steep hill for the Twins to climb, but the teams still had 10 games left with each other with six at the Metrodome.

Twins starter Johan Santana did his part, allowing no runs and just four runners to get on base (three hits and a walk). He was helped in part by outfielders Shannon Stewart and Lew Ford, who made terrific catches. For seven innings, his counterpart, Freddy Garcia, was even better, giving up a pair of walks to catcher Joe Mauer and allowing only one other base runner (on an error).

So it was understandable that the crowd of 33,572 was a bit agog (and perhaps a bit awed) by the state of affairs when Jacque Jones strode to the plate to open the eighth inning.

Jones had been performing with a heavy heart. A favorite uncle had passed away the day before and Jones was leaving the team the next day to attend the funeral. "When you get on the field, everything else goes out the door," he told reporters. "None of that other stuff matters when you cross the lines."

Well, one thing inside the lines did matter. That was Garcia's 1–2 pitch, a curve ball that Jones smoked 423 feet over the center-field fence for the Twins' first hit—and, as it turned, the game's lone run of the night—to open the eighth inning.

Joe Nathan entered in the ninth and surrendered a walk but fanned the final two batters to put the lid on an old-fashioned 1–0 pitchers' duel that kept playoff hopes alive (Minnesota trailed wild-card leader Cleveland by three games as well). "It was really a playoff atmosphere tonight," said Minnesota manager Ron Gardenhire after the game. "I'm still sweating."

It marked the second time in team history that Minnesota's only hit of the game had been a game-winning home run. ⁓

At a Glance

WP: Santana (13–6)

S: Nathan (32)

HR: Jones (18)

Key stats: Jones ninth-inning HR; Santana 3 hits, 7 Ks in 8 IP

A Debut Worthy of a Broadway Hit

For someone who always described himself as an everyman sort of guy, Kent Hrbek sure had a flair for the dramatic. There was his grand slam homer that broke open Game 6 of the 1987 World Series. There was his wrestling-like move that eliminated Atlanta's Ron Gant from the bases at a key moment in Game 2 of the 1991 Fall Classic.

Those were memorable moments, to be sure. But the genesis of all that may have started on a Monday night in a place far, far away from Minnesota. In his first major league game, Hrbek offered a preview of coming attractions when he conked a 12th-inning home run at Yankee Stadium to lift the Twins to a 3–2 win. Angelo Giuliani, the legendary local scout who had first spotted Hrbek playing for Bloomington Kennedy High School, put things in his usual wry perspective. "I was the catcher when [Joe] DiMaggio broke in at Yankee Stadium," Giuliani said after watching Hrbek's homer on TV back in the Twin Cities. "He got three hits that day but that doesn't match this for a first time out."

> ## At a Glance
>
> **WP:** O'Connor (3–2)
>
> **HR:** Hrbek (1)
>
> **Key stat:** Hrbek's MLB debut is a GW home run to lead off the top of the 12th inning

The second half of the strike-ravaged 1981 season wasn't going well for the Twins. They had dropped eight of nine games and were on a long road trip. Changes seem inevitable. Still, many folks were surprised when regular first baseman Ron Jackson was dealt to Detroit. Those same folks were further surprised when the call went to Class A Visalia to get the big first baseman who was hitting .379. Among the list of surprised folks was Hrbek himself. "I'm confident I can hit at that level but I didn't expect the call this early," he said after being summoned. His manager Billy Gardner, however, was confident, saying, "I think the kid can make the jump."

When he first arrived at "The House That Ruth Built," Hrbek had an instant impression. "Left center field looked 4,000 feet away," he said. "It's an awesome building."

As a matter of protection as much as anything, Gardner put Hrbek eighth in the batting order. ("I didn't want him going 0-for-4 in his first game," Gardner explained later.) In his second at-bat, Hrbek recorded his first RBI with a single off Yankee starter Tommy John that tied the game at 1-all. New York took the lead in the seventh, but Dave Engle's RBI-single the next inning re-tied the game at 2–2.

Both teams had chances but the game remain deadlocked until Hrbek jumped on George Frazier's 2–2 offering and sent it far into the New York night. Hrbek danced around the bases while Gardner had a different reaction. "When he hit that home run, I reached for the smelling salts," he said later. "Then, I congratulated him."

Jack O'Connor, the Twins' third pitcher of the night, gave up a one-out single but retired the next two batters (the last one, ironically, was another Minnesotan, Dave Winfield) to end an opening worthy of opening night on Broadway.

Hrbek's long, happy night wasn't over. In a pre-cell phone era, he stayed up until 3 a.m. talking to his parents, his girlfriend, and probably half of Bloomington from his hotel room. "It's worth the cost," he said later.

No disagreement there.

A Chance to Get into First Place

By late August, it seemed every game in the American League had some kind of bearing on the wild four-team dance between the Twins, Red Sox, Tigers, and White Sox. On nights like this one, when the Twins were playing a twi-night doubleheader at Cleveland's Municipal Stadium, there was more time spent watching the out-of-town scoreboard than, say, eating hot dogs.

This was Minnesota's third doubleheader in four days and manager Cal Ermer's pitching staff was wearing a bit thin. It didn't help that the first game was an exhausting affair that ended up with four pitchers being used in a 6–5, 10-inning victory.

What Ermer and the Twins really needed in the nightcap was for a starter to go the distance. Even though he was working on just two days' rest after getting shelled in a game at Detroit, Dean Chance took this idea to heart. He didn't have his best stuff, walking five batters and allowing a first-inning run. But he got the outs when he really needed them and retired the last 10 batters in a row to pitch a no-hitter in a 2–1 victory. The win vaulted the Twins a half-game ahead of the Red Sox and White Sox, who split a doubleheader against each other that same day.

It wasn't Chance's first Ohio no-hitter. He tossed 18 of them in high school in Wooster, some 50 miles from Municipal Stadium. As was the case in high school, Chance's parents were in the stands watching. "The fact that the game was so close and we're in the pennant race took some of the pressure off throwing a no-hitter," he said later. "I was thinking only of winning."

As was often the case in this wild race, winning took a lot of work. In the first inning, the Indians loaded the bases on a pair of walks and an error by third baseman Cesar Tovar. Chance then hurt the cause by heaving a wild pitch for the game's first run.

Minnesota tied the game quickly in the second inning when Tony Oliva singled and scored all the

Twins	AB	R	H	RBI
Carew 2b	5	0	1	0
Uhlaender cf	4	0	1	0
Tovar 3b	4	1	1	0
Oliva rf	3	1	2	0
Killebrew 1b	3	0	2	0
Valdespino lf	4	0	0	0
Zimmerman c	3	0	0	0
Hernandez ss	3	0	0	0
Reese ph	1	0	0	0
Versalles ss	0	0	0	0
Chance p	3	0	0	0
Totals	**33**	**2**	**7**	**0**

Indians	AB	R	H	RBI
Maye lf	2	1	0	0
Davalillo cf	3	0	0	0
Hinton rf	3	0	0	0
Horton 1b	4	0	0	0
Alvis 3b	3	0	0	0
Azcue c	3	0	0	0
Fuller 2b	1	0	0	0
Whitfield ph	1	0	0	0
Gonzalez 2b	0	0	0	0
Brown ss	3	0	0	0
Siebert p	1	0	0	0
Wagner ph	1	0	0	0
Culver p	0	0	0	0
Totals	**25**	**1**	**0**	**0**

```
MIN  0 1 0 0 0 1 0 0 0 - 2 7 1
CLE  1 0 0 0 0 0 0 0 0 - 1 0 1
```

Twins	IP	H	R	ER	BB	SO
Chance W(17–9)	9	0	1	1	5	8

Indians	IP	H	R	ER	BB	SO
Siebert L(6–11)	8	7	2	2	2	7
Culver	1	0	0	0	1	1
Totals	**9**	**7**	**2**	**2**	**3**	**8**

E—Minnesota Tovar. Cleveland Maye. DP—Minnesota 2. Cleveland 1. 2B—Minnesota Carew. SH—Cleveland Siebert. HBP—Minnesota Chance. LOB—Minnesota 8. Cleveland 3. Attendance—10,519.

way from first base when Cleveland left fielder Lee Maye misplayed Harmon Killebrew's single. The game remained stuck at 1-all until the sixth, when the threat of speed led to a run. With one out, Tovar singled to left, and moved to third when Tony Oliva singled to right.

Cleveland pitcher Sonny Siebert was well aware that this was the best possible speed combination the Twins could muster. Too aware of that fact, as it turned out. He balked on a move toward Oliva and Tovar was sent home with the deciding run.

Given a lead, Chance shut the Indians off the rest of the night, finishing with eight strikeouts and a very efficient total of 95 pitches. His catcher, Jerry Zimmerman, wasn't surprised. "Dean has no-hit stuff almost every time he goes out these days," he said. Early Wynn, a 300-game winner serving as the team's pitching coach that season, noticed another good trait. "I saw [Bob] Feller, [Bob] Lemon and [Sonny] Siebert pitch no-hitters and they were calm all the way through," Wynn said. "So was Chance tonight."

> An established top pitcher when he was acquired from the Angels, he was a workhorse in 1967 as the Twins chased Boston to the final day of the season, winning 20 games and throwing a no-hitter. He led the league in starts, complete games, and innings pitched that season (and even recorded one save). He was still very good the next season, winning 16 games and recording a 2.53 ERA.

Dean Chance

Ermer was always a bottom-line guy. In two sentences, he summarized Chance and his team's night on Lake Erie. "A no-hitter and we move into first place on the same night," Ermer marveled. "Imagine that." —⁓—

Pitching on two days' rest in Game 2 of a doubleheader against the Tigers, Dean Chance threw a no-hitter to lift the Twins into first place in the American League. Chance grew up in Wooster, Ohio, only 50 miles from Municipal Stadium in Cleveland.

Kralick Dazzles Them

On August 21, Jack Kralick shackled the Washington Senators on no hits until Joe Hicks broke up the spell with a sixth-inning single. Five days later, Kralick's magic lasted longer—and nearly ended with the first perfect game in the American League in 40 years.

A ninth-inning walk was the only blemish on the southpaw's record that day in Minnesota's 1–0 victory over Kansas City at Met Stadium. That's pretty good work for a guy who discovered in the bullpen his curveball wasn't working. Thus, Kralick divided his 97-pitch output between fastballs and sliders.

"I've seen him with better stuff but never better control," said his catcher, Earl Battey.

It would be nice to say the crowd of 23,224 came to the ballpark inspired by Kralick's previous outing or by the Twins' high standing (they trailed the first-place Yankees by just four games.) But it was Camera Day at the Met (when fans were allowed on the field to take pictures of the players) and it played a small part in Kralick's career outing.

The picture taking caused Kralick to be a little rushed in his pregame warm-ups. As a result, he didn't feel good when he left the bullpen to start the game. His mood, however, began to improve when he retired the first 10 batters he faced. Third baseman Ed Charles then stroked a ball to right that looked like it might be a home run. Bob Allison, however, had other ideas, racing back and snagging the ball just before it got over the wire. From that point on, Kralick knew he might be on to something special.

"I knew I had a no-hitter going but I never looked at the scoreboard," he said after the game.

His mound opponent, Bill Fischer, was giving up a lot of base hits but the Twins did nothing with them until the

At a Glance

WP: Kralick (10–8)

Key stats: Kralick no-hitter, 1 BB, 3 Ks

seventh inning. Bernie Allen led off with a single. Zoilo Versalles then dropped an unsurprising bunt, but Charles' throw to second was too late to get Allen.

Kralick dropped another bunt down, and the runners moved up a base. All Lenny Green had to do was get the ball to the outfield. He did that with a deep fly ball to center fielder Bobby Del Greco that easily scored Allen.

All that was left was to see if Kralick could get the first no-hitter in Twins' history. It was almost an afterthought that he was also pursuing the first perfect game in the AL since Chicago's Charlie Robertson tossed one in 1922.

With one out, pinch-hitter George Alusik ended that dream by taking a 3–2 fastball for a walk. There was no question the pitch was high. Kralick could only shake his head and concentrate on keeping the A's off the board. He did better than that—he didn't let them put the ball in fair territory. Pinch-hitter Billy Consolo and Del Greco fouled out to first baseman Vic Power and Kralick's no-hitter was history.

Ironically, it came on a day when team owner Calvin Griffith was missing his first home game ever. Griffith was in Charlotte scouting prospects and got reports on the game via the telephone.

Even Minnesota Governor Elmer Andersen got into the act, sending Kralick a congratulatory message that included a mini pep talk as well. "Congrats on a great performance," the note read. "Now let's catch those Yankees and have us a World Series." —ᴡᴡ—

Did You Know?

Although they have been victimized twice for perfect games, the Twins have never been no-hit in nearly 4,000 games at home. The closest a visiting pitcher came was April 23, 1980, at Met Stadium when Ken Landreaux doubled with one out in the ninth inning off California's Bruce Kison. Kison retired the next two batters for the 17–0 win. This continued a trend from the team's past. Although the Senators fell victim to four no-hitters before moving to Minnesota, all were on the road. Four of the five no-hitters in Minnesota history (including Dean Chance's five-inning perfect game) were played at home.

Worth the Wait

Twins	AB	R	H	RBI
Powell rf	8	0	1	1
Castino 3b-ss	7	0	2	0
Smalley ss	5	0	0	0
R. Jackson 1b	1	0	0	0
Adams dh	4	1	1	0
Rivera ph-dh	2	0	0	0
Wynegar c	5	1	1	0
Cubbage 1b-3b	7	1	1	0
Landreaux cf	5	2	2	0
Sofield lf	3	1	2	0
Morales ph	1	1	1	3
Edwards lf	2	0	1	1
Wilfong 2b	1	0	0	1
Mackanin ph-2b	4	0	1	1
Totals	55	7	13	7

Blue Jays	AB	R	H	RBI
Griffin ss	7	1	3	0
Bailor lf	3	1	1	0
Braun ph	0	0	0	0
Cannon pr-lf-rf	3	0	0	0
Garcia 2b	4	1	2	1
Velez 1b	5	2	2	2
Stieb lf	1	0	0	0
Ault dh	2	0	1	0
Mayberry ph	1	0	1	1
Iorg pr-dh-lf-1b	2	0	2	0
Howell 3b	5	0	0	0
Moseby rf	6	0	0	0
Ainge cf	5	0	1	0
Whitt ph	1	0	0	0
Davis c	6	0	0	0
Totals	51	5	13	4

MIN 0 0 0 0 1 0 1 3 0 0 0 0 0 0 2 - 7 13 1
TOR 0 0 4 0 0 0 0 1 0 0 0 0 0 0 0 - 5 13 2

Twins	IP	H	R	ER	BB	SO
D. Jackson	7	8	4	4	2	5
Corbett	4	3	1	1	2	3
Verhoeven W(2-3)	3	1	0	0	2	1
Williams S(1)	1	1	0	0	1	0
Totals	15	13	5	5	7	9

Blue Jays	IP	H	R	ER	BB	SO
McLaughlin	6	6	2	2	1	1
Willis	0.1	1	0	0	0	1
Barlow	1.1	1	2	2	1	0
Garvin	2.2	3	1	1	0	0
Schrom	3.2	1	0	0	2	1
Jefferson L(4-13)	1	1	2	1	1	0
Totals	15	13	7	6	5	3

E—Minensota Landreaux. Toronto Griffin, Velez. DP—Minnesota 3. Toronto 2. 2B—Minnesota Sofield 2. Toronto Iorg. 3B—Minnesota Castino. HR—Minnesota Morales (7). Toronto Velez (20). SH—Minnesota Edwards, Landreaux, Mackanin. Toronto Garcia, Iorg. SF—Minnesota Wilfong. LOB—Minnesota 12. Toronto 10. SB—Toronto Ainge, Garcia. Attendance—14,035.

Quick question: What is the longest winning game in Twins' history?

Quick answer: It depends on your point of view.

Some would say it was the 5–4, 22-inning marathon decision over the Indians in 1993. That game went 6 hours, 17 minutes (a 17-inning game in 1995 in Cleveland actually went six hours, 36 minutes. But the Twins lost that one, 10–9.)

But you could make a case as well for this 7–5, 15-inning win in 1980 at Toronto's Exhibition Stadium. It ended roughly 24 hours after it started and featured a rare save by a Twins starting pitcher while the opposing team's top mound winner was playing left field.

It started with an unusual Thursday afternoon series opener. The game was being played in the daytime because the Canadian National Exhibition (the country's version of a state fair) was going on next door to the ballpark. As part of the CNE, there was a daily nighttime concert on a stage erected next to the stadium. Hence, it was declared no inning could start after 5 p.m.

Early on, time didn't appear to be an issue. Otto Velez hit a two-run homer as part of a four-run third inning that gave the Blue Jays a 4–0 lead. But Minnesota rallied to take a 5–4 lead when pinch-hitter José Morales redirected a Jerry Garvin forkball for a three-run homer in the eighth inning. Doug Corbett was summoned to save the game for starter Darrell Jackson. However, John Mayberry's RBI single tied the game at 5-all in the bottom of the eighth.

Corbett stayed on until the 12th inning when he gave way to John Verhoeven, who got into instant trouble. In the inning, Damaso Garcia was batting with a 2–2 count and Alfredo Griffin was on second base with two outs. As Verhoeven delivered a pitch, Griffin suddenly broke for third base. Catcher Butch Wynegar reacted late and threw wildly past third baseman Mike Cubbage. Griffin trotted home and the grounds crew quickly headed for the stage.

But Cubbage had noticed something that had escaped Wynegar and the Blue Jays' attention. Home plate umpire Ted Hendry had signaled the pitch was a strike. Thus, the inning was over and the grounds crew retreated quickly to their former space.

The teams played two more scoreless innings before running into the odd curfew. The show must go on.

Things had changed slightly when the teams reconvened the next afternoon. Toronto's Velez and Minnesota outfielder Bombo Rivera had been together in a car that was in an accident late Thursday night. Rivera had replaced DH Glenn Adams during the game but was in no condition to play. Velez was injured enough that his season was over. The Jays were out of position players so pitcher Dave Stieb, scheduled to start the originally scheduled game, trotted out to left field when play resumed on Friday afternoon.

As often happens in these cases, the game ended quickly and unexpectedly. Wynegar led off the 15th with a walk and moved to second when Cubbage was safe on an error by Griffin. One out later, outfielder Dave Edwards, who hadn't entered the game until the eighth inning and had just one RBI in the previous month, singled to score Wynegar. Later, second baseman Pete Mackanin squeezed home another run to make it 7–5.

In the bottom of the inning, Al Williams, normally a starter, gave up a hit and a walk but no runs to end one of the weirdest games in team history. Minnesota then won the regularly scheduled game as well, 5–2, behind Geoff Zahn's complete-game nine-hitter. The losing pitcher? Dave Stieb. ⎯⚬⎯

Home Run Derby

The 1963 Minnesota Twins were the most power-packed lineup in team history. Their 225 home runs were 40 more than the year before, and they still stand as the highwater mark for four-baggers. So it only makes sense the team record for most home runs in a game came in the same season. It is even more logical when you consider the venue and opponent.

It was a true clash of opposites when the Twins entered D.C. Stadium for a makeup twi-night doubleheader. Minnesota led the league in runs scored while the Senators had allowed the most tallies. Neither team changed their positions after eight home runs that resulted in a 14–2 victory in the opening game.

Minnesota wasted no time taking command. Vic Power and Bob Allison each went deep in the first inning for a quick 3–0 lead against Sens starter Don Rudolph. Pete Burnside was in the game when Harmon Killebrew hit his 30th of the season in the fifth. The game was well out of hand by the sixth when Power and Killebrew found pitches from Ron Moeller they liked and distributed them among the 2,161 fans on hand.

Jimmie Hall hit home run No. 6, a solo shot off Moeller, in the eighth inning. In the ninth, Ed Roebuck entered and, in a span of four pitches, watched Bernie Allen and Rich Rollins take the tour. It marked just the second time in AL history a team had hit eight long-balls in a game. It also set a Twins team record that still stands for most total bases in a game (47).

At a Glance

WP: Stange (8–4)

HR: Power 2 (8), Allison (29), Killebrew 2 (31), Hall (26), Allen (6), Rollins (16)

Key stats: Twins hit 8 HRs; Power 4-for-6, 2 HRs, 4 RBIs; Killebrew 3-for-4, 2 HRs, 3 RBIs

The only happy pitcher was Minnesota starter Lee Stange, who scattered eight hits to get the win. It was a lot more relaxing than Stange's previous start at Baltimore. In that game, he dodged bullets for a 1–0 win. (The only tally: a Hall home run, of course.) "The guys told me they did this game out of guilt for that 1–0 game," Stange joked afterward.

The barrage didn't seem to tire the lads much. In the second game, there were four more home runs and a 10–1 win. ―w―

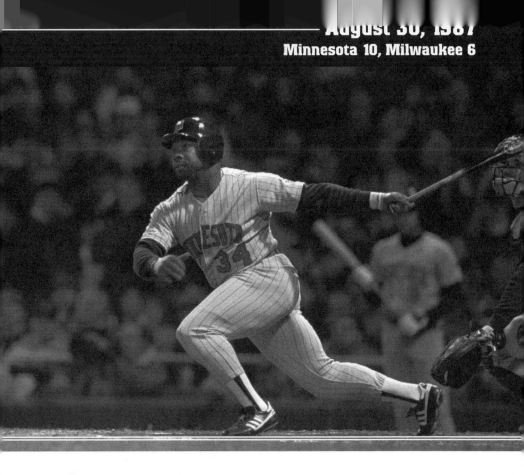

Puckett Stands 10 Feet Tall

Tom Kelly, a master of the understatement, summarized Kirby Puckett's afternoon work at County Stadium this way: "There is not much more you can do in a game. He makes a great catch and he makes things happen when he is swinging good."

This is what Kelly meant by swinging good:

- Six hits in six at-bats (two singles, two doubles, two home runs)
- Four runs scored
- Four RBIs

Kirby Puckett went 6-for-6 with two singles, two doubles, and two home runs in a 10–6 victory over Milwaukee on August 30, 1987.

- One disjointed scorecard
- One discouraged Milwaukee pitching staff

Minnesota's 10–6 victory moved the team back into first place a game ahead of the A's. Combined with a 12–3 win the night before (when Puckett went 4-for-5 with a pair of home runs), it gave the team its first two-game winning streak in two weeks. In the process of going 10-for-11, Puckett elevated his batting average 13 points to .328.

"Tony Oliva [hitting coach] told me I have been losing some of my aggressiveness at the plate," Puckett told reporters after the Sunday outburst. "That's not me. I'm usually up there hacking."

Puckett's big games and the team's two wins came out of the blue. Minnesota trudged to Milwaukee on a skid, having lost seven of its last eight games. In the series opener, the Twins managed just two hits in a 1–0 loss that knocked them out of first place. The bats came back for 16 hits the next night to end the skid.

But that was the hors d'oeuvre for Sunday's main dish. The opening entree was Puckett's RBI single in the first inning off Brewer starter Juan Nieves. In the third inning, Puckett homered to left to make it 2–0.

On many occasions, this was often enough for Minnesota starter Frank Viola. On this day, however, catcher Bill Schroeder clubbed a three-run homer in the fourth inning to give the Brewers a 3–2 lead and end Viola's day a bit early.

Not to worry. Puckett's single to lead off the next inning sparked a complete turn through the batting order that produced three runs and a 5–3 Minnesota lead. This meant the center fielder would lead off the next inning. He did so with a ringing double.

The Brewers could swing the bat themselves. Now they turned on Juan Berenguer, driving him from the game. His replacement, Keith Atherton, struggled as well. By inning's end, Milwaukee was ahead 6–5.

Greg Gagne opened the eighth with a single and scampered to third on Puckett's second double (and fifth hit) of the afternoon. This led to Gary Gaetti getting an intentional walk. One out later, Kent Hrbek's sacrifice fly tied the game and moved

Twins	AB	R	H	RBI
Newman dh-ss	5	1	2	1
Gagne ss-rf	6	2	2	0
Puckett cf	6	4	6	4
Gaetti 3b	5	2	2	0
Brunansky lf	3	0	0	0
Hrbek 1b	3	0	0	1
Davidson rf	3	1	1	1
Bush ph-rf	1	0	0	0
Larkin ph	1	0	1	2
Lombardozzi 2b	4	0	1	0
Laudner c	3	0	0	0
Totals	40	10	15	9

Brewers	AB	R	H	RBI
Molitor dh	4	1	2	0
Yount cf	3	0	0	1
Braggs rf	4	0	3	1
Manning rf	1	0	0	0
Deer lf	4	0	0	0
Brock 1b	5	1	2	0
Sveum ss	4	1	1	0
Schroeder c	3	1	1	3
Riles 3b	4	1	2	0
Castillo 2b	2	1	0	0
Totals	34	6	11	5

MIN	1	0	1	0	3	0	0	3	2	-	10 15 1
MIL	0	0	0	3	0	3	0	0	0	-	6 11 1

Twins	IP	H	R	ER	BB	SO
Viola	3.1	7	3	3	2	4
Berenguer	2.1	3	3	2	1	2
Atherton W(5–4)	1.1	1	0	0	2	0
Reardon S(25)	2	0	0	0	1	3
Totals	9	11	6	5	6	9

Brewers	IP	H	R	ER	BB	SO
Nieves	4.2	10	5	5	3	5
Crim L(5–6)	2.1	3	3	3	4	1
Plesac	2	2	2	0	0	2
Totals	9	15	10	8	7	8

E—Minnesota Gagne. Milwaukee Riles. DP—Minnesota 1. Milwaukee 1. 2B—Minnesota Lombardozzi, Gaetti, Puckett 2. Milwaukee Sveum. HR—Minnesota Puckett 2 (21). Milwaukee Schroeder. SH—Milwaukee Castillo. SF—Minnesota Hrbek. Milwaukee Yount. HBP—Minnesota Lombardozzi. LOB—Minnesota 12. Milwaukee 9. SB—Minnesota Gaetti, Davidson. Milwaukee Braggs, Molitor. Attendance—22,417.

all runners up a base. Gene Larkin followed with a pinch-hit two-run single to break the tie one last time.

It looked like Puckett's day was destined to end at 5-for-5 when the first two Twins went out in the ninth inning. Gagne fanned for a potential third out but Schroeder missed the ball. Gagne scrambled safely to first base. Given an opening, Puckett poured through with a two-run homer. After going 17 games without a four-bagger, Puckett now had four in two games. "There were times when I felt I was hitting the ball well and I felt it was coming back to me," said Puckett, whose batting average had fallen from .354 on July 4 to .315 after the 1–0 loss. "But that feeling would only last for a few days. It would come and go. Maybe it will stick around for a while this time."

In a way, it did just that. Puckett used his big two-day binge in Milwaukee to jumpstart an eight-game hitting streak. He kept on hitting the rest of the season, finishing with a .332 batting average and leading the league in hits with 207.

There may have been better statistical performances (Pittsburgh's Rennie Stennett once had seven hits in a 22–0 win at Chicago), but Puckett's performance ranks as one of the top all-time single-game efforts in MLB history. 〜

Kirby Puckett

He had four hits in his first game with the Twins and hit perhaps the most famous home run in team history. Although small in stature, everything Kirby Puckett did on the field loomed large. His career was cut short by an eye ailment but it didn't stop him from being a first-ballot choice for baseball's Hall of Fame in his first year of eligibility. In theory, he went in because of his .318 lifetime batting average and his excellent defense. In reality, he went in because he was the game's most dynamic player for his entire 12-year career.

Baker Toys with History

It had already been an unusual day at the Metrodome. In the afternoon, the Twins had played the makeup of a game against Kansas City that had been postponed after the collapse of the I-35W Bridge. Unfortunately, the locals played like they didn't know what time the game was supposed to start, committing three errors in an ugly 9–4 loss.

But all of that was forgotten by 9 p.m. or so that night. That's because righthander Scott Baker was completely stifling the visitors. Baker was in such complete control of the game that the Royals hadn't even mustered a loud out. After a flurry of early strikeouts (nine total), Baker was retiring Kansas City hitters handily on slow rollers and pop-ups.

When the ninth inning began, Baker had a 5–0 lead and was three outs away from that baseball rarity, the perfect game.

The top of the Metrodome, however, seemed to sag when John Buck walked to open the ninth inning, reviving slightly when Esteban German forced him at second for the first out of the inning.

At a Glance

WP: Baker (8–6)

Key stats: Baker 1-hitter, 1 BB, 9 Ks

Mike Sweeney stepped in as a replacement for shortstop Tony Pena. Sweeney was considered a better hitter than his .245 average would indicate. Due to an injury, this was his first at-bat in more than two months. Baker tried to go inside with a fastball and Sweeney got just enough of the bat on it to loop a single to short center. In a split second—and a matter of about 150 feet—the no-hitter was gone. "It was the right pitch," Baker said afterward. "It just wasn't meant to be."

There was still the matter of finishing what he had started. Baker did so, retiring the final two hitters of the game, ending the long day on a happy note. "I wasn't nervous at all [before or after Buck's walk]," Baker told reporters later. "What was there to be nervous about? I had pitched a great game already . . . even if it didn't work out."

"We went from playing our worst game of the year to almost perfect," said manager Ron Gardenhire. "It was simply a great performance by Baker." —⁓—

Bluegill Survives a Snag to Get a Win

Jim "Bluegill" Hughes was one of the pleasant stories of the 1975 season. He had just two major league appearances under his belt when he made the Opening Day roster as a starter. He went on to lead the staff with 16 victories. None were stranger or perhaps harder to achieve than his effort that ended in a 5–3 victory over the Rangers at Arlington Stadium.

Hughes allowed a commendable three hits in 7 2/3 innings. But he also walked eight and survived a leaky defense that produced five errors, including three by first baseman Johnny Briggs. Fortunately for the Twins, they also hit three home runs, including back-to-back jobs by Rod Carew and Briggs in the fourth inning that produced a lead they never lost.

There were innings like the sixth. The Twins were clinging to a 4–3 lead when the Rangers put runners on first and second. Roy Howell beat out an infield roller for a hit, but second baseman Jerry Terrell caught Jim Spencer going too far around third and tagged him out in a rundown.

At a Glance

WP: Hughes (13–12)

S: Burgmeier (7)

HR: Ford (15), Carew (13), Briggs (10)

Key stats: Hughes 7 Ks, 8 BBs in 7 2/3 IP

In the ninth, Tom Grieve was safe on an error to lead off the inning but was promptly wiped out in a double play. Lenny Randle then singled. Briggs then committed his third error of the night when he dropped Joe Lovitto's foul fly. Reliever Tom Burgmeier sighed and then retired Lovitto on a fly ball to center to end the exhausting game.

"They tried like hell to give it to us," said Texas manager Frank Lucchesi afterward. But some fish are just harder to hook. —⁓—

Did You Know?

Jim Hughes finished the 1975 season with a solid 16–14 record. He won nine games the next season but lasted just two games in 1977.

Hisle Leads the Way

At the time, the deal was a head scratcher. Late in 1972, the Twins sent Wayne Granger, who had saved 19 games and had four victories out of the bullpen, to the Cardinals for two players who hadn't done much recently. Pitcher John Cumberland won nine games one season for the Giants and outfielder Larry Hisle didn't even play in the majors in 1972.

Cumberland ended up a washout and was released at the end of spring training. Hisle, who had hit 20 homers in his first full season in the majors, turned out to be a solid outfielder. In five seasons here, he was a rarity—a fellow with power and speed. Hisle's star never shone brighter than it did on this night at Royals Stadium when he recorded the only five-hit game of his career, including one in a seven-run ninth inning rally that produced an 11–5 victory.

> ## At a Glance
>
> **WP:** Campbell (2–1)
>
> **HR:** Darwin (16)
>
> **Key stats:** Hisle 5-for-5, 2 RBIs; Oliva 3-for-6, RBI; Twins 7 runs, 6 hits in ninth

For eight innings, it was a rollicking game. In the eighth, Hisle doubled for his fourth hit of the night and raced home on Tony Oliva's single to tie the game at 4-all. The deadlock lasted just two batters into the bottom of the inning. At that point, Paul Schaal homered off Bill Campbell.

Joe Lis' led off the Twins' ninth with a walk and Danny Monzon ran for him. Gene Garber, the Royals' closer, must have been unnerved by this because he promptly threw a wild pitch. Rich Reese followed with a single to center that scored Monzon to tie the game at 5-all. One out later, Eric Soderholm doubled to score Reese and Minnesota was ahead, 6–5.

After Jerry Terrell grounded out, Hisle had one last crack at things. Although he was having a good season, his manager, Frank Quilici, had been telling him for weeks he could raise his average even higher if he would quit trying to pull everything. This time, Hisle listened to the advice and slapped a ball into the right-center alley, scoring Soderholm with an insurance run. Rod Carew followed with a single to score Hisle. Bobby Darwin then capped the outburst with a three-run homer and the Royals' pennant hopes went on hold for a night.—⁓—

Larry Hisle

A bright offensive light in an often dim era, Hisle hit 109 doubles and 87 home runs during his tenure here and was an underrated (and often unnoticed) base runner, swiping 92 bases in that same period. In his final season here, Hisle led the AL in RBIs with 119. He saw the majority of his action in left field but also handled center when required. In 1976, he led all AL outfielders in assists with 16.

Preview of Upcoming Attractions

As the 1990 season was headed for the home stretch, it was clear the Twins were looking ahead. At the end of May, Minnesota was nine games over .500 and in the thick of the AL West race. By the end of June, the club was five games under .500, 13 games out of first place and there was already talk of doing better in 1991. Even when things ended up well—as was the case in a 7–1 win over the Brewers at County Stadium for the team's first four-game winning streak since May—there was a dark cloud hanging around.

In this case, the cloud hovered over pitcher David West. Considered one of the key acquisitions from the Mets in the Frank Viola trade, West finally seemed to be coming out of the malaise that had affected him most of the summer. Given a 2–0 lead before he even hit the field, West hadn't allowed a hit into the third inning when he delivered a pitch to Bill Spiers and—SNAP!—his hamstring gave out on him. Just like that, West's season was over.

Fortunately for the Twins, Tim Drummond was there to pick him up. The right-hander had been used mainly in mop-up duty and had a 4.54 ERA. But he stepped in like an old pro and silenced the Brewers on just four hits in 5 2/3 innings. His teammates were doing some lusty swatting, banging out a season-high 19 hits to make things go easier. Pedro Munoz and Gary Gaetti had four hits each. Kent Hrbek had three hits and two RBIs, while Kirby Puckett and Nelson Liriano had two hits each. All except Liriano (who ended up in Kansas City) would become key members the next season when the Twins rose from last to first to win their second World Series championship.

At a Glance

WP: Drummond (3–4)

HR: Sorrento (4)

Key stats: Munoz 4-for-6; Hrbek 3-for-6; Gaetti 4-for-5, 2 RBIs

Manager Tom Kelly took note of the unusual outburst. "We had a few balls fall for us and had some good at-bats," he said. "The bottom line is, though, tonight we pitched good and the hitters responded to that."

West would recover from his hamstring pull and be part of the 1991 ride as well, although his World Series contribution was subdued. (He appeared in two games, faced six batters and didn't retire any of them.)

Drummond didn't have such a happy ending. He was released by the team after the season and never pitched again. But he'll always have County Stadium to remember. —⁓—

(Co-) Rookie of the Year

The comparisons were uncanny. Although John Castino swore it wasn't by design, his play and mannerisms at third base reminded folks of another hot corner guy who had recently retired. Unlike that fellow (who batted just .091 in his first look at the major leagues), Castino was hitting up a storm. That player—Brooks Robinson—went on to become a solid hitter and fielder extraordinaire in a 23-year career that earned him a spot in the baseball Hall of Fame.

Castino didn't make it that far, but games like his 4-for-4 night in an 8–3 win over the Kansas City Royals at Met Stadium helped him earn a share of the AL Rookie of the Year honors.

"Gene [Mauch, Twins' manager] said he'd be happy if I hit .230," Castino said after getting the first four-hit game of his life. "But I never doubted my ability to get hits. I'm very happy to be having the season I'm having."

On this night, Castino and company roughed up Royals starter Paul Splittorff for five runs in just 1 2/3 innings of work. Minnesota scored a run in the first when Bobby Randall walked and was sacrificed to second by Castino. One out later, Ron Jackson tripled to right for the early lead. In the second inning, Minnesota had a runner on first and two outs when Butch Wynegar, Randall, and Castino had consecutive singles, producing two more runs. José Morales' only triple of the season plated another pair and it was 5–0.

That finished Splittorff but Castino was just getting warm. He tripled in the fourth but was left stranded. He followed this up with two more singles, the latter of which drove in another run. By the time the night was complete, Castino had scored twice, knocked in two runs and had caused his manager to alter his expectations considerably. "He's *my* Rookie of the Year. I know that," Mauch said.

> ## At a Glance
>
> **WP:** Goltz (13–10)
>
> **Key stats:** Goltz 10-hitter, 5 Ks; Castino 4-for-4, 2 RBIs

At the end of the season, the Baseball Writers Association Of America agreed—sort of. For the only time in the history of the award, there was a tie for the honor. Castino, who finished with a .285 batting average, shared the award with Toronto shortstop Alfredo Griffin.

A SHORT BUT FUN RUN

In theory, there was no sophomore slump for Castino. He posted a .302 batting average the following season, hitting a career-high 13 home runs. But he began to have back problems near the end of the 1980 season, moving over to shortstop for a few games. In 1981, he led the AL in triples with nine. When the team moved indoors to the Metrodome for the 1982 season, Castino was shifted to second base. His average fell considerably but he rebounded nicely at the plate in 1983. However, the back issues simply weren't going away. By early May 1984, Castino was told he would need a fused disc to continue playing. He went 3-for-4 in a game at California and then gave up the ghost.

In 666 career games for Minnesota, Castino recorded 646 hits, ending his major league career with a solid .278 mark. —〜—

Did You Know?

Although Met Stadium was never considered a home run haven along the lines of Tiger Stadium, Fenway Park or Yankee Stadium, it was home to some serious power in the early 1960s. The Twins led the league in home runs in 1963 with 225 and followed that up with a league-best 221 the next season. In the latter season, the Twins had an astonishing six players hit 20 or more longballs. Killebrew led the league with 49 homers (10 more than second-place Boog Powell and a tie for his career best). Bob Allison and Oliva were next on the list with 32 each. Hall hit 25, two more than Don Mincher (who did it in just 287 official at-bats). Zoilo Versalles also had a career high 20 four-baggers. In doing this, the Twins became members of a select group. The only other team to have six players hit 20 or more home runs in a season was the 1961 New York Yankees.

Streakbusters

Although they were well on their way to a Western Division title (with a 13-game lead over second place Chicago), the Twins felt they had some unfinished business to take care of as the A's came to town to open a three-game series. It was bad enough the A's came riding in with the third-longest winning streak in modern baseball history—20 straight wins. But three of those triumphs had come at the Twins' expense the previous weekend in Oakland. The last of those three was a bitter pill to accept. Minnesota had hit three ninth-inning home runs to take a 5–4 lead only to go down in defeat when Miguel Tejada tagged a three-run homer off Eddie Guardado in the bottom of the inning.

It was a matchup that required a team to be at their best from the start. Brad Radke was the perfect man for the job. The veteran righty made his 100th career win a truly memorable one, retiring 19 of the last 21 batters he faced to finish with a six-hit, one-walk shutout. Corey Koskie went 3-for-3 with a pair of RBIs and the Metrodome turf performed some accustomed magic.

Suddenly, the A's had a one-game losing streak by a lopsided 6–0 count.

But it wasn't as easy as it sounds.

In the third inning, Minnesota led 1–0 when the A's placed runners on first and third with one out. Eric Chavez, who already had 31 home runs to his credit, tagged a Radke high and deep toward left field. At the last second, it wavered just foul. "When that happened, I thought, 'Wow, this is going to be our night,'" Radke said.

Sure enough, Chavez struck out. Jermaine Dye then grounded out to end the inning and the A's never got a runner past second for the rest of the night.

The Metrodome gods then got into the action. In the bottom of the inning, second baseman Luis Rivas drove a ball to right-center that picked up speed on the Astroturf and skipped past center fielder Terrence Long for a triple. One out later, Rivas scored on an infield out and now it was 2–0.

Koskie hit a solo homer in the sixth but it was still only 3–0 when another Metrodome bounce finished matters for the night. A. J. Pierzynski was on second when Jacque Jones hit a high chopper toward Tejada at short. There

Brad Radke

The epitome of the term "professional pitcher," Radke won 11 games in his first season in the bigs. Two years later, he won 20 games on a team that went just 68–94 overall. In 2002, he authored a pair of wins in the American League Division Series victory over Oakland. By the time he retired four years later, Radke was firmly entrenched in several top 10 all-time categories, including second in starts (377).

was no way he could throw Jones out. Then Tejada spotted Pierzynski running full blast for the plate. His throw came too late. Now it was 4–0. Micah Bowie replaced starter Cory Lidle on the mound and fared no better. Cristian Guzman promptly doubled to left to make it 5–0.

Game over.

"That's why we like playing in the dome because we're built for this kind of stuff," Pierzynski said.

Radke took over from there, finishing with his first shutout of the season. It was a big relief for the Twins' horse, who had missed two months of the season with a groin injury.

At a Glance

WP: Radke (7–4)

HR: Koskie (11)

Key stats: Radke 6-hit shutout with 5 Ks; Koskie 3-for-3, 2 RBIs

Twins manager Ron Gardenhire admired Radke's performance and Oakland's accomplishment. "That's an amazing thing they've done," he said. "But we had business to do. And that's taking care of things in our ballpark."

As it developed, history repeated itself a month later. The Twins faced the A's in the first round of the 2002 AL playoffs, winning the final game 5–4 in Oakland. The winning pitcher? Brad Radke. —⁓—

Did You Know?

The Twins are the only team in major league history to turn two triple plays in one game. It happened on July 17, 1990, at Boston. On both occasions, third baseman Gary Gaetti, second baseman Al Newman and first baseman Kent Hrbek hooked up to turn the trick. Unfortunately, it wasn't enough as Minnesota lost, 1–0.

A Debut to Remember

Question: Which Twins' player doubled and homered in his first two at-bats in the major leagues?

Hint: It wasn't Rod Carew, who singled and grounded out in his 1967 debut. It wasn't Tony Oliva, who fanned as a pinch-hitter in a 1962 game in Detroit. It wasn't Kirby Puckett, who grounded out and then singled in his 1984 opening in Anaheim.

Hint No. 2: He wasn't in the starting lineup in the Twins' 8–3 win over Milwaukee.

Hint No. 3: He ended up the winning pitcher in the game, less than 24 hours after arriving in town.

Answer: John Harold Haydel.

Even diehard Twins' fans can be excused for missing this one.

Hal Haydel's tale is one of the most unusual in team history. Originally signed by the Braves as a teenager in 1962, he had made 253 appearances in five different farm systems before finally getting his call to the major leagues.

He arrived in the Twin Cities the night before the Twins were scheduled to face the Brewers in a Labor Day doubleheader at Met Stadium. Haydel spent the first game watching Brant Alyea supply all the offense with a grand slam and a three-run homer in a 7–6 victory.

Luis Tiant started the nightcap but left after one inning with a pulled arm muscle. Minnesota manager Bill Rigney knew very little about Haydel but wanted to get him into a game. So, the call went out and Haydel was now officially a big leaguer. "I was really nervous. But after I threw the first pitch, I felt better," Haydel said later. "When I got an out [Jerry McNertney flied to center], I wasn't nearly as nervous."

> ### At a Glance
>
> **WP:** Haydel (1–0)
>
> **S:** Perranoski (29)
>
> **HR:** Haydel (1)
>
> **Key stats:** Haydel gets win and home run in MLB debut

In the bottom of the second, Haydel trudged to the plate for the first time. Although he had been a .091 hitter at Evansville, Haydel remembered he had homered in his minor league plate debut in 1962. "Pitchers aren't supposed to be good hitters so I wasn't too worried how I looked," he said. "I go up and get my rips. I never walk."

True. Haydel doubled to left off Milwaukee starter Al Downing, dancing home on Cesar Tovar's single to give Minnesota a 2–1 lead.

Back on the mound, Haydel allowed a solo homer to Tommy Harper in the top of the third but his teammates got that run back in the bottom of the inning. In the fourth, the right-hander retired the Brewers in order. In the bottom of the inning, he stunned Downing and (likely) the 19,964 fans on hand with a home run to left to push the lead to 4–2.

The Brewers got a run back in the sixth and finally retired Haydel at the plate on strikes to end the bottom of the frame. At that point, Rigney decided he had seen enough, sending in ace reliever Ron Perranoski to protect the one-run lead. Helped by an error and a wild pitch, Minnesota scored four in the bottom of the inning, sailing to victory from there.

Haydel had allowed two runs on four hits (but no walks) in five innings of relief, ending up with the win. All in all, it was a very good effort for a first game in the major leagues. Afterward, Haydel revealed his secret for mound success. "On the way in from the bullpen, I told myself that all I had to was keep the ball down," he said.

Simple game, isn't it?

TOUGH ACT TO FOLLOW

It would have been a hard thing to top under any circumstances. But Haydel never matched his stunning first effort as a major leaguer. He did gain one more win before the end of the 1970 season. He went back to the minors at the start of 1971 but was called back in late June, recording a 4–2 record with a 4.28 ERA in 31 relief outings. Despite that promising start at the plate, Haydel only batted three more times in the bigs, getting one hit. Thus, he retired with a lifetime batting average of .500 (3-for-6). But that's a quiz for another day. ⸺

Go-Go Twins

The season was growing late. Trailing first-place Oakland by 4½ games with only 23 games to play, Minnesota could afford few slipups the rest of the way. Taking advantage of playing at the Metrodome, and taking care of last-place Seattle, was almost considered mandatory.

Manager Tom Kelly generally didn't take time to explain his reasons for various lineups. Thus, when the starting lineup listed Kirby Puckett as the designated hitter (a role he had not filled in two years), little-used Darren Reed in left field, and Terry Jorgensen at first base, and flipped around shortstop Greg Gagne and third baseman Scott Leius to bat second and ninth (instead of the other way around), nobody said a word.

At a Glance

WP: Tapani (15–10)

S: Guthrie (4)

Key stats: Puckett 2-for-3, 2 RBIs

Instead, the Twins went out and set a team record for stolen bases with half a dozen in a 6–2 win. The thievery wasn't by design. "When you have a chance to run, you do it," Kelly said. "When your pitcher sets a good tempo, it allows you to do a few things."

That pitcher would be Kevin Tapani, who retired the first six batters in a row. The Twins responded with a quick 3–0 lead. In the fourth, the Mariners came to life for a pair of runs but center fielder Shane Mack's strong throw nailed Jay Buhner at the plate to preserve the lead.

That's when the greyhounds went to work. Jorgensen singled, stole the first base of his career in the bottom of the inning, and rode home on Leius' RBI single. The next inning, Mack was on third and Puckett was on first when the latter broke for second. The double steal worked to perfection, and Minnesota now led 5–2. In the seventh, Puckett singled another run home (and stole another base). "I didn't have to worry about running to my position," Puckett smiled later. "So I relaxed a little and let loose."

Tapani rolled with the flow from there, going 8 2/3 innings to get his 15th win of the season and revenging himself on Mariners rookie Dave Fleming, who had bested him in a 1–0 duel a couple of months before. The Twins just hadn't unleashed their secret weapons yet. —⁓—

Long Night's Journey Ends Successfully

Had it been no more than the win that put the Twins at the .500 mark for the first time since early May, Minnesota's exhausting 8–7, 15-inning victory over the White Sox at Met Stadium might be celebrated as one of the great triumphs in the team's history. Manager Frank Quilici may have been overstating it slightly when he said "This is beating the National League in Game 7 of the World Series" but any win that sees a team rally from behind three times in extra innings rates as one to remember and savor.

> ## At a Glance
>
> **WP:** Johnson (1–0)
>
> **HR:** Darwin (24), Thompson (4), Kusick (8)
>
> **Key stats:** Brye 3-for-8; Hisle RBI single in 15th

For most of the evening, it appeared that Bobby Darwin's two-run homer and Danny Thompson's solo shot off Sox starter Wilbur Wood that built a 4–1 lead would be sufficient to move the Twins to 71–71. Then, Brian Downing stunned Minnesota closer Bill Campbell for a three-run homer in the top of the ninth to tie it up, and the game started to take on a new flavor.

Downing became a real villain to the local fans when he singled to lead off 11th inning and scored on Bucky Dent's two-out single. The visitors' joy was short-lived, however, because Craig Kusick hit the first pitch in the bottom of the inning into the left-field seats. Dent did it again two innings later, hitting another two-out RBI single for a 6–5 lead.

Eric Soderholm and Kusick walked to open the bottom of the inning. Thompson dropped down an unsurprising bunt but Sox pitcher Terry Forster's throw to get Soderholm was too late and the bases were loaded. Glenn Borgmann singled sharply to left to score Soderholm. But it turned out Borgmann hit it too hard because Jerry Hairston's throw nailed Jerry Terrell (who was running for Kusick) at home.

It was the time of night when teams begin to run out of options. Quilici decided the top of the 14th inning was a good time to have pitcher Tom Johnson make his major league debut. The St. Paul native got off to a good start by striking out third baseman Eddie Leon, but Jorge Orta followed with a single. Johnson tried to pick Orta off first but threw the ball away for an error. One out later, Sox rookie Nyls Nyman—the only player on their roster Johnson knew (from their days in the Southern League)—singled home Orta for a 7–6 lead.

Things looked bleak when the first two Twins were retired in the bottom of the inning. Soderholm stopped folks from exiting the stands with a grounder that deflected off Leon's face into left field. Pinch-hitter Tony Oliva returned them to their seats with a double that chased Soderholm off with the tying run.

Johnson now settled in and pitched a perfect 15th. In the bottom of the inning, Rod Carew walked with one out and then stole his third base of the night. Larry Hisle had been hitless in his last 12 plate appearances but his bad luck ended with a ball that took a bad hop and bounced over Leon's head. Carew never stopping running, ending the four-hour-plus affair on a happy note. Quilici's second summary of the night was succinct. "That's one of the toughest . . . and best comebacks I have ever seen," he said. —⁓—

Milton Answers the Wake-Up Call

It is a tradition that dates back to the first year of the franchise at Met Stadium. Every September, the Twins would play one or more Saturday morning home games. In the Met Stadium days, this occurred whenever the University of Minnesota had a home game at Memorial Stadium. This enabled WCCO-AM, which aired both teams, to carry both games in their entirety.

When the Twins moved to the Metrodome, the need for breakfast ball continued. That's because the Golden Gophers, who shared the joint with the Twins and Vikings, would sometimes be scheduled for a night game.

At a Glance

WP: Milton (7–11)

HR: Hocking (7)

Key stats: Milton no-hitter with 2 BBs, 13 Ks

As the 1999 season wound down, the Twins were buried in third place in the AL Central, 29 games out of first place. Their opponents, the Angels, were last in the West, 28 games from the lead. This explains why a semicapacity crowd of 11,222 showed up for this 11:05 a.m. start. Those who came were treated to a game for the ages. Manager Tom Kelly called it a "yeoman effort." Eric Milton had pitched a career game, a 7–0 no-hitter with a baker's dozen worth of strikeouts.

The home team wasted little time at the plate. Catcher Terry Steinbach tripled home a run in the first inning. Minnesota scored three more in the second and two more in the fifth inning on Denny Hocking's two-run home run.

Thus, the lone drama left was Milton's bid. The southpaw was nearly perfect. Orlando Palmeiro worked a first inning walk but never left first base. Jeff DaVanon drew a two-out walk in the third. DaVanon attempted to steal second but Steinbach's rifle throw dismissed him. That was the final base runner the Angels got for the day.

Milton simply overpowered an Angels' lineup filled with inexperienced players and rookies who couldn't handle his 125-pitch assortment of fastballs and sliders. There was a minidrama before the eighth inning began. The between inning promotion featured the following question: "Which Twin threw the first no-hitter in history?" Kelly and others who were respecting the tradition of not mentioning a no-hitter swallowed their gum in disbelief but Milton didn't even notice it.

"I'm pretty numb," he said later. "It's probably the greatest day of my life. There is not much else I can say." —ᴍ—

Mr. Kelly Takes Over

Tom Kelly suspected something was up when Twins public relations director Tom Mee pulled him aside about noon to give a piece of news. Despite a win the night before, the team hierarchy had decided to fire Ray Miller and elevate Kelly, the third base coach, to the top job.

Ten hours later, Kelly seemed to be in a small state of shock but still could celebrate his first win as the team's manager, 4–2, over the Texas Rangers at the Metrodome. "A couple of times, I started out to coach third base and had to catch myself," he said after the game. "Your first win as a manager in the big leagues is something special."

Kelly had managed many of his new charges in the Twins' minor league system. Although he didn't criticize his predecessor, he quickly made a few noticeable changes.

Before being let go, Miller had made out a lineup for that night's game. Although he had no guarantees on the subject, Kelly was already thinking ahead to 1987. So, he moved catcher Mark Salas up in the order and inserted young outfielder Billy Beane into the game. Neither player got a hit (although Beane did walk and steal a base) but Kelly made his point: it was now his team and he would run it the way he wanted to.

Fortunately for him, there were some folks who could be left alone. Kirby Puckett stayed at the top of the batting order, going 2-for-4 with two runs scored. His three-run homer in the fifth inning provided the winning runs in the game. It also gave Kelly some new insight into his new place with the team. "It was difficult to see Puckett's home run because everybody jumped up in the dugout," he said. "I had to take somebody's word for it."

> ## At a Glance
>
> **WP:** Heaton (7–13)
>
> **S:** Atherton (10)
>
> **HR:** Puckett (28)
>
> **Key stats:** Heaton 6 1/3 scoreless IP; Puckett 2-for-4, 3 RBIs

Neal Heaton pitched 6 1/3 shutout innings before giving way to a three-pronged bullpen that closed the game out. The Rangers kicked up their heels with a pair of solo home runs in the ninth inning, but Keith Atherton induced Darrell Porter to ground out to end the game.

Kent Hrbek, another mainstay left untouched in the order, brought in a bottle of Dom Perignon with a note that read, "The first of hopefully many." Later, Hrbek, whose first major league manager was Billy Gardner, was asked what he thought the difference in managers might do for the team. "It seems like it was a happier place back then," he said, his voice trailing off. What was left unsaid spoke volumes.

FAST TRACK TO SUCCESS

Kelly's second game as manager didn't go as well—a 14–1 loss. But he guided the team to a 12–11 record the rest of the season and was indeed given the job the following season. The Twins won their division handily, dispatched Detroit in five games and then held off St. Louis to win their first World Series in seven games. Four years later, the team followed a similar formula, dismissing Toronto in five games and edging Atlanta in a thrilling seven-game series. Although Kelly stayed in the job until after the 2001 season and had some very good years, the Twins never advanced to the postseason again. Kelly retired as the winningest manager in team history with a 1,140–1,244 win-loss regular season mark. He now works for the team as an advisor. —

Did You Know?

Two fellows who set pitching records while working for the Twins—Bert Blyleven and Mike Marshall—were part of one of the oddest games in team history. On June 22, 1977, Eddie Stanky left the University of South Alabama and took over as manager of the Texas Rangers before a game at Met Stadium. Blyleven started for the Rangers but only lasted 3 1/3 innings, giving up four runs on four hits. His teammates rallied for a 10–8 win with Marshall getting the final two outs for the save. The next day, Stanky changed his mind, resigned, and returned to his old job at South Alabama. The Twins won the next night, 12–2.

Taking No Chances

The *New Yorker's* Roger Angell summarized the harried 1967 American League pennant race: "It seemed that whoever was in first place depended on what edition of the newspaper you bought."

The broadcasters at ESPN would have gone out of their collective minds as the Twins, Red Sox, Tigers, and White Sox climbed over and around each other in the final month of the season. Every game was crucial. As a result, there was no move too unorthodox for a manager to try.

Exhibit A: Minnesota's taut 3–2 win over the Senators at D.C. Stadium. Manager Cal Ermer pulled several levers to salvage this game, including replacing an injured Tony Oliva in the ninth inning and sending in the team's top winner to garner a save.

For eight innings, it appeared no such drama was necessary. Harmon Killebrew had started things on the right foot with a two-run homer before starter Jim Kaat threw a pitch. In the fourth, Tony Oliva singled and Bob Allison tripled to right to make it 3–0.

That looked like plenty for Kaat, who was enjoying a resurgence at just the right time as part of a streak of seven straight wins down the stretch.

On this night, Kaat took a six-hit shutout into the ninth—then things got a bit dicey. The Senators opened with back-to-back singles by Frank Howard and Paul Casanova. Center fielder Fred Valentine then smoked a ball to deep right. Oliva took off in hot pursuit and caught up to the ball just as he crashed into the fence. The ball squirted free, and one run scored.

> ## At a Glance
>
> **WP:** Kaat (13–13)
>
> **S:** Chance (1)
>
> **HR:** Killebrew (39)
>
> **Key stats:** Chance 2 Ks in ninth for save; Kaat 2 ER, 9 Ks in 8 IP

Ermer went out to inspect the damage. Oliva would have to leave the game (he was replaced by Carroll Hardy), eventually taking three stitches in his left knee. But it took a while to get him off the field, allowing more warm-up time for Kaat's replacement, Dean Chance.

Yes, the team's leader in wins, who had been roughed up for five unearned runs in three innings two days before, trudged in to try to keep the Twins in their flatfoot tie with the Red Sox for first place. The first man he faced, Rich Coggins, lifted a fly ball that Sandy Valdespino (a defensive replacement) tracked down. But Cananova scored to make it 3–2.

Chance then really bore down and struck out Mike Epstein and Cap Peterson to end the game. Afterward, Ermer credited Oliva with the big play of the night. "It kept the tying run off third base," he said. —⁓—

Party Time

The issue wasn't whether the Twins would win the American League Central Division race. They entered this Sunday afternoon game at Jacobs Field owning a 12-game lead over the White Sox with 13 games remaining.

The question was when and how would the Central race would officially end.

It took a while—and the end came in an odd manner—but the celebration of the Twins' return to the postseason was still heartfelt.

Kyle Lohse took care of his obligation, tossing six innings of two-hit, shutout ball. Minnesota had a hard time solving Cleveland starter Cliff Lee, a hard-throwing southpaw who was making his major league debut. Minnesota held a tenuous 1–0 lead until Denny Hocking drove in two more with a seventh-inning single. Hocking's jolt did more than put the game out of reach—it apparently triggered a rainstorm that delayed the game 65 minutes.

While the Twins waited, they observed the scoreboard that showed Chicago ahead in their game in New York, and that, too, was in a rain delay. Eventually, it stopped raining in Cleveland. Johan Santana and Eddie Guardado finished up what Lohse had started in what would become a 5–0 victory.

By now, the Yankees had gone ahead of the White Sox 8–4, but the game was in its third rain delay. "How else could this end?" asked first-year manager Ron Gardenhire after the players had quietly congratulated themselves. "We finally play a great ballgame and get a shutout, and then we have to wait on the Yankees. Isn't that what everybody in baseball does—wait on the Yankees?"

Players milled about until Santana looked up at a TV screen and noticed the Yankee postgame show was on. The game had been officially stopped. At 5:07 p.m., the wait was officially over, and Minnesota had a divisional championship to celebrate. T-shirts and champagne bottles appeared out of nowhere.

At a Glance

WP: Lohse (13–8)

Key stats: Lohse 8 Ks in 6 scoreless IP

Now his club had dethroned the defending division champs because of guys like Lohse, who had won 13 games in his first full season with the team. "Man, we've come a long way," Gardenhire said. "This is a big party but I think we might have a couple more this year."

That prediction only turned out to be partially correct. Minnesota eliminated Oakland in five games but fell to Anaheim in the ALDS, four games to one. —⁓—

Hometown Fellow Makes Real Good

In 1992, Dave Winfield had achieved his first goal when he was a member of the Toronto Blue Jays' World Series championship team. A year later, he was back home with another goal in mind. There was never a doubt that Winfield would reach the 3,000-hit plateau. As it turned out, he did so in vintage Winfield fashion—coming up with a clutch hit. Although he wasn't part of the three-run rally in the last of the 13th that produced a 5–4 win over Oakland, this was still Winfield's night. "It feels like the weight of the world is off me," Winfield said.

As the 1993 season headed toward the homestretch, the pressure had been starting to build on Winfield. In the first half of the season, his average had been in unchartered waters, hanging in the .260 range, roughly 25 points below his career numbers. He began to surge a bit in mid-July but then began to struggle again. He was back at .260 as this game began.

The A's scored twice in the top of the first. Rookie Miguel Jimenez shut the Twins down for six innings. In the seventh, Winfield banged out hit No. 2,999—a single—off reliever Kelly Downs. But it was still 2–0 when A's ace closer Dennis Eckersley started the last of the ninth. Kirby Puckett greeted Eckersley with a booming triple to right. After Chip Hale fanned, it was Winfield's turn. Eckersley worked the count to 1–2 and tried to slip a fastball on the inner half of the plate. Winfield, however, was waiting and quickly redirected it into left field to become the first player to reach the 3,000-hit plateau in a Twins uniform. The crowd of 14,654 cheered, but his teammates, aware they were still behind 2–1, were a little unsure as to what to do. "The game was so close they didn't know whether to run on the field or not," Winfield said.

At a Glance

WP: Hartley (1–2)

Key stat: Twins score three in bottom of 13th

As it turned out, there was a lot of baseball left to be played. Scott Stahoviak's two-out single scored Winfield to send the game into extra innings. Oakland scored twice in the 13th but the Twins maneuvered two hits, three walks, a wild pitch and a ground out into three runs to pull the game out.

At long last, Winfield was able to relax and enjoy his big night, noting "When I look back on this night, I will be very happy I did it in a Minnesota Twins uniform." He wasn't alone in that view. —ᴍ—

St. Paul native Dave Winfield delivers his 3,000th major league hit in front of the hometown fans.

Reardon Quietly Goes into the Record Books

He did it the way he normally went about his business. Jeff Reardon was one of the quietest fellows around. Most of the night, he was as invisible as a 6-foot-tall bearded fellow could be. But if the game was on the line in the late innings, Reardon was suddenly the center of attention. When he threw a perfect ninth inning to finish off a 3–1 victory over the White Sox, Reardon became a member of a very exclusive club. He was the first player to record 40 saves in both leagues. "This qualifies as my best individual record because no one had done it before," Reardon observed later. "But saving the seventh game of the World Series [as he did in 1987] still ranks as the best moment ever."

Reardon had led the NL with 41 saves for Montreal in 1985. He had rescued 31 in his first season in Minnesota, the celebrated World Series title year. The next season, he had more saves in fewer innings worked. "If I save a game, any game, that means we've won," Reardon said. "That is always the most important thing to me."

> ### At a Glance
>
> **WP:** Anderson (14–9)
>
> **S:** Reardon (40)
>
> **HR:** Gaetti (28)
>
> **Key stats:** Anderson 5 hits, 1 ER in 8 IP; Reardon perfect inning

On this night, Allan Anderson had held off the Sox on a solo run and five hits for eight innings. Gary Gaetti's two-run homer in the sixth inning broke a 1-all deadlock for good. By the time the ninth rolled around, Reardon was raring to go.

He set about his work quickly, using just nine pitches to dispatch Jerry Hairston, Daryl Boston, and Ozzie Guillen in order. "My first pitch was a changeup and I hadn't thrown one in two weeks," he mused. "I don't feel I have to throw that hard to get people out." But get them out he did. —⁓—

The Dome Damages
One Last Opponent

For most of the summer of 2009, the AL Central race reminded folks of the battle between the tortoise and the hare. Detroit lumbered into the divisional lead in May and stayed there the rest of the way. The Twins would have outbursts of power and mini-streaks where runs were abundant. Then they would slip back, and the Tigers would gradually increase their divisional lead.

By the time Detroit came for a mid-September weekend visit to the Metrodome, the Twins trailed by four games in the standings. But they knew they had seven games remaining with leaders—still time to make their move. In the first game of the series at the Metrodome, rookie Brian Duensing outdueled his more celebrated first-year foe Rick Porcello and, thanks in great part to a two-run Michael Cuddyer homer, came away a 3–0 winner.

The next day proved a more difficult task. Detroit ace Justin Verlander seemed on his game and carried a 2–1 lead into the bottom of the eighth inning. At that point, the Metrodome's quirky roof came into play, and the race tightened accordingly.

The eighth started innocently enough as second baseman Nick Punto struck out. Left fielder Denard Span singled to left. Shortstop Orlando Cabrera, who had performed well since being acquired from Oakland, then lifted what looked like a routine fly ball to left. But Detroit left fielder Don Kelly, who had entered the game for defensive purposes, was immediately puzzled and had no initial idea where the ball was. When he spotted it falling near the foul line, he dove for it unsuccessfully. The ball bounced off Kelly and rolled behind him. Punto scrambled to third and Cabrera gratefully checked in at second base.

> ### At a Glance
>
> **WP:** Crain (6–4)
>
> **HR:** Mauer (28), Cuddyer (28)
>
> **Key stats:** Pavano 2 ER in 7 IP; Span, Cabrera, Young two hits each

As the crowd of 43,338 roared its approval, Verlander sighed and intentionally walked catcher Joe Mauer, hoping to induce right fielder Jason Kubel to hit into a double play. But once the roof gods got into the act, there was no turning back. Kubel lifted a soft, broken-bat blooper that Kelly had no chance to catch. Punto scored easily and Cabrera, breaking quickly, came in right behind him to give Minnesota a 3–2 lead. Broken-hearted, Verlander left in favor of reliever Brandon Lyon.

It took just three pitches to seal the deal. Cuddyer turned on a 1–1 pitch and hammered it into the center field seats to put the game out of reach. —

Perry Puts Division Title within Close Range

On July 4, the idea that Jim Perry could make it to the 20-win plateau for the first time in his 10-year major league career seemed insane. The big right-hander was 6–4 with a 3.68 ERA. But then he pitched a complete-game five-hitter in a win over Oakland. Things only got better from there. His six-hit complete-game effort in a 3–2 win over Seattle lifted him to the top of the mountain with a 20–6 standard.

It did something else, too. It clinched a tie for first place in the first year of the American League's Western Division.

Perry's 20th win got off to a rocky start. John Kennedy's two-run homer in the second inning gave the expansion Pilots an early 2–0 lead. When ex-Twin Ron Clark followed Kennedy's big blow with a four-pitch walk, Twins manager Billy Martin decided it was time to have

> ### At a Glance
> **WP:** Perry (20–6)
>
> **Key stats:** Perry 6-hitter with 8 Ks; Uhlaender 3-for-5; Carew 3-for-4, RBI

a chat with Perry. "He told me I wasn't throwing the ball the way I did when I won the first 19," Perry said after the game. "But he told me to settle down because he knew I was going to win 20."

Perry listened and obeyed. He allowed only three singles the rest of the way.

It took his teammates (to be specific, Rod Carew and Tony Oliva) a while to make Martin's prophecy become accurate. Seattle still led 2–0 in the seventh when Ted Uhlaender hit a one-out triple. Carew singled off Seattle starter Gene Brabender to score Uhlaender with the Twins' first run of the afternoon. Oliva followed with a single to send Carew to second and Brabender to the showers in favor of reliever Diego Segui. Harmon Killebrew struck out but Rich Reese singled to score Carew and tie the game at 2-all.

In the ninth, Carew singled. As Oliva came to the plate, Perry noted that there was a huge gap in left-center field. "If Tony hits that way, the game is over," he said to his catcher, John Roseboro. Oliva must have listened because he did just that. Carew scored easily and the game was, indeed, over.

Minnesota could officially clinch a tie if Oakland lost its game that night. Martin seemed unconcerned. Asked if he was going to try to find out how things were going on the west coast, he smiled. "I'm going home to take my son fishing."

As it developed, Oakland lost its game and the Twins officially clinched two days later in a win at Kansas City. —⁓—

Killer Goes Deep Thrice

It should not come as a major surprise to discover that Harmon Killebrew once hit three home runs in a game at Boston's cozy home field, Fenway Park. But it may come as a bit of revelation that it was the only time in Killebrew's 22 seasons that he ever did so. It also marked the only time in his career he ever had a multi-homer game at Fenway. It was part of a big day for Harmon. He hit his troika in the first game of a doubleheader—a 13–4 win—and added a solo shot in the nightcap. "I never hit four in one day before," Killbrew said. "Not even in the minors, high school, or sandlot days."

Fenway Park may be a welcome sight for many right-handed hitters. Killebrew wasn't necessarily one of them. "I've never had great success here until now," he said after his big day. "I really don't know why."

Things got off to a good start when the big fellow took a Bill Monboquette pitch into the screen for a solo home run in the first inning as Minnesota sprinted to a quick 3–0 lead. Minnesota still had a three-run cushion (at 5–2) in the fifth inning when Killebrew hit number two—another solo shot, this time off Pete Smith. The game was getting out of hand by the eighth inning. Arnold Earley was Killebrew's final victim, with a three-run drive that ended the day's scoring.

The outburst gave Killebrew the league lead for home runs over Boston first baseman Dick Stuart by one (43–42). Killebrew would add two more homers (one in that second game and another the next afternoon) to claim the third of six home run crowns he would win. Stuart, who would never come so close again, seemed to view his home turf as a disadvantage. Referring to Met Stadium, he grumbled, "Nothing against Harmon but I'd have hit 100 if I have played in that bandbox." —〰—

At a Glance

WP: Stange (11–5)

S: Dailey (20)

HR: Banks (2), Killebrew 3 (43), Mincher (17)

Key stats: Killebrew 3-for-5, 3 HRs, 5 RBIs; Allen 3-for-6, HR, 3 RBIs

Tovar the Multitasker

It was the final home game of the season and owner Calvin Griffith was looking for ideas to get a few extra people into the Met Stadium stands. Cesar Tovar was approached with the idea of playing all nine positions—something that had happened only once before in the history of Major League Baseball. In his career with the Twins, Tovar had already appeared at six different positions. What's three more? He could borrow a glove to play first base and catch. But pitching? Tovar said no problem. "I've got a fastball, curve, and slider," he said. When told that, his manager, Cal Ermer, smiled. "None are them are very much," he said softly.

Ermer knew this sounded easier than it was. Tovar's multi-tasking would require several other moves as well, requiring substitutes and other players to move around. But Ermer was a good company man. So it was that Tovar worked his way around the diamond in a 2–1 win over the A's. He was productive at the bat, going 1-for-3, stealing a base and scoring the game's first run. He fared well in the field, too, making a nice play at first base to save a run, finishing with five putouts and an assist.

On the mound, he achieved something that eluded many other American League pitchers—he retired Reggie Jackson.

It was decided that Tovar would start the game at pitcher. Ironically, the

> ### At a Glance
>
> **WP:** Hall (2–1)
>
> **S:** Worthington (17)
>
> **Key stats:** Tovar plays all nine positions, pitches scoreless first inning

first guy he faced was the only other man to perform this feat—Campy Campaneris. Campaneris popped out, bringing up Jackson. Tovar fanned Jackson for the second out. Apparently tiring, Tovar walked Danny Cater and then balked him to second base. But Sal Bando popped out to end the threat.

In the second inning, Tovar went behind the plate. Despite the fact the shin guards were so long they dragged on the ground, he handled reliever Tom Hall's offerings just fine. There was also a pair of walks but no runs scored.

In the third inning, Tovar went to the other position he had never played before—first base. With one out, Jackson smashed a shot to the right side. Tovar flagged it down and tossed it to Hall covering for the second out. Perhaps relieved he would now be returning to familiar territory the rest of the way, Cesar led off the bottom of the third with a single, stole second, and scored on Bob Allison's triple.

From there, it was another day at the office. Griffith had a few more people than usual on hand to watch it. A crowd of 11,340 might not sound like much. But it was the second-largest house among the final 10 home games.

Griffith was very appreciative of Tovar's effort. He gave him a gift of a new color television. —∿—

Youth Shall Be Served

Although he was barely 19 years old, Dave Boswell had been one of the last cuts by the team in spring training. With the Twins out of the pennant race in September—and rumors rampant that manager Sam Mele's job was in jeopardy—he decided to give the youngster a look-see. His first outing didn't inspire confidence (the Red Sox roughed him up for three runs in three innings).

> **At a Glance**
>
> **WP:** Boswell (1–0)
>
> **S:** Grant (1)
>
> **Key stats:** Boswell 1 ER, 9 Ks in 8 IP

Things went better in his second appearance. The righty was nicked for three singles by Larry Stahl but just two hits by the remainder of the Kansas City A's in a victorious eight-inning effort that ended in a 2–1 win at Municipal Stadium. In the process, Boswell, who had received a $20,000 bonus to sign, outdueled Lew Krausse, whose 1961 bonus totaled $100,000 more. He walked two batters and struck out nine. His bid for a shutout was ruined when Dick Green led off the ninth inning with a homer. Stahl's subsequent single led a triumvirate of one-batter relievers, the last of whom was Jim Grant, who retired pinch-hitter Bill Bryan on a pop-up to shortstop to end the game.

Afterward, Boswell sounded like a wise old pro instead of a precocious teen who had started the season in the Northern League. "The higher the classification, the easier the work," Boswell said. "The catchers are better. The players play better behind you."

Boswell even helped out at the plate. In the third inning, second baseman Bill Bethea led off with a walk. In just his second big league at-bat, Boswell bunted him to second base, leading to a run.

A CAREER CUT SHORT BY ODD HAPPENINGS

In 1965, Boswell made the team out of spring training, but a bout with mononucleosis shortened his season to 27 appearances. By 1966, however, he moved into the rotation, staying there for the next four seasons. The 1969 season was his most memorable—on and off the field. On the field, he won 20 games to help the Twins win the first Western Division championship. Off the field, he was involved in a brawl with manager Billy Martin outside a Detroit tavern. In Game 2 of the ALCS that year, he gave up just seven hits in 10 2/3 innings of work but was saddled with a 1–0 loss at Baltimore.

In 1970, Boswell started off badly, losing his first five starts. He then went through a series of mishaps, including an altercation with a fan in the parking lot, a snakebite, and a hand injury courtesy of a fishing knife. His season ended prematurely when he took a 22-stitch cut in his pitching hand during a "scuffle" with catcher Paul Ratliff. —m—

One Very Loud Comeback

In both of their World Series appearances, much ado was made about the noise in the Metrodome. Perhaps the loudest regular season outburst came on this night when the Twins shrugged off a six-run inning and added another chapter to the Chicago White Sox's miserable memories of games at the Metrodome.

Alexi Casilla's 10th-inning single was the final blow in a wild 7–6 victory. But how the Twins got to this point is a story unto itself. The White Sox had come to town with a 2½-game lead. Minnesota won the first game easily 9–3 and then grinded out a 3–2 win. The lead was now just a half-game as 43,601 fans piled in for the finale. Sox starter Gavin Floyd had three wins against Minnesota in 2008, including a near no-hitter. But Joe Mauer's RBI double in the first inning sent the crowds into a tizzy with a quick 1–0 lead.

Minnesota starter Kevin Slowey came out of the gates firing, retiring the first 10 batters he faced. Then, Orlando Cabrera homered and the game turned

Alexi Casilla smacks a game-winning single in the 10th inning to give the Twins a 7–6 victory over the White Sox. The Twins trailed 6–2 before the rally, which gave them a half-game lead on the White Sox in the AL Central.

dramatically. After a Jermaine Dye single, notorious Twin killer Jim Thome doubled to center. Paul Konerko's groundout scored Dye to make it 2–1. If Twins pitcher Kevin Slowey had cut it off there, things would have been fine. Instead, there was a walk, a single, and a hit by pitch. So it was 3–1 and the bases were loaded with two out when Jose Uribe came to bat.

Uribe lined a ball off Slowey's hand. Slowey recovered to field the ball but threw wildly past first baseman Justin Morneau. By the time the play ended, three runners had scored to make it 6–1 and Slowey was done for the night with an injury. Matt Guerrier replaced him and fanned Dewayne Wise. A new trend was set in motion.

The White Sox managed just four base runners the rest of the night against six Minnesota relievers. In the bottom of the fourth, Carlos Gomez tripled home one run and scored on Denard Span's double.

6–3.

In the sixth, Gomez tripled again. Span dropped a perfect suicide squeeze bunt down to score him, and hope began to swell around the Dome.

6–4.

It was still 6–4 in the eighth when Brendan Harris led off with a double. After Nick Punto grounded out, Sox manager Ozzie Guillen went for the jugular, bringing in closer Bobby Jenks to get five outs. This was a rarity (Jenks only had two such outings all season) but the divisional lead was on the line.

The decibel level increased sharply when Gomez singled to right and Harris scored. The noise went through the roof after Span roped a ball into the right field corner for a triple that scored Gomez.

6–6.

Jenks, however, refused to give in and retired Casilla and Joe Mauer to keep the game tied.

The ninth inning was uneventful. The Sox went up and down in order in the top of the 10th. Jenks,

White Sox	AB	R	H	RBI
Wise lf	5	0	0	0
Cabrera ss	5	1	2	1
Dye rf	4	1	1	0
Thome dh	4	1	2	0
Konerko 1b	5	0	0	1
Griffey cf	3	1	0	0
Anderson cf	0	0	0	0
A. Ramirez 2b	4	1	1	1
Pierzynski c	3	1	0	0
Uribe 3b	3	0	1	1
Swisher ph	1	0	0	0
Fields 3b	0	0	0	0
Totals	37	6	7	4

Twins	AB	R	H	RBI
Span rf	4	1	3	3
Casilla 2b	5	0	2	1
Mauer c	5	0	3	1
Morneau 3b	5	0	0	0
Kubel dh	3	0	1	0
Cuddyer ph-dh	2	0	0	0
Young lf	5	0	0	0
Buscher 3b	2	1	0	0
Harris ph-3b	2	1	1	0
Punto ss	4	1	1	0
Gomez cf	5	3	4	2
Totals	42	7	15	7

```
CHI  0 0 0 6 0 0 0 0 0 0 - 6 7 0
MIN  1 0 0 2 0 1 0 2 0 1 - 7 15 1
```

White Sox	IP	H	R	ER	BB	SO
Floyd	5.2	11	4	4	1	4
Thornton	1.2	1	1	1	0	1
Jenks L(3–1)	2.1	3	2	2	2	2
Totals	9.2	15	7	7	3	7

Twins	IP	H	R	ER	BB	SO
Slowey	3.2	5	6	4	1	3
Guerrier	1	0	0	0	2	1
Reyes	0.1	0	0	0	0	1
Bonser	1	0	0	0	0	0
Crain	1	2	0	0	0	0
Breslow	1	0	0	0	0	1
Nathan W(1–2)	2	0	0	0	0	2
Totals	10	7	6	4	3	9

E—Minnesota Slowey. 2B—Chicago Thome. Minnesota Mauer, Gomez, Span, Harris. 3B—Minnesota Gomez 2, Span. HR—Chicago Cabrera (8). SH—Minnesota Casilla, Span. HBP—Chicago Pierzynski. LOB—Chicago 5. Minnesota 11. SB—Chicago Cabrera. Attendance—43,601.

who hadn't worked more than two innings in two seasons, was still in there. Nick Punto worked a one-out walk in the bottom of the inning, moving to second on Gomez's grounder.

Jenks uncorked a wild pitch that sent Punto to third and the crowd into spasms. Span, who had three hits and three RBIs, was passed intentionally. That brought up Casilla, who ended the harried night with a clean single through the box that sent the Twins back into first place in the West.

Afterward, the winners were overjoyed but a bit stunned by it all. "I can't even breathe," gasped manager Ron Gardenhire. "This was the most intense series I have ever been a part of." Joe Nathan, who had a rare two-inning effort of his own and ended up the winning pitcher, sounded likewise. "Probably the best game I've been a part of in my career," he said.

Unsurprisingly, Guillen saw it another way. "We wasted 26 innings in this town," he sighed. ―⚹―

Twins Seal First Pennant

Earl Battey, one of the few members of the Twins who could speak with knowledge on the subject, surveyed the madhouse going on in the locker room at D.C. Stadium after that day's game and smiled, "You guys act like you have never done this before."

He was right.

The Twins' 2–1 win over Washington a bit earlier sealed the deal. It was official: Minnesota was the American League champion, the first pennant for the organization in more than three decades.

Minnesota had taken command of the AL race at midseason and never released its grip. By September, only the Orioles and White Sox held any hope of catching them. A sweep of a Saturday twin bill officially finished the White Sox. A combination of the old and the new worked together to get the Twins to their 99th victory to eliminate their last standing rival, Baltimore.

Fittingly, Jim Kaat, one of the seven players who had been with the team in its final year in Washington, pitched a complete game to gain the victory. "They had been after me about not finishing games lately. I know they considered pitching [Jim] Perry today," he said. "So I had plenty of incentive to show them what I could do."

It was a vintage Kaat effort—an eight-hitter with no walks and 10 strikeouts. The Senators had at least one runner on base in each of the first four innings. But the only time they scored came in the third inning on, of all things, a throwing error by Kaat, winner of 16 Golden Gloves for fielding excellence.

As the sixth inning began, the Twins had as many hits off Pete Richert as the Senators had runs. That changed quickly. Zoilo Versalles led off with his league-leading 12th triple of the season, scoring after Don Zimmer, an infielder who had been transformed into a catcher in his final season in the bigs, allowed a passed ball.

The deadlock remained until the eighth. Second baseman Frank Quilici, whose midseason call-up

Twins	AB	R	H	RBI
Versalles ss	3	1	1	1
Nossek cf	3	0	0	0
Oliva rf	4	0	1	0
Killebrew 3b	3	0	0	0
Battey c	4	0	0	0
Allison lf	4	0	0	0
Mincher 1b	2	0	0	0
Quilici 2b	3	1	1	0
Kaat p	3	0	0	0
Totals	29	2	3	1

Senators	AB	R	H	RBI
Brinkman ss	4	0	1	0
McMullen 3b	4	1	1	0
Howard lf-rf	4	0	3	0
Kirkland pr-rf	0	0	0	0
Held rf-lf	4	0	0	0
Lock cf	4	0	0	0
Nen 1b	4	0	1	0
Zimmer c	4	0	1	0
Blasingame 2b	3	0	1	0
Richert p	3	0	0	0
Totals	34	1	8	0

MIN	0	0	0	0	0	1	0	1	0	-	2	3	1
WAS	0	0	1	0	0	0	0	0	0	-	1	8	0

Twins	IP	H	R	ER	BB	SO
Kaat W(17–11)	9	8	1	0	0	10

Senators	IP	H	R	ER	BB	SO
Richert L(15–11)	9	3	2	2	3	8

E—Minnesota Kaat. DP—Minnesota 1. 2B—Minnesota Quilici. 3B—Minnesota Versalles. SF—Minnesota Versalles. LOB—Minnesota 4. Washington 6. Attendance—8,302.

from Denver added a needed body to the infield, led off with a double. Richert moved him to third with a wild pitch. Kaat, a very good hitter for a pitcher, struck out. As befitting a guy who would be named the league's Most Valuable Player, Versalles sent a fly ball deep enough to center field to plate Quilici.

The stage was set for Kaat to end the suspense. He gave up a couple of hits in the eighth but was aided by a double play to get out unscathed. In the ninth, he needed no such help, whiffing Dick Nen and Zimmer to put the exclamation point on the season. "I felt sluggish as I warmed up but I felt good once the game started," Kaat said later.

The success even affected guys like hitting coach Jim Lemon, who played 12 years without ever seeing a postseason game. "Most of us have never finished first before," he said a bit apologetically amid the wild celebration.

Manager Sam Mele, who narrowly missed going to the World Series as a player when the Red Sox lost a one-game playoff to Cleveland in 1948, couldn't stop beaming. "We came through the front door," he said. "We didn't want to back in."

Ironically, the man who may have been most responsible for the win, owner Calvin Griffith, was absent from the celebration. Due to litigation over his family pulling the team out of Washington, Griffith couldn't be on hand and had to watch the triumph on TV while sitting in a booth at Met Stadium at a Vikings game. "The big satisfaction is that we proved when we had the money to compete, we could develop a winning team," he said with a relieved smile. "Am I disappointed at not being there? Hell, yes. The last time it happened for us was 1933." —⁓—

Manager Sam Mele (left), who guided the Twins to the 1965 World Series, chats with Casey Stengel (center) and Dodgers manager Walter Alston at the Fall Classic.

Confidence Builder

Nobody was willing to say so out loud, but the Twins' confidence appeared a bit shaken. With just nine games left, Minnesota had a six-game lead over second-place Oakland in the AL Western Division heading into a weekend series with Kansas City at the Metrodome. But George Brett knocked in three runs and old nemesis Jamie Quirk homered in a 6–4 Royals win Friday night. The next day, Danny Tartabull hit a three-run homer in the ninth inning off Jeff Reardon for a 7–4 win.

Suddenly, the Royals were now in second place, five games out with seven to play. With the Twins heading out for a six-game road trip to finish (the last three of which would be in Kansas City), there appeared to be reason for concern.

There were 53,106 folks at the Metrodome who wanted to believe otherwise, though. They started roaring before the team took to the field and never stopped until the 8–1 victory was complete. The victory didn't officially end the race (that happened the next night at Texas), but the West was won that afternoon. Even the normally placid manager, Tom Kelly, noticed the din before the game. "I was a little surprised at it," he said. "I thought we're going to have some fun today. It was unbelievable."

Bert Blyleven, one of the few Twins with postseason experience, threw a complete-game five-hitter to earn the victory. But he—and nearly everybody else on hand—agreed the turning point of the game might have come on an extraordinary play that happened before his teammates ever came to bat.

The Royals had picked up where they had left off the previous two days. Leadoff man Willie Wilson walked, moving briskly to third on Kevin Seitzer's single. That brought up Brett, who was in his 15th season and was still one very dangerous hitter. Brett rapped a smart grounder to third baseman Gary Gaetti, who threw to second baseman Al Newman to force Seitzer. Wilson delayed and broke for the plate. Out of the corner of his eye, Newman saw it and, instead of throwing to first, fired to catcher Tim Laudner, who tagged out the stunned Wilson for a rare 5–4–2 twin killing.

"That play made the game," Kelly said.

In the bottom of the inning, the Twins tattooed nearly everything pitcher Charlie Leibrandt threw at them. With one out, Newman doubled. Kirby Puckett homered. Gaetti was up next and followed suit. One out later, DH Don Baylor, acquired for the stretch drive in situations like this, singled. Hrbek hit the third homer of the inning as the building rocked with noise. Leibrandt was done for the day, and so were the Royals.

Blyleven, who had been pressed into action on three days' rest because of Joe Niekro's bad hip, cruised along, walking two, fanning eight, allowing only a Danny Tartabull solo home run. "If Newman's play and a five-run inning doesn't pick you up, nothing will," he said. "As the game went on, I got more and more pumped up."

So did Hrbek, who sensed the tide had turned for good. "This is great, the best feeling I have ever had," he said. "I'd have liked to have been a fan cheering us on. I probably would have run on the field." —∾—

At a Glance

WP: Blyleven (15–11)

HR: Puckett (28), Gaetti (31), Hrbek (34)

Key stats: Blyleven 5-hitter, 8 Ks

Foreshadowing Things to Come

It was the type of game the Twins had in mind when they lured Jack Morris home. All year long, the sturdy right-hander had answered the bell for them, eating up innings when they were most needed. Now, with his new team on the verge of winning the Western Division, they were counting on him to cement a postseason berth.

Officially, Minnesota didn't claim its Western Division title until the next afternoon when the White Sox lost to Seattle. The day before, however, Morris and his teammates gave an effort that friends and foes alike could only marvel at. "He took a lot of wear and tear off our bullpen this year," said manager Tom Kelly of the St. Paul native who had signed a one-year contract after 14 seasons in Detroit. "He's led the way all year for the starters."

On this afternoon, Morris and Toronto's Tom Candiotti went toe-to-toe for four scoreless innings. Candiotti blinked first. Greg Gagne's RBI double broke the scoreless tie. When Shane Mack dashed home after a bad throw, it was 2–0. A walk, a stolen base, and Chuck Kno-blauch's two-run single pushed the lead to 4–0 before the inning ended, giving Morris more than enough of a cushion. Minnesota pushed across a ninth-inning walk as a bonus.

> ## At a Glance
> **WP:** Morris (18–12)
> **Key stat:** Morris 6-hit shutout

In the first six innings, Morris allowed six hits and three walks, but no runners ever reached third base. With a tie for the division flag in sight, he bore down, retiring the last 11 Toronto hitters in a row. "I don't care what anybody says," he noted later. "It's easier to pitch with runs." As his teammates readied for the celebration that would come soon, Morris said, "I can't say when I signed with the Twins, I knew we could win the division. I did know the Twins were not a last place team."

Twenty-nine days later—in Game 7 of the World Series—Morris threw another complete game. This time, he had to work one more inning and didn't get as many runs. But he allowed the same total as he did that afternoon at SkyDome. To Jack Morris, the final result—no matter how you got there—is all that mattered. —⁓—

Kooz Hits the 20-Win Mark on His Last Turn

Jerry Koosman knew chances like this don't come up very often. He had crossed the 20-win mark only one other occasion in his 12-year career. So, when he was told he would get the ball for the season finale at Met Stadium, Koosman wanted to be ready from the start. "It was my last chance to get there," he said. "So I had to put my game on the line and hope for the best."

Koosman's best was just good enough. The Brewers hadn't been blanked in 214 games. But Koosman gave them something to think about all winter, allowing nine hits but no runs in a 5–0 victory that pushed his record to 20–14. "I didn't have good stuff at first," he reflected after the game. "I had Lady Luck and John Castino on my side all day."

Luck came in the second inning when Jim Wohlford slipped during a pickoff attempt and was eventually tagged out, becoming Koosman's 14th pickoff victim of the year. Still, Lenn Sakata's ensuing double now did no damage. There was more luck later. With one runner on base and two outs, Gorman Thomas, who was leading the league with 45 home runs and already had two hits in the game, was at bat. Thomas, however, was also one away from tying Dave Nicholson's AL standard of 175 whiffs in a season. Thomas took a half-swing at a Koosman curve. Umpire Derryl Cousins said Thomas went too far and called him out on strikes. Thomas went wild with protest and was dispatched from the premises.

Castino, on his way to earning co-Rookie of the Year honors, finished in style with three sterling defensive gems. He scored a run and knocked one in as part of the five-run fifth inning that was the Twins' offense for the afternoon.

At a Glance

WP: Koosman (20–13)

Key stat: Koosman 9-hit shutout

All in all, it made the final record of 82–80 palatable and sent Koosman to his nearby farm in a very happy frame of mind. He had pushed the Mets to trade him to the Twins and he seemed happy he did so. His contract was up, though. "I expect to negotiate with them shortly on next year," he said. (He went on to pitch two more seasons before being traded to the White Sox.)

The lefty felt so good he offered solace and comfort to the enemy. Asked about Thomas' record-setting strikeout, he said, "I set the record for pitchers one year [62 strikeouts in 1968]. More than [Sandy] Koufax, [Dean] Chance and all those other lousy hitters. Tell Gorman not to worry about it. He had a helluva good year." So did Koosman. —〜—

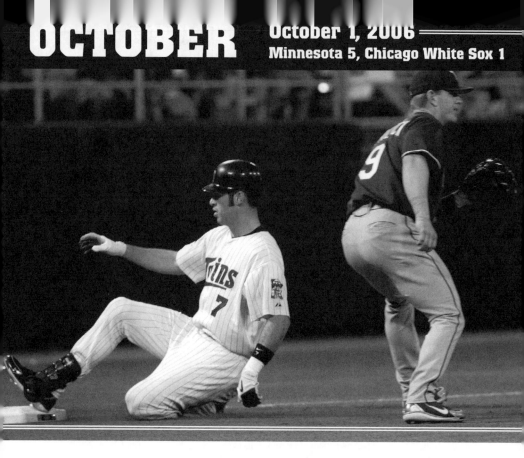

With Help, Twins Take the AL Central

In the end, it was one of the loudest and happiest days the Minnesota Twins have ever spent at the Metrodome. In the beginning, however, it looked like it would be a long and unhappy one.

At approximately 1:15 p.m., things seemed grim. Oh, the Twins knew they had clinched a playoff spot. But they needed a win over the White Sox plus a Kansas City win at Detroit to avoid facing the dreaded Yankees, who had clinched the AL East crown. This scenario would also place them at home instead against AL West champ Oakland.

The Tigers and Twins were tied for the AL Central lead. But Detroit held the tiebreaker by virtue of an 11–8 margin in head-to-head games. The early news from Detroit, whose game started an hour before the Twins-White Sox affair, was not good. The Tigers had skipped out to a 6–0 lead and had 14-game winner Jeremy Bonderman pitching. It appeared the only interesting storyline of the day would be Joe Mauer's bid to become the first catcher to win an AL batting crown. Mauer had entered the day with a one-point lead over the Yankees' Derek Jeter, .346 to .345.

To make matters worse, the Sox, who had already won the first two games of the series, jumped to a 1–0 lead in the top of the first inning. As Minnesota came to bat in the bottom of the fourth inning, it was still 1–0. But the news out east was encouraging. The Royals were worming their way back into the game and trailed 7–4 in the sixth inning.

Mauer, aware that Jeter was 1-for-3 on the day, doubled to open the bottom of the fourth. One out later, Justin Morneau did likewise to tie the game. Torii Hunter then homered to make it 3–1. That was all Minnesota would need. Carlos Silva was in fine form. After giving up two hits in the first inning, he scattered three more until leaving in the sixth. By then, the Twins had a fourth run (Mauer had singled to help the rally) and the 45,182 on hand were positive they would force Detroit's hand.

The out-of-town scoreboard had never received such scrutiny. The crowd became almost oblivious to the on-field action when it was revealed that Kansas City had scored four eighth-inning runs to take an 8–7 lead. Jeter went hitless in his final two trips to the plate and Mauer's title seemed assured.

As a series of relief pitchers mowed the White Sox down, Detroit subdued the crowd with a tying run in the eighth inning. Their game went into extra innings as Joe Nathan entered the game in the ninth inning. Nathan gave up a leadoff double, but retired the next three Sox in order to cap the 5–1 win.

Mauer had his batting title with a .347 final mark. Now all eyes turned to the scoreboard to watch the goings on in Detroit. In the 11th, the Tigers loaded the bases with one out but Kansas City reliever Jimmy Gobble became an instant local hero by retiring the next batter.

Finally, the Royals pushed across a pair of 12th-inning runs. Gobble gave up a two-out walk but

White Sox	AB	R	H	RBI
Sweeney rf	5	1	1	0
Ozuna 2b	4	0	2	0
Gload 1b	4	0	1	1
Thome dh	3	0	0	0
Fields 3b	4	0	1	0
Pierzynski c	2	0	0	0
Stewart c	1	0	0	0
Cintron ss	4	0	1	0
Mackowiak lf	3	0	2	0
Anderson cf	4	0	0	0
Totals	34	1	8	1

Twins	AB	R	H	RBI
Castillo 2b	4	0	2	0
Punto 3b	4	1	0	0
Mauer dh	4	1	2	0
Cuddyer rf	3	0	2	1
Morneau 1b	4	1	1	1
Hunter cf	4	1	1	2
White lf	3	0	1	0
Ford pr-lf	1	1	0	0
Redmond c	4	0	0	0
Bartlett ss	4	0	2	1
Totals	35	5	11	5

CHI	1	0	0	0	0	0	0	0	-	1	8	1
MIN	0	0	0	3	1	1	0	0	x	-	5	11	0

White Sox	IP	H	R	ER	BB	SO
Vazquez L(11–12)	4.2	8	4	4	0	7
Cotts	0.1	0	0	0	0	0
Haeger	3	3	1	1	2	2
Totals	8	11	5	5	2	9

Twins	IP	H	R	ER	BB	SO
Silva W(11–15)	5.1	5	1	1	2	3
Reyes	0.2	1	0	0	1	0
Rincon	1	0	0	0	0	1
Crain	1	1	0	0	0	2
Nathan	1	1	0	0	0	2
Totals	9	8	1	1	3	8

E—Chicago Ozuna. DP—Chicago 1. Minnesota 1. 2B—Chicago Mackowiak, Fields, Cintron. Minnesota Mauer, Morneau. HR—Minnesota Hunter (31). LOB—Chicago 9. Minnesota 8. SB—Chicago Ozuna. Attendance—45,182.

retired Sean Casey to end the game. The Twins, who had been 12½ games out in late May, were alone on top of the AL Central for the first time all season. As the Metrodome roared its approval, Mauer breathed a sigh of relief. "I'm just happy to sleep in my own bed tonight," he said. For a long time he had been telling reporters he wasn't paying a lot of attention to the batting race. Now he fessed up. "I lied to you guys," he said. "It's hard not to think of it when you hear about it so often."

His teammates were still trying to grasp what had happened. "I'm having a hard time believing this," Justin Morneau admitted. "I was in shock watching the Detroit game."

His manager, Ron Gardenhire, recalled what had been happening on the Metrodome turf. Silva had received a standing ovation when he left the game in the sixth inning. Gardenhire felt that was justifiable. "This set the tone for us going into the playoffs," he said. "It was a great performance."

So was the entire day. —⚡︎—

Did You Know?

In 2009, Joe Mauer became the fifth Minnesota player to win the American League Most Valuable Player award. His teammate Justin Morneau won the honor in 2006. Rod Carew (1977), Harmon Killebrew (1969) and Zoilo Versalles (1965) also have been MVPs.

Follow the Bouncing Ball

Perhaps no team suffered more inside the Metrodome than the Chicago White Sox. Even in years such as 1986—when neither the Twins nor the Sox were involved in a divisional race—odd things occurred in their games.

It was the second-to-last night of the season and there was little to play for but personal statistics and pride. By the time Minnesota's 7–3 win was completed, Twins shortstop Greg Gagne's statistics had improved and Sox outfielder Daryl Boston's pride was bruised.

The fun started in the second inning. The score was 1–1 lead when catcher Tim Laudner lifted a high pop-up near first base. What comes up usually comes down. The ball did come down, but the Sox infielders didn't see it. It bounced on the spongy infield near first base and rolled foul. Laudner stood on first base a bit sheepishly until he was informed that, since the ball rolled foul before it crossed the bag, it was simply a strike and he had to return to the plate.

At a Glance

WP: Blyleven (17–14)

HR: Laudner (10), Gagne 2 (12)

Key stats: Blyleven 9-hitter; Gagne 3-for-4, 2 HRs, 4 RBIs

Sox starter Floyd Bannister tried another pitch and Laudner walloped it into the left field seats for a home run.

The crowd was still buzzing when Gagne lifted what appeared to be an innocent fly ball toward Boston in center field. But Boston never saw it go up and he had no idea where it came down until he was told the ball was behind him and rolling to the center field fence. By the time Boston retrieved it, Gagne had sprinted around the bases for an inside-the-park home run.

When Gagne returned to the plate in the fourth inning, Minnesota led 3–1 with two runners on base. This time, he shot a line drive toward Boston that skipped off the turf and hit the edge of his glove. Once again, the ball rolled to the fence and everybody scored. After looking at the replay, official scorer Bob Beebe decided Boston was an innocent victim and awarded Gagne a second home run. Thus, he became the first American Leaguer to hit two inside-the-parkers in one game since Dick Allen of the White Sox did it in 1972 (ironically, against the Twins). "It took a Dome hop," Beebe explained at the time. "You can't give him [Boston] an error because he got the tip of his glove on a ball that took an unnatural bounce."

In the sixth inning, Gagne added to Boston's nightmare with another fly ball that disappeared in deep right-center field. This time, Boston scrambled back and held him to a triple. A fielder's choice scored Gagne, and the offense was complete. Minnesota starter Bert Blyleven gave up nine hits but went the distance to get the win. —⌇⌇—

Mr. Kelly Leaves as He Came In

In hindsight, it was vintage Tom Kelly.

In his final game as manager, the Twins defeated the White Sox 8–5 with one of his favorite players—Brad Radke—pitching a strong 8 1/3 innings to get the decision. At the time, however, only Kelly knew for sure this was his farewell appearance.

After years in the wilderness, the Twins had shown great improvement in 2001, finishing a solid second place to Cleveland with an 85–77 record. Denny Hocking seemed to speak for many when he said, "What we did this year will make the guys hungrier for next year. There are still steps we have to take—I think everyone agrees with this—but they are not dramatic steps."

Radke, not a fellow prone to dramatic pronouncements, added, "Cleveland is still the team to beat but we're right behind them now."

That day's win was a good example. Minnesota shook off a Jose Valentin homer in the top of the first to whack four doubles and 11 hits off four pitchers. They stole four bases. The top four hitters in the batting order (Jacque Jones, Luis Rivas, Corey Koskie, and Matt LeCroy) went a combined 7-for-15 with six runs scored and five RBIs. It was the type of effort at the plate Kelly preached about so often—hammer away at the opposition piece by piece if necessary.

Meanwhile, Radke mowed the Sox, taking an 8–1 lead into the ninth inning before Eddie Guardado squashed a mini-rally.

There had been speculation about 2002, but Kelly, who had been on the job since 1986, would only say, "Me and Mr. [Carl] Pohlad will talk. We have already talked three times and I think everything will work out just fine." Then he reviewed the season. "We finished in second place and that's very good because no one expected us to be there," Kelly said. Five days later, Kelly announced his retirement. —

Tom Kelly

His playing time was brief—just two months. When he returned eight years later, it was for a longer period. He took over as manager late in 1986. The next year, he led his team to a World Series championship. Four years later, the Twins repeated the feat. He stayed in the dugout for another decade and is the team's all-time leader in managerial wins with 1,140. After retiring from the dugout, he has remained with the team as an advisor to the general manager.

Having the Last Laugh

It was an ending so preposterous that even Hollywood would have pooh-poohed it. In a logical world, Joe Mauer, finishing off the best hitting season ever for a major league catcher, or Michael Cuddyer, who had so ably replaced the injured Justin Morneau at first base, or Jason Kubel, the 100-RBI man, would have produced the winning hit and Joe Nathan would do his usual yeoman work and the Minnesota Twins would defeat Detroit in the one-game playoff for the AL Central title. All one day after the Metrodome hosted its final regular-season game, preparing for the Twins to move across town to Target Field in 2010. The Metrodome magic, however, was not ready to be put to rest.

But baseball is often illogical. So it was that two of the lightest hitting Twins—Alexi Casilla and Carlos Gomez—played the hero roles. Casilla's single to right scored Gomez to cap a wild 6–5, 12-inning victory, sending 54,088 fans into hysterics and the Twins to a playoff date with the Yankees. "I said, 'I'm going to be the hero tonight,'" Casilla told the media as the champagne flowed in the locker room after the exhausting four-and-a-half-hour game was over. "I don't know. I was just feeling it."

A week before, it seemed so improbable. Minnesota went into Detroit knowing they needed at least a split of a four-game series to stay alive. They dropped two of the first three games but kept the Tigers from closing them out by winning the fourth game to stay within sight. Still, a little help was needed. Minnesota took care of their business, disposing of Kansas City three straight times. They got the necessary help when the White Sox routed Detroit two games in a row. On the final day, Detroit won to force a playoff game.

Normally, these games are played on the day after the season. But the Metrodome was booked for a football game. So, both teams sat for a day. Thus, the starting pitchers—Rick Porcello for Detroit and Scott Baker for Minnesota—came in well-rested.

The game veered off script early. The Tigers roughed Baker up for three third-inning runs.

Tigers	AB	R	H	RBI
Granderson cf	5	1	2	0
Polanco 2b	6	0	1	0
Ordonez rf	5	2	2	2
Thomas rf	1	0	0	0
Cabrera 1b	5	1	2	2
Guillen dh	3	0	0	0
Ramirez pr-dh	0	0	0	0
Huff ph	0	0	0	0
Kelly pr-dh	1	1	1	0
Raburn lf	4	0	2	0
Inge 3b	5	0	1	1
Laird c	6	0	0	0
Santiago ss	4	0	1	0
Everett pr-ss	1	0	0	0
Totals	**46**	**5**	**12**	**5**

Twins	AB	R	H	RBI
Span cf-rf	5	0	1	0
Cabrera ss	6	1	1	2
Mauer c	4	0	2	0
Kubel rf	4	1	1	1
Gomez cf	2	1	1	0
Cuddyer 1b	5	1	1	0
Young lf	5	0	1	0
Morales dh	2	0	0	0
Harris ph-dh	1	0	0	0
Casilla pr-dh	1	0	1	1
Tolbert 3b	5	1	2	1
Punto 2b	4	1	1	0
Totals	**44**	**6**	**12**	**5**

```
DET  003 000 010 100 - 5 12 1
MIN  001 001 200 101 - 6 12 0
```

Tigers	IP	H	R	ER	BB	SO
Porcello	5.2	4	2	1	2	8
Miner	0.2	4	2	2	0	1
Ni	0.1	0	0	0	0	0
Lyon	1.2	0	0	0	1	1
Rodney L(2–5)	3.0	4	2	2	3	1
Totals	**11.1**	**12**	**6**	**5**	**6**	**11**

Twins	IP	H	R	ER	BB	SO
Baker	6.0	6	3	3	2	2
Rauch	0.2	0	0	0	0	0
Mijares	0.0	1	0	0	0	0
Guerrier	0.2	1	1	1	2	0
Nathan	1.2	2	0	0	0	2
Crain	1.1	1	1	1	0	2
Mahay	0.1	0	0	0	0	1
Keppel W(1–1)	1.1	1	0	0	2	1
Totals	**12.0**	**12**	**5**	**5**	**6**	**8**

E—Detroit Porcello. DP—Detroit 1. Minnesota 2. 2B—Detroit Cabrera, Inge. Minnesota Mauer. 3B—Minnesota Cuddyer. HR—Detroit Cabrera (34), Ordonez (9). Minnesota Kubel (28), Cabrera (9). S—Minnesota Span. LOB—Detroit 12. Minnesota 12. Attendance—54,088.

Minnesota responded in the bottom of the inning, getting a run on Porcello's errant pickoff throw. Kubel's solo homer in the sixth cut the score to 3–2 and late-season acquisition shortstop Orlando Cabrera seemed to settle matters for good with a two-run homer in the seventh that gave Minnesota a 4–3 lead.

Matt Guerrier was in the game in the eighth inning to set the stage for Nathan to seal the deal. But Detroit's Magglio Ordonez, who had been criticized at home for a lack of power, launched a homer to left that tied the game at 4–4. Guerrier walked two more batters, forcing Nathan to make a rare eighth-inning appearance to get out of the mess.

In the ninth, Detroit put runners on first and third with one out. Nathan, however, wiggled away when Ordonez's line drive was snagged by Cabrera, who picked Curtis Granderson off first base to end the inning.

In the first extra inning, it appeared the locals had run out of miracles. First, Detroit pinch-hitter Aubrey Huff was hit by a pitch. One out later, Brandon Inge doubled into the left field corner for a run that pushed Detroit ahead 5–4.

In the bottom of the inning, however, Cuddyer led off with a laser to left that eluded Detroit's Ryan Raburn and rolled to the fence for a triple. After a ground out and an intentional walk, Matt Tolbert singled through the box to re-tie the game at 5–5. The next batter—second baseman Nick Punto—nearly ended the game with a fly ball to left. But Raburn gunned a bullet to the plate and nipped Casilla (who had entered as a pinch-runner) by a hair, and the game went on.

In the 12th, Detroit tried again, loading the bases with one out and the dangerous Brandon Inge at the plate. The first pitch was well inside. Inge thought it hit him and headed for first base. Home plate umpire Randy Marsh thought otherwise. Four pitches later, Punto grabbed Inge's slow roller and threw one runner out at the plate. Bobby Keppel then struck out Gerald Laird and another threat was squashed.

Gomez, a .229 hitter, bounced one through the left side to lead off the bottom of the inning. Cuddyer grounded out to Inge at third, moving Gomez to second base. Delmon Young, a late-season hero, was intentionally walked, bringing up Casilla, who had started the season with the team but was sent to the minors twice and had just two-at-bats since September 11.

Naturally, Casilla's grounder found a hole in the right side and Gomez sprinted easily across the plate as the Metrodome went mad.

Minnesota manager Ron Gardenhire knew a classic when he saw one. "This game's going to live forever," he said. "People are going to talk about this forever." —⁓—

Joe Nathan celebrates after pitching 1 2/3 innings of scoreless relief in the Twins' 6–5 victory over Detroit. The win in the one-game playoff gave the Twins the American League Central Division title.

Well Worth the Wait

It is hard to imagine now just how big of an event the 1965 World Series was. The Twins—and their ballpark, Met Stadium—still weren't used to having the spotlight on them even though they had run through the AL fairly easily, finishing a solid seven games in front of the field.

One got the impression the immensity of the event still hadn't quite registered locally as Minnesota prepared to play Game 1 against the Los Angeles Dodgers at Met Stadium. By the end of the day, however, after the Twins had thoroughly roughed up Don Drysdale for an 8–2 win, everybody around town had become baseball experts. "I think we proved today that we're a good ball club," said Minnesota manager Sam Mele. "I've been saying that all season but I know a lot of people weren't convinced. Maybe after today, they will be."

Drysdale, who had drawn the series opener nod because his celebrated teammate Sandy Koufax was observing Yom Kippur, was a quick convert to Mele's way of thinking. First baseman Ron Fairly gave the Dodgers a second-inning lead when he hit a solo homer. But Twins first baseman Don Mincher offered Drysdale a preview of upcoming attractions when he did likewise in the bottom of the inning.

In the third, the Twins tore into Drysdale and put the game away. Shortstop Zoilo Versalles offered the first big blow. After the first two runners of the inning reached base, Versalles unloaded a three-run homer to left to make it 4–1. Left fielder Sandy Valdespino doubled, and after an out, went to third on third baseman Harmon Killebrew's single. There was another out and a walk to load the bases when catcher Earl Battey came up. Unknown to most National Leaguers, Battey showed why he had been on the All-Star team earlier that year with a single to right that scored two runs. When second baseman Frank Quilici followed with his second hit of the inning to make it 7–1, Drysdale was done—and so were the Dodgers.

Dodgers	AB	R	H	RBI
Wills ss	5	0	2	1
Gilliam 3b	5	0	1	0
Davis cf	4	0	1	0
Fairly rf	4	1	1	1
Johnson lf	4	0	1	0
Lefebvre 2b	4	1	1	0
Parker 1b	3	0	1	0
Roseboro c	4	0	1	0
Drysdale p	1	0	0	0
Reed p	0	0	0	0
Crawford ph	1	0	0	0
Brewer p	0	0	0	0
Moon ph	1	0	0	0
Perranoski p	0	0	0	0
LeJohn ph	1	0	0	0
Totals	37	2	10	2

Twins	AB	R	H	RBI
Versalles ss	5	1	2	4
Valdespino lf	4	1	1	0
Oliva rf	4	0	0	0
Killebrew 3b	3	1	1	0
Hall cf	3	0	1	0
Mincher 1b	3	2	1	1
Battey c	4	0	1	2
Quilici 2b	4	1	2	1
Grant p	3	2	1	0
Totals	33	8	10	8

											R	H	E
LA	0	1	0	0	0	0	0	1	-		2	10	1
MIN	0	1	6	0	0	1	0	0	x	-	8	10	0

Dodgers	IP	H	R	ER	BB	SO
Drysdale L(0–1)	2.2	7	7	3	1	4
Reed	1.1	0	0	0	0	1
Brewer	2	3	1	1	0	1
Perranoski	2	0	0	0	2	0
Totals	8	10	8	4	3	6

Twins	IP	H	R	ER	BB	SO
Grant W(1–0)	9	10	2	2	1	5

E—Los Angeles Lefebvre. DP—Los Angeles 1. 2B—Minnesota Quilici, Valdespino, Grant. HR—Los Angeles Fairly (1). Minnesota Mincher (1), Versalles (1). SH—Minnesota Grant. LOB—Los Angeles 9. Minnesota 5. SB—Minnesota Versalles. Attendance—47,797.

Twins catcher Earl Battey and pitcher Mudcat Grant celebrate a victory over the Los Angeles Dodgers in the 1965 World Series.

Zoilo Versalles

Although he is best known for his MVP season in 1965 (he led the AL in runs, doubles, and triples), Zoilo actually hit for a better average in his initial season with the team (.280). Despite his size (5-foot-10, 146 pounds), he had good power, registering four consecutive seasons with double-digit home runs. Zoilo also appeared in a pair of All-Star Games (1963, 1965).

The six runs were the most Los Angeles had allowed in an inning all season.

It was plenty for Minnesota starting pitcher Jim "Mudcat" Grant, who gave up 10 hits but went the distance to get the victory. Although Grant didn't always show the form that produced his 21–7 regular season win-loss record, Mele was still impressed. "He [Grant] didn't have his best stuff because his breaking ball wasn't working very well," Mele said. "But he had his at-em ball working and, as anybody who played some ball knows, that's a heckuva good pitch."

This was the first World Series game ever played at Met Stadium and the first for the Griffith organization since 1933. It was Minnesota's day in every way possible. Not only did the Twins win easily, but the weatherman's prediction of rain was right on the nose. Just as the locals had said it would, it rained heavily that day. The rain started two hours after the game ended and stopped in plenty of time for Game 2. ⟶〰⟵

Did You Know?

The Twins hold an odd distinction. Before the advent of interleague play, they are believed to be the only team in major league history to play a regular season and World Series game on the road in the same ballpark. In 1965, the Angels were still playing home games at Dodger Stadium. Minnesota went 4–5 against the Angels there during the regular season. In the World Series, they lost all three games to the Dodgers there.

Finally, the Twins Are World Series Champs

By the time Game 7 of the 1987 World Series arrived, there were few Twin Cities baseball fans left who could speak above a rasp. The first five games had been tense but sedate affairs. A series of loud explosions in Minnesota's 11–5 Game 6 victory, including a memorable Kent Hrbek grand slam home run that nearly wiped out a TV cameraman in center field, set the stage for one of the most memorable Sunday nights ever.

For once, fate was on the Twins' side. They had their ace, Frank Viola, starting on the mound against a raw but talented rookie, Joe Magrane. The noise level in the Metrodome was reaching 120 decibels. Still, there was a game to be played and if the Cardinals' rabbits struck first, the quiet in the Dome would be deafening.

St. Louis did strike first, scoring a pair of second-inning runs. As often happened in this series, it wasn't the big sticks that did the damage. Rather, it was DH Tony Pena, a .214 hitter, who doubled home one run and catcher Steve Lake, a .251 swatter, who knocked in another.

This may have quieted the crowd, but center fielder Kirby Puckett was still confident. "We never doubted that if we could get somebody on base, we could do something good," he said.

The answer came instantly. Don Baylor was plunked with a pitch to start the bottom of the second. No surprise there—Baylor is the all-time MLB leader in that department. Right fielder Tom Brunansky singled him up a base. One out later, catcher Tim Laudner singled and Baylor lumbered toward the plate. But St. Louis left fielder Vince Coleman was ready and threw a bullet home. Umpire Dave Phillips called Baylor out, although replays indicated otherwise.

No problem. Second baseman Steve Lombardozzi singled and Brunansky scored to cut the Cards' lead to 2–1. Magrane labored into the fifth before veteran Danny Cox took over to face Puckett with a runner on first base. Later, Twins GM Andy MacPhail noted, "When you are talking about the

Cardinals	AB	R	H	RBI
Coleman lf	4	0	0	0
Smith ss	4	0	0	0
Herr 2b	4	0	1	0
Lindeman 1b	3	1	1	0
Ford ph	1	0	0	0
McGee cf	4	1	1	0
Pena dh	3	0	2	1
Oquendo rf	3	0	0	0
Lawless 3b	3	0	0	0
Lake c	3	0	1	1
Totals	32	2	6	2

Twins	AB	R	H	RBI
Gladden lf	5	0	1	1
Gagne ss	5	1	2	1
Puckett cf	4	0	2	1
Gaetti 3b	3	0	0	0
Baylor dh	3	0	1	0
Brunansky rf	3	2	1	0
Hrbek 1b	3	0	0	0
Laudner c	3	1	2	0
Lombardozzi 2b	2	0	1	1
Smalley ph	0	0	0	0
Newman pr-2b	1	0	0	0
Totals	32	4	10	4

											R	H	E
STL	0	2	0	0	0	0	0	0	-	2	6	1
MIN	0	1	0	0	1	1	0	1	x -	4	10	0

Cardinals	IP	H	R	ER	BB	SO
Magrane	4.1	5	2	2	1	4
Cox L(1–2)	0.2	2	1	1	3	0
Worrell	3	3	1	1	1	2
Totals	8	10	4	4	5	6

Twins	IP	H	R	ER	BB	SO
Viola W(2–1)	8	6	2	2	0	7
Reardon S(1)	1	0	0	0	0	0
Totals	9	6	2	2	0	7

E—St. Louis Lindeman. 2B—St. Louis Pena. Minnesota Puckett, Gladden. HBP—Minnesota Baylor. LOB—St. Louis 3. Minnesota 10. SB—St. Louis Pena. Minnesota Gaetti. Attendance—55,376.

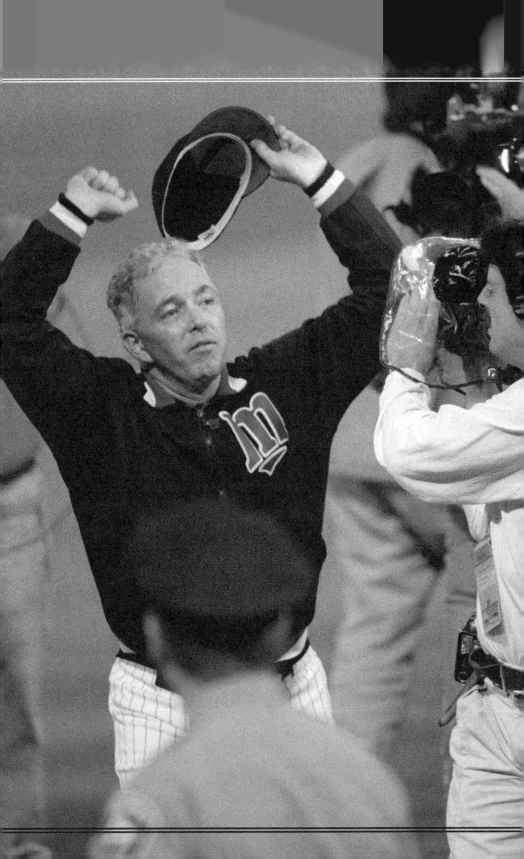

guy who has been the number-three hitter in your order most of the season, you are talking about the guy who is your team's most productive player." Which is a longwinded way of noting Puckett tied the game by hitting Cox's first pitch for an RBI double.

One inning later, the game was untied. After three walks, shortstop Greg Gagne legged out an infield hit that scored a run to make it 3–2.

While all this was going on, Viola was doing what he had done all year, efficiently keeping the Cards in line. After his second-inning difficulties, he allowed just two more hits for the rest of the night. As the Dome grew louder in noise, the southpaw seemed to get stronger and the 3–2 lead seemed like 11–2. For good measure, however, the Twins added an eighth-inning run on a Laudner single and left-fielder Dan Gladden's run-scoring double.

When the ninth inning arrived, Viola still felt strong but he knew what was going to happen. ("We all know who gets the ball in the ninth inning," said manager Tom Kelly later.) Jeff Reardon, who had been a sea of stability all season long in the closer's role, took over and did his thing one last time. The final out was Willie McGee's grounder to third baseman Gary Gaetti. The club that had lost 100 games just five years before now stood as the undisputed World Series champs.

"We've come so far since 1982. This is simply unbelievable," Viola said as the mad clubhouse celebration went on. "I was hyper as hell before the game but I knew I would be okay once I had the ball." —⟿—

Manager Tom Kelly found reason to celebrate after the Twins won the 1987 World Series. It was the first World Series title for the Twins, and the first for Kelly.

'And We'll See You Tomorrow Night'

By the time Game 6 of the 1991 World Series rolled around, the country was captivated. Three of the five games between Atlanta and Minnesota, the first pair of teams to rise from the cellar the year before to get to baseball's biggest stage, had been decided on the winning team's last at-bat. Despite having two teams from "small" markets, the ratings for the games were among the highest ever recorded.

Game 6 did nothing to hurt that status. There were as many turning points in this one as some teams get in an entire season. When Kirby Puckett's 11th-inning homer ended the nearly four-hour affair, CBS-TV's Jack Buck ended the night with his memorable phrase that is the title of this chapter.

There have been longer World Series games, but few captured the drama of the event better.

Long before his ball landed in the left-center field seats, the entire country now knew what Minnesotans had known for nearly a decade—that the barrel-legged center fielder was one of the few guys capable of controlling the game by himself.

Puckett's heroics started early. In the first inning, Puckett tripled into the left-field corner (scoring Chuck Knoblauch, who had singled) and it was quickly 1–0. Minnesota scored another run in that inning, but the lead seemed in jeopardy in the third. Lonnie Smith was on first base with one out when Ron Gant crashed a Scott Erickson fastball on a solid line toward the left-center field seats. But the ball had more speed on it than height. Puckett chased it down and pulled it in before it could hit the glass above the seats.

In the fifth inning, Terry Pendleton drilled a ball that neither Puckett—nor anybody else—could

Braves	AB	R	H	RBI
Smith dh	3	1	0	0
Pendleton 3b	5	1	4	2
Gant cf	5	0	0	1
Justice rf	4	0	0	0
Bream 1b	4	0	1	0
Mitchell pr-lf	0	0	0	0
Hunter lf-1b	5	0	0	0
Olson c	5	0	0	0
Lemke 2b	4	1	2	0
Belliard ss	2	0	1	0
Gregg ph	0	0	0	0
Blauser ph-ss	2	0	1	0
Totals	**39**	**3**	**9**	**3**

Twins	AB	R	H	RBI
Gladden lf	4	1	0	0
Knoblauch 2b	5	1	1	0
Puckett cf	4	2	3	3
Davis dh	4	0	0	0
Mack rf	4	0	2	1
Leius 3b	3	0	2	0
Pagliarulo ph-3b	1	0	0	0
Hrbek 1b	4	0	0	0
Ortiz c	2	0	0	0
Harper ph-c	2	0	0	0
Gagne ss	4	0	1	0
Totals	**37**	**4**	**9**	**4**

ATL 0 0 0 0 2 0 1 0 0 0 0 - 3 9 1
MIN 2 0 0 0 1 0 0 0 0 0 1 - 4 9 0

Braves	IP	H	R	ER	BB	SO
Avery	6	6	3	3	1	3
Stanton	2	2	0	0	0	1
Pena	2	0	0	0	0	2
Leibrandt L(0–2)	0	1	1	1	0	0
Totals	**10**	**9**	**4**	**4**	**1**	**6**

Twins	IP	H	R	ER	BB	SO
Erickson	6	5	3	3	2	2
Guthrie	0.1	1	0	0	1	1
Willis	2.2	1	0	0	0	1
Aguilera W(1–1)	2	2	0	0	0	0
Totals	**11**	**9**	**3**	**3**	**3**	**4**

E—Atlanta Hunter. DP—Atlanta 2. Minnesota 2. 2B—Minnesota Mack. 3B—Minnesota Puckett. HR—Atlanta Pendleton (2). Minnesota Puckett (2). HBP—Atlanta Smith. LOB—Atlanta 7. Minnesota 5. SB—Minnesota Gladden, Puckett. Attendance—55,155.

"And we'll see you tomorrow night." Those words were all Twins fans needed to hear after Kirby Puckett's home run in the 11th inning in Game 6 against the Braves forced a Game 7.

catch for a two-run homer to tie the game at 2–2. As was their wont during the championship season of 1987, the Twins came right back in the bottom of the inning. Dan Gladden walked, stole second, went to third base on Knoblauch's out to deep right, and scored on a sacrifice fly by Puckett.

Gant got a form of revenge in the seventh inning. With the bases loaded and one out, he hit into a fielder's choice that produced the tying run. Reliever Carl Willis prevented further trouble when he whiffed David Justice to end the threat.

Atlanta kept getting chances off Willis and his successor, Rick Aguilera. In the ninth and 10th innings, they saw runners eliminated on double plays. In the 11th, pinch-runner Keith Mitchell was tossed out trying to steal second. It was a game that cried out for a dramatic end, and the Twins had just the man who could do it.

Veteran southpaw Charlie Leibrandt entered the game for Atlanta to start the bottom of the 11th on the mound. The first man he faced was Puckett. The two knew each other well from Leibrandt's six-year term with Kansas City and his appearance as the Braves' starter in Game 1. But he rarely worked in relief. As a result, Puckett expected Leibrandt would probably start with his best effort—a circle changeup. Leibrandt didn't disappoint and dropped it on the corner for strike one. When the next two pitches were wide, Puckett, a notoriously free swinger, had a pretty good idea what was coming.

Sure enough, Leibrandt sent in another circle changeup and Puckett turned on it with a vengeance. The ball quickly shot out to left-center, disappearing almost directly over the spot where Puckett had broken Gant's heart earlier that night. The Metrodome crowd of 55,155 exploded in joy and the country exhaled, too. "I finally did something I said I was going to do," Puckett said after the game. "I'm such an aggressive hitter that I swing at anything."

In the first five games of the series, Puckett had managed just three hits and one RBI. In Game 6, he had three hits, three RBIs and a new legion of fans across the country. "This is a game I'll never forget," he said.

He is not alone in that department. ⌐ᴡᴡ⌐

Saving the Best for Last; Morris Tosses a Gem

There have been pitchers who threw more innings and recorded more strike-outs than Jack Morris did in Game 7 of the 1991 World Series. But no pitcher ever dominated so much with the season on the line. When he ended up on the winning side of a 1–0, 10-inning complete-game victory over Atlanta that gave the Twins their second World Series title in five years, Morris joined such fellows as Don Larsen (perfect game), Bob Gibson (17 strikeouts), and Mickey Lolich (three complete game wins in eight days) in the category of unforgettable efforts.

"He could have gone 25 innings if needed," said a fellow who had a good view of Morris all night, Twins first baseman Kent Hrbek. "That man is a horse."

It was a vintage Morris effort. He scattered seven hits and two walks effectively. Twice, the Braves moved a runner to third base with one out. On both occasions, Morris quickly subdued the threat. "In a game like this, concentration isn't the problem," he said. "It's what you do with your pitches. Early on, I had a good fastball and slider. My forkball came back around the sixth inning."

Still, there were scary moments. In the top of the eighth, the bases were loaded with one out when Atlanta's Sid Bream rapped a sharply hit grounder at Hrbek, who fired home and got back to the bag in time for an unusual 3–2–3 double play that squashed the threat.

Atlanta starter John Smoltz was Morris' match, and then some. In his first seven innings of work, the Twins advanced to third base just once. In the eighth, however, pinch-hitter Randy Bush led off with a single. Al Newman ran for him, moving to third base on Chuck Knoblauch's one-out single. Mike Stanton entered to face Hrbek.

Hrbek was having a rough series but he tried to make amends with a line drive to the right side. But the ball went straight to second baseman Mark Lemke, who turned it into an inning-ending

Braves	AB	R	H	RBI
Smith dh	4	0	2	0
Pendleton 3b	5	0	1	0
Gant cf	4	0	0	0
Justice rf	3	0	1	0
Bream 1b	4	0	0	0
Hunter lf	4	0	1	0
Olson c	4	0	0	0
Lemke 2b	4	0	1	0
Belliard ss	2	0	1	0
Blauser ph-ss	1	0	0	0
Totals	**35**	**0**	**7**	**0**

Twins	AB	R	H	RBI
Gladden lf	5	1	3	0
Knoblauch 2b	4	0	1	0
Puckett cf	2	0	0	0
Hrbek 1b	3	0	0	0
Davis dh	4	0	1	0
Brown pr-dh	0	0	0	0
Larkin ph-dh	1	0	1	1
Harper c	4	0	2	0
Mack rf	4	0	1	0
Pagliarulo 3b	3	0	0	0
Gagne ss	2	0	0	0
Bush ph	1	0	1	0
Newman pr-ss	0	0	0	0
Sorrento ph	1	0	0	0
Leius ss	0	0	0	0
Totals	**34**	**1**	**10**	**1**

ATL	0	0	0	0	0	0	0	0	0	-	0	7 0
MIN	0	0	0	0	0	0	0	0	1	-	1	10 0

Braves	IP	H	R	ER	BB	SO
Smoltz	7.1	6	0	0	1	4
Stanton	0.2	2	0	0	1	0
Pena L(0–1)	1.1	2	1	1	3	1
Totals	9.1	10	1	1	5	5

Twins	IP	H	R	ER	BB	SO
Morris W(2–0)	10	7	0	0	2	8

DP—Atlanta 3. Minnesota 1. 2B—Atlanta Hunter, Pendleton. Minnesota Gladden 2. SH—Atlanta Belliard. Minnesota Knoblauch. HBP—Minnesota Hrbek. LOB—Atlanta 8. Minnesota 12. Attendance—55,118.

double play. Morris handled the ninth without issue. The Twins placed their first two runners on base to open the last of the ninth, but Stanton's replacement, Alejandro Pena, wriggled off the hook to send the season into extra innings.

In the Minnesota dugout, there was surprisingly little question as to who was coming out for the 10th inning. "I told [manager Tom] Kelly I had a lot left," Morris reported. "My fastball was still very alive."

Kelly is a man who prides himself on knowing his players' limits. Going overtime was nothing new to Morris, who had pitched 10 innings eight times in his career before this game. He shrugged his shoulders and okayed Morris' request, saying, "What the heck, it's just a game." He knew what he was talking about, retiring the Braves in quick 1–2–3 order. (Later, Kelly was asked what it would have taken to take Morris out of the game. "Probably a shotgun," he replied.)

But his team still needed a run. Dan Gladden brought the crowd to life with a leadoff double, moving to third on Knoblauch's obligatory sacrifice bunt. Taking no chances, the Braves walked Puckett and Hrbek to load the bases. Gene Larkin, who had hit .286 during the regular season but only had batted three times in the World Series, now entered as a pinch-hitter. "I had butterflies in my stomach the whole game," he would say later. "I lost them, however, when I got to the plate."

Larkin quickly made the Braves feel queasy, lifting a drive into the left-center field gap to easily score Gladden and give the Twins the World Series. In presenting the trophy afterward, MLB commissioner Fay Vincent said, "This was probably the greatest World Series ever."

Twins DH Chili Davis, however, may have been speaking for the players when he said, "You can ask me all the questions you want and I'll tell you the same thing every time," he said. "It's done." —ᄴ—

Jack Morris

The St. Paul native only pitched one season for the Twins. But what a year it was. In addition to stabilizing the pitching staff with an 18–12 win-loss mark and a 3.43 ERA during the regular season, he won a pair of American League Championship Series games against Toronto and two more in the World Series against Atlanta. The second of those wins was the famous 10-inning effort that helped earn him MVP honors for the series.

Jack Morris' 10-inning, 1–0 victory over the Atlanta Braves in Game 7 of the 1991 World Series remains one of the greatest games ever played in the Fall Classic.

ACKNOWLEDGMENTS

All authors have those who inspired them to get at it. To that end, forgive me for giving a shout-out to some former mentors. Father Ronald Cullen, my high school English teacher, consistently harped on me to use better grammar. When I moved to Minnesota, the late Father James Whalen, who started the Journalism Department at St. Thomas, picked up the cudgel and continued the assault. I can hear their words . . . and sharp comments on my writings . . . still ringing in my ears today. Reno Bertoia, known in Minnesota as a trivia answer (name the man who was the team's original third baseman and later was the first player to be traded), was my high school history teacher. He was the person who told me to go to school in Minnesota, a move that I am eternally gratefully for.

This effort could not have been done without the support of my wife, Lynne, who has told me for years I had a book in me. My friend Stephanie Harris read the entire first draft, patiently offering invaluable advice and suggestions. I cannot thank those two enough for their support.

And I need to acknowledge two people who are no longer with us—my late Uncle Cletus, who taught me so much about baseball, and my mother-in-law Colleen Larkin, who recounted what she remembered of witnessing Jack Kralick's 1962 no-hitter at Met Stadium.

Bob Temple at Red Line Editorial is the fellow who decided this was a worthy project. Since (like me), Bob had covered many games for the wire service, he was able to bring sharp insight and observations that gave the book better focus. Don Gulbrandsen at Triumph Books answered a rookie author's questions patiently and did a lot of the quiet work that rarely gets attention but is critical to the success of the project.

REFERENCES

A historical narrative such as this can only be accomplished with the help of research. To that end, I wish to give heartfelt thanks and gratefully acknowledge the following sources:

- The Minnesota History Center, which houses nearly every issue of the *St. Paul Pioneer Press*, *St. Paul Dispatch*, *Minneapolis Tribune*, *Minneapolis Star*, and the current *Star-Tribune*. Their files were extensively culled for the past results and many of the quotes used in this book came from articles in those papers.

- *Retrosheet.org*. This wonderful source has boxscores of games, dating back to 1871, and play-by-play data going back as far as 1911. Every game used in this book was examined on this website. There are also fairly complete listings of players' big league careers, including separate listings for top achievements. In addition, there is a listing for "special events" such as no-hitters or the game in which the Twins hit out of order four times in one night.

- *Nationalpastime.com*. This historical site offered information and tidbits that were not available in other sources in their "This Day In Baseball History" section.

- *The Cool of the Evening* by Jim Thielman. This recap of the Twins' first pennant in 1965 was most helpful.

- *Once There was a Ballpark* by Joe Soucheray. I culled a few historical facts and figures from this book that was written roughly at the same time the Twins moved to the Metrodome.

- The *New York Times* archives. It was interesting and instructive to get a view of the Twins from an eastern source.

- The Minnesota Twins' media guides, skillfully edited by media relations guru Mike Herman. Much of the statistical information (as well as many ideas for games) came directly from these books.

- The many former writers who covered the team at various points and allowed me to pick their brains. In particular, retired *Pioneer Press* scribbler Gregg Wong was particularly helpful with recollections from the team's World Series runs. Former *Star-Tribune* writer Jon Roe provided insights from his time on the beat as did current staffer Howard Sinker, who covered the team during one of its drier spells. In many cases, these guys confirmed information and added insights that didn't make it into print.

ABOUT THE AUTHOR

Dave Wright is a Detroit native who emigrated to Minnesota in 1972 to attend college (on the recommendation of ex-Twin Reno Bertoia) and has been there almost nonstop since. He has covered pro and college games for the Associated Press and UPI and works about 100 high school and college games a year as a public address announcer. When he is not writing (or talking), he lives in St. Paul with his wife Lynne and dog Pete.